Edinburgh's Transport

FRONT COVER

In the late summer of 1955 the western sun lights up Edinburgh Corporation tram car 69 as it ascends the Mound. It is *en route* to Craiglockhart, the short-lived final terminus of route 27. Looking down austerely over the scene is W.H. Playfair's facade of New College with, behind, the General Assembly Hall of the Church of Scotland, the temporary first home of Scotland's newly devolved Parliament. After an absence of nearly three hundred years the Parliament has returned to Scotland's capital. Could a modern electric passenger tramway also return, to assist Edinburgh break free from the stranglehold imposed on the city centre by the private car and convoys of buses? *(Chris Banks Collection, Colour-Rail IR230)*

EDINBURGH'S TRANSPORT

Volume Two
THE CORPORATION YEARS
1919 – 1975

D. L. G. HUNTER CEng FIMechE FCIT

Published by
ADAM GORDON

A catalogue entry for this book is available from the British Library.
ISBN 1 874422 23 0

Published by Adam Gordon
Priory Cottage, Chetwode, Buckingham MK18 4LB
Tel: 01280 848650

Printed by Drogher Press
Unit 4, Airfield Way, Christchurch, Dorset BH23 3TB

Typesetting by Trevor Preece, Gawcott, Buckingham

CONTENTS

Inside back cover: Edinburgh Coporation Tramways and Motors map
c 1927

INTRODUCTION

I was pleased to have been asked by David Hunter to edit his second volume of 'Edinburgh's Transport' for publication by Adam Gordon. I knew David for over forty years and through this time he assisted and fostered my growing interest in transport history. It is therefore with a sense of privilege that I was able to edit his text to prepare it for publication.

Volume One of this work ('Edinburgh's Transport – The Early Years' published in 1992 by Mercat Press) covered the period starting with the origins of public transport in Edinburgh, up to the take-over of the cable tramway system by the Corporation on 30 June 1919. Further chapters dealt in detail with the tramways of Leith Corporation, the Musselburgh Electric Tramways, plus other proposed tramways in the area. There were also chapters dealing with early motor buses and the advance of local railways. That first volume was, in itself, an extended account of the early years of Edinburgh's transport, which had been covered by David in the original 1964 'Edinburgh's Transport' published by The Advertiser Press of Huddersfield. Various elements which were covered within the original, single, volume, have now been dealt with in expanded form by David in separate works, hence there is in this volume no coverage of the later years of the SMT motor bus company. This is recorded fully in David's 1987 work 'From SMT to Eastern Scottish' published by John Donald Ltd. Likewise the story of the decline and fall of the suburban railways has been omitted.

This volume concentrates upon the period from 1919 to 1975 when the transport undertaking was run by Edinburgh Corporation. The previous volume saw the start of Edinburgh's tramways; this volume covers the change from cable to electric operation – a massive undertaking in its own right – up to the fall from grace of electric tramways. Then followed an obscene rush to close down and remove from sight any vestige of a system which had efficiently and profitably carried millions of passengers. It was seen to be an anachronism in a society hell-bent in following the American error of placing local public transport into dependency on imported fuel, subject to vagaries of world, not national or local, interests. Forty years later consideration is again being given to re-creation of an effective public transport system with, initially, a guided bus way as a possible precursor to a light rail transit system – a progressive policy to get private car congestion away from Edinburgh's spacious streets.

This book has used as many as possible of the fine photographs taken by Edwin O. Catford ('EOC'). EOC was head of the motor department of the Corporation Tramways and fulfilled the role of official photographer – although he was not employed as such (nor was anybody else!). The highly skilled results of his work are preserved on hundreds of glass plates which were given to David Hunter by EOC, and by David to myself. The quality of EOC's work is apparent in almost every scene and it is my pleasure that further prints (for which no negatives now exist) were passed on for inclusion in this work by EOC's grandson, Kenneth. David also photographed the Edinburgh transport scene. His photographs were taken as record views of the vehicles only and he would be the first to acknowledge that they lacked the quality and depth of the EOC compositions. Without these views, the historic record of Edinburgh's Transport would be poorer.

Unfortunately not all of EOC's negatives survived, it is even rumoured that some, with the image removed, went to make green houses! If any reader knows of any others I would be glad to hear of their whereabouts.

There are few tangible relics of Edinburgh's tramway history. Car 35 which was retained by the Corporation has had several homes over the years, but is presently on display at the National Tramway Museum in Derbyshire. Car 226 (the first) has been retrieved from its second life as a holiday home at Hume Castle in the Borders and is at this time beginning a lengthy restoration programme. Perhaps some day in the future they may both be available in Edinburgh for the interest of future generations.

David was a prolific historian, searching for information long before the interest in transport history became widespread. Without these delvings much less of the history of Edinburgh's transport would be on record. His other interest was the history of the Highland Railway, and on the subjects closest to his heart he wrote and had published some ten volumes.

Thanks must be recorded to the people who have assisted in completing the publication of this, the second part of 'Edinburgh's Transport' – Ken Catford, Alastair Gunn, Adam Gordon, Gavin Booth and many, many others.

A. W. Brotchie
Aberdour
April 1999

D.L.G. Hunter CEng FIMechE FInstT
30 March 1909 – 25 February 1998

Chapter 1

THE NEW CORPORATION TRANSPORT DEPARTMENT

1 July 1919 may be regarded as the actual start of Corporation operations, as on that day the Tramways Department of the City (as it was then called) commenced to function under the managership of Mr R Stuart Pilcher. The lease of the tramway system to the District Tramways Co. expired on 30 June, and the auspicious occasion was marked by a lunch in the City Chambers. The Council had decided on conversion of the cable tramways (the complexities of which are described in volume 1) to electric traction. The Edinburgh Corporation Order Confirmation Act 1919 (passed 20 November 1919) provided for this being carried out in sections. All existing staff were transferred to the City's employment, except for the old Company's manager, Mr Cox. Arrangements were, however, made to dispense with the conductresses who had served during the war. Male staff were fitted out with new uniforms and caps of the 'cheese-cutter' style. On 20 January 1920 responsibility for permanent way was transferred from the Burgh engineer to the new Tramways Department.

The council was now giving thought to the method to be adopted for the electrification, particularly in respect of Princes Street, and also to a programme of conversion. It had been suggested that the Northern routes should be electrified first, but the track required reconstruction, hence it was proposed that motor buses should be run until this could be accomplished. Meanwhile the Pilrig to Nether Liberton route could conveniently be dealt with. An important aspect of the electrification programme was the availability of power supplies.

At this time there were two power generating stations in the city, at Dewar Place and McDonald Road. Leith had its own station but also took power from Edinburgh. The output of these stations, and the distribution network, was fully loaded and a scheme for a high tension generating station and distribution network had been prepared before the First World War. Suspended in 1916, it was agreed that a new generating station at Portobello should be pressed forward. High Tension cables were to be laid to converting stations located at Cowgate, Causewayside, Morningside, Robertson Avenue and Granton. The two existing generating stations would cease to function. Power for the electric tramways in Edinburgh was thus inexorably linked to progress of the Corporation electricity undertaking.

Mr Pilcher planned to use most of the existing equipment, converting depots and rebuilding rolling-stock. Obviously it would be some time before conversion would be completed, hence short-term steps were taken to improve the cable system. Before the Company's lease expired the Corporation had accepted tenders for forty top covers for cable cars and also for three motor charabancs and twelve buses. The Company crest disappeared from the cars, being replaced by the City coat of arms, and there followed much repainting of existing rolling-stock. Some of the oldest Northern cars had already been withdrawn. Enamelled plates (of the same colour as the service number boards) but

Princes Street West End, probably during the first year of Corporation operation of the cable tramway system. The three top covered trams were typical of those operated latterly by the Company, although 201 on the left was soon to be fitted with a new Hurst Nelson top deck. It is running on service 9 from Craiglockhart to Pilrig as is 118 in the distance. Car 46 on the right is on service 5 from Abbeyhill to Morningside Station. The 'kink' in the cable slot rail – just where the perambulator (with sunshade!) is being propelled – shows how the gripper was diverted at junctions. Note also the passenger-loading island for eastbound cars. (FC Inglis)

showing only the terminus, were screwed on to destination boards used on numbered services. After the war the financial position was difficult, but penny fares were introduced as had been promised, and several 1½d transfer fares were reinstated.

The three charabancs arrived in August 1919, and ran two circular tours covering respectively the north and south sides of the city, from the Mound. The buses commenced a route from Ardmillan Terrace to Abbeyhill on 29 December 1919 via Fountainbridge, Bread Street, High Street, and Canongate. Details of tram and bus rolling-stock are given later. These services filled a need and the Corporation soon ordered further vehicles. Even the charabancs were pressed into traffic on Saturdays for football crowds. One problem was splashing from the solid tyres as they trundled over the setts on a wet day. Several types of brush hanging outside the wheels were tried in an effort to address complaints, but none proved adequate.

The Edinburgh Boundaries Extension and Tramways Act, 1920 (adopted 4 August 1920) provided for extensions to the City boundaries, and more fundamentally achieved the incorporation into the City of the Burgh of Leith. On 2 November 1920 the Leith electric system passed into control of the Tramways Department. The Leith manager, Mr F. A. Fitzpayne, became deputy manager of the combined undertaking. Until through services were achieved the Leith accounts were kept separate. Lettering on the Leith cars was changed from 'Leith Corporation' to 'Corporation Tramways' and fleet numbers

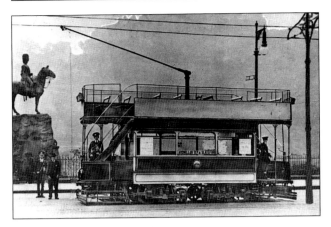

Not what it seems – a Company Slateford electric car 'under the wires' in Princes Street, but a completely falsified view to illustrate the appearance of overhead wires in the famous thoroughfare! The inspector holding the trolley rope to locate the trolley correctly has been 'touched out' and the pole and wires skilfully added. Behind is Edinburgh Castle and the equestrian Royal Scots Greys monument opposite the foot of Frederick Street. (via K Catford)

were increased by adding 230. Cable cars did not carry any such lettering, while buses and charabancs, which had been lettered 'Corporation Tramways' or 'Edinburgh Corporation Tramways' were altered to 'Corporation Motors'. Buses were lettered on sides and back, charabancs on the back only.

The Act of 1920 included powers to construct tramway extensions – from the Nether Liberton terminus to Liberton crossroads; from Seafield Place to Kings Road; from Pilrig Street up Dryden Street to form a rear entrance to Shrubhill Depot, plus the vital connection between the Edinburgh and Leith systems at Pilrig. Powers existed under the 1916 Act to construct a tramway to Corstorphine, plus a siding into ground on the south side of the road near the terminus; a terminal spur into Hope Street at the West End; and the Braids to Firrhill tramroad. In the 1920 Bill the Corporation sought further powers to run buses outside the City boundary (East Lothian was particularly in mind). The SMT Co, not surprisingly, objected to this, and an agreement was reached (12 May 1920) where the City dropped these clauses and the SMT Co agreed to provide services on specified routes, including Gilmerton – as a monopoly – and to charge protective fares on tramway routes within the City. The agreement was initially for seven years, but was continued until 1954.

With costs post-war rising it was found that the penny stages could not be maintained.

The first Corporation chara-banc (Leyland B8725) arrived in August 1919, and operated from here at the foot of the Mound, on tours of either the northern or southern suburbs, fare 1s 0d. As can be seen, these were immediately popular. Behind the vehicle is the Sailors and Soldiers Rest Hut which served a vital need at the end of the First World War. (EOC)

September 1920 saw the introduction of a bus service extending from the cable car terminus at Craiglockhart to Colinton village – soon extended to Juniper Green. Leyland SG1650 (fleet number 23) is proceeding west along rural Colinton Road past the newly-built Redford Cavalry Barracks. This became route 8 when numbers were introduced early the next year. (EOC)

On 31 December 1919 the 1½d minimum was reintroduced (the new 1½d ticket white with a red stripe). Several changes to fares followed. On 22 May 1920 the 2d and 3d fares were increased by a half-penny, and then on 7 September 1920 there was a further upward revision, but a short penny stage was included, and a 4d maximum applied on the cable system. Transfer fares were mostly eliminated. Workmen's returns at 1d more than the single fare were available for the 2d, 3d and 4d stages on the tramways (the return being allowed on the top deck only). Further revision followed on 27 October 1921 with a longer average journey. Leith had, however, continued on its old fare basis. Tickets in the format of the Company and Leith Corporation continued in use on the two sections until about 1922.

An unusual incident was recorded on 4 October 1919 when a Comely Bank car failed to stop at Frederick Street terminus: the bogies sheared off and the body slid on under its own momentum into Princes Street!

In February 1920 it was decided that as the Northern cable section was worn out and uneconomic, it should be closed down and replaced temporarily by buses. In view of the gradients involved, powerful vehicles were ordered – AECs with 40-50 hp engines and improved brakes.

The first tramway route to be withdrawn, however, was the electric service from Ardmillan Terrace to Slateford, which suffered from its isolation. The Ardmillan Terrace to Abbeyhill buses had been extended to Easter Road Station on 21 March 1920, and from 18 October a proportion of these were extended from Ardmillan Terrace to Slateford and the electric cars withdrawn. On 31 October the Mound to Tollcross cars were temporarily replaced by a bus service, and on 2 December the Comely Bank tram route closed, also replaced by a bus service. About a fortnight afterwards these Comely Bank buses were extended from Frederick Street to St. David Street, proceeding inwards via George Street and outwards via Princes Street. At Comely Bank the buses continued to Fettes Avenue to turn, but in April 1921 the bus terminus was brought back to the old car terminus. On 29 December 1920 the Tollcross and Mound buses were extended across Princes Street, down Hanover Street to Goldenacre replacing the Hanover Street cable cars, leaving only the Broughton Street cable operated from Henderson Row cable power station.

Some new bus services started in 1920. First was a morning rush hour and afternoon service between Craiglockhart car terminus and Colinton from 4 September, which was extended to Juniper Green on 21 September. At that time this was quite a country route. Next was from 27 September; West End to Bonnington Toll via Dean Bridge, Henderson Row and Broughton Road, which was extended by Henderson Street to the Shore, Leith, on 17 March 1921. Meantime the Easter Road Station terminus of the first bus route had been extended to the foot of Easter Road on 27 November 1920. An afternoon service had also operated between Murrayfield car terminus and the Zoo from 16 May 1920, but on 17 January this became a morning 'rush' and afternoon service to Corstorphine (with the terminus at Victor Park). The terms of the 1920 Act, however, called for provision of through travel facilities by tramcar or bus to the new suburbs, and Corstorphine residents complained of having to change at Murrayfield. For a time the Corporation refused to conform, retorting that most Corstorphine people used the train. Following a ratepayers' petition it was agreed on 23 November 1921 that a through service be run, and a bus was put on to run approximately hourly from Waverley Bridge to Corstorphine.

Staff trouble was brewing and in November 1920, arising from grievances about shifts, cable car crews threatened to strike, showing their feelings by refusing to take standing passengers. On 12 November the Corporation revoked the Byelaws, also the licences of drivers and conductors, which it had provided for in the 1916 Act. The following week-end there was considerable delay as drivers refused to start until standing passengers were removed. The climax came on Monday 15 November when some employees were

Tram services were reduced early in 1921 to save fuel as a consequence of a strike by miners. Operation of some early morning runs was taken over by buses. Number 182 (AEC SG2330 with body by E & H Hora of London) was operating over the Leith system, and is seen at Newhaven harbour. (EOC)

sacked on the spot. All other crews ran their cars into the depots and a strike commenced at 9pm. For the next two days only a skeleton service was run (Portobello, Leith, and the buses continued to run normally). Private buses were hired to help out, mostly in the western suburbs. On 17 November agreement was reached and services returned to normal.

On 24 January 1921 Henderson Row power station was closed down and route 9 cars were diverted from Broughton Street to Pilrig. To replace these a bus service was run from St Andrew Street via Leith Street and Broughton Street to Goldenacre, via York Place on the inward journey. At this time the Henderson Street – Bonnington – West End route was extended along George Street, York Place, and Broughton Street to Goldenacre also, while on 17 February this was further extended from Goldenacre via Trinity Road to Stanley Road. Henderson Row depot was converted to a bus garage, relieving pressure on the overcrowded yard at Shrubhill (hitherto their home).

On 28 February 1921 a new 'country' service commenced from Surgeon's Hall to Newcraighall serving the then outlying villages of Craigmillar and Niddrie. Initially this also was a morning and afternoon service only. Routes were now numbered as follows, with the colours of the bus window boards:

1	Easter Road and Ardmillan Terrace	Brown
2	Easter Road and Slateford	Brown
3	Goldenacre and Tollcross	White
4	St David Street and Comely Bank	Green
5	Leith – Bonnington – West End – Broughton Street – Goldenacre – Stanley Road	Yellow
6	St Andrew Street and Goldenacre	?
7	Surgeon's Hall and Newcraighall	Blue
8	Craiglockhart and Juniper Green	Red
9	Waverley Bridge, Murrayfield and Corstorphine	Brown

In early 1921 there was a prolonged strike in the mining industry and to save coal Tollcross power station was adapted to burn oil fuel, and some early morning cars were replaced by buses. Some charabancs were temporarily converted to lorries to assist in moving coal and ten buses were loaned to the War Department. From 9 May car services were curtailed, and the Grange cable was stopped from 13 May to 10 June, with the Mound route buses temporarily extended to Marchmont as a replacement. All services returned to normal from 14 June.

Further expansion of bus services continued with a Wednesday, Saturday and Sunday afternoon service from the Mound to Cramond via Barnton starting 18 April 1921. The fare was 8d, a bright brown ticket being used. The buses, if full, often returned direct via Quality Street, Davidson's Mains. In those days a good deal of liberty was sometimes taken en route, but it appears that this service was at that time being operated without the requisite licence, which resulted in a complaint from the SMT Co. On 20 June the Council decided to operate this service daily. The Magistrates offered a stance in George Street, but buses continued to run from and to the Mound and eventually the Mound stance was agreed. The route was now via Corbiehill Road, in both directions, numbered 11, with a red side window board. The fare was reduced to 5d.

When tarring was in progress on Queensferry Road it was usual for buses to divert by Orchard Brae and Craigleith Road, or occasionally by Ravelston Terrace and Queensferry Terrace. In the spring of 1922, during repairs at the Dean Bridge, Belford

Approaching the end for cable cars at Gorgie. Car 119 on route 2 is working under the newly-erected overhead in Gorgie Road at Delhaig. (EOC)

Road was used. The SMT Co's drivers generally followed these diversions too.

Another afternoon route on Saturdays and Sundays from Seafield to Portobello start-ed on 18 June 1921. It ran all day every day from 29 June as number 10 (which was dis-played as X). In September this was extended to Bernard Street and from 19 February 1923, to Niddrie crossroads (Milton Road). As traffic was normally light, some buses were altered to front entrance (beside the driver), who thus collected fares from passen-gers as they boarded. A tour around Arthur's Seat and a longer circular suburban tour were added to the 1921 summer season.

An innovation in 1922 was two AEC open-top double deck buses of the latest London 'S' type. Their licences precluded use on the Mound, Hanover Street, Frederick Street, east of the Tron church, and also the Cramond route, because of the steep hills or low bridges. The starting point for the tours was transferred from the Mound to the south side of St Andrew Square in April 1922.

While all this was going on the cable car services were being improved by the rebuild-ing of several open-top cars with new top covers. Other changes were made, in an endeavour to simplify the system and reduce costs. The auxiliary cables had always been a major source of trouble (as they were relatively easily dislodged from their pulleys).

Completion of overhead wiring of the first section to be undertaken, Pilrig to Nether Liberton, just a few days prior to the commencement of electric operation. At the foot of North Bridge, facing Register House and the Wellington statue, are the first two tower wagons. SG5077, on the left is a 1922 Tilling-Stevens, WS194 on the right a Halley formerly of Leith Corporation dating back to 1914. A Sunday morning, to judge by the absence of other traffic. (EOC)

Experiments were made and it was found that satisfactory operation could be obtained by leading the main cables round the curves, the cars proceeding with the gripper slightly open thus reducing speed. Accordingly the auxiliary cables from Leith Street to Princes Street and to North Bridge were removed and the main cable taken from its tunnel and put in place under the slot from Leith Street to North Bridge. The third auxiliary cable from Princes Street to North Bridge had to remain in use, but it is not clear what provision was made for cars proceeding from Princes Street to Leith Street (number 9 service). It would seem that a long fly-shunt was required. This arrangement left the trailing crossover at the foot of the North Bridge without cable power, and in order to maintain facilities for turning cars back towards Nether Liberton, a facing crossover was added, making a scissors crossing, worked both ways by gravity. The main cable slipping through the partly open grippers in these arrangements did not cause undue wear, and the practice was extended where possible. It seems probable that the auxiliary cable was removed and the main cable also extended round the curve at Salisbury Place junction (also perhaps at London Road junction and Haymarket, but not, apparently, at Kings Theatre junction). The Craiglockhart, Grange, and Murrayfield cables were now speeded up to 10½ mph. The crossover at the east end of Morrison Street was removed at this time and the practice of running the Gorgie cars to that point, when there was a stoppage of the Princes Street cable, ceased. Extra cars were put on between Post Office and Piershill from 3 November 1921.

Much welding of track joints was undertaken by the 'Thermit' process in 1920 and 1921, and the Sandberg process of hardening the surface of the rails was also utilised. Some of the Morrison Street rails were lifted at this time and used for repairs elsewhere. On the Leith section an enlargement of the depot was undertaken. Electric and cable tracks were connected up at Pilrig, a triangular double junction being formed, and a single line was laid up Dryden Street to the rear entrance of Shrubhill depot.

In April 1921 Mr Pilcher submitted a detailed Report on his plans for the first stage of electrification with poles and overhead equipment from Pilrig to Nether Liberton, and along Grange Road to Churchhill. Picardy Place to St Andrew Street, and London Road to Abbeyhill were also equipped. The old cast-iron centre poles for lighting in Leith Walk south of Pilrig were replaced by tramway centre poles uplifted from Junction Street and Commercial Street (complete with their bases bearing the Leith coat-of-arms). The Electricity Department now had 550 volts DC power available at McDonald Road, Cowgate, and Causewayside substations, and feeder cables were laid and the rails bonded for return current. New crossovers for electric cars were laid at Surgeons Hall and Newington Station. At this time the plans to electrify the whole tramway system faced opposition from a section of the public who advocated delay, in the hope that better buses would be forthcoming. However, on 29 December 1921 a special meeting of the Town Council decided to proceed with the electrification.

Chapter 2

ELECTRIFICATION AND THE END OF THE CABLE SYSTEM

The inauguration of electric cars in Edinburgh to and from the Leith system ending the Pilrig 'muddle' of the previous twenty-two years, was arranged for 20 June 1922. At noon that day, the official first electric car, number 123, with Lord Provost Hutchison and a select party aboard, came up from Leith, and amidst a large crowd of spectators, broke a blue ribbon at Pilrig to proceed on to the former cable system. All went decorously until the car reached the University where it became surrounded by students determined to get aboard. As they had no official invitation, they felt slighted. In the melee which developed bags of flour were flung and some of the councillors and their friends suffered. Police appeals were unheeded and the car proceeded to Nether Liberton with difficulty, carrying an augmented and unauthorised load including a large number on the roof! Some injuries were suffered and there was a Court sequel at which it appeared the students had felt aggrieved at their exclusion from the original select party.

Service cars followed from Leith and as each one went into service between Nether Liberton and Stanley Road via Pilrig Street route 7, and between Churchhill and Stanley Road via Junction Street, route 11, a corresponding cable car ran into Shrubhill depot. The Murrayfield, Craiglockhart, and Marchmont cars were turned at Waverley Steps, or

Official party, 20 June 1922, at Leith Depot before starting the first through journey. R Stuart Pilcher is in the centre of the photograph in front of the right hand saloon window pillar. (AWB Collection)

St Andrew Street, but the Braids and Gorgie ones continued – via York Place – to Pilrig. The service on London Road to Abbeyhill was replaced by electric cars, 15 running to Salisbury Place, and 16 to St Andrew Street (via York Place). The Granton Circle cars were extended up to St Andrew Street (via York Place) and numbered 13 and 14 on the outer and inner circuit. The Seafield to Stanley Road service was altered to run from Seafield to Nether Liberton, and numbered 12, and 'part-day'* cars

The Pilrig scene at mid-day on 20 June 1922 when car 123 with the official party came up from Leith Depot to cross the former boundary into Edinburgh, ending the Pilrig change from electric to cable car. Large crowds gathered to witness the event. (EOC)

ran between Newington Station and Bernard Street or Newhaven, numbered 17. To compensate for the withdrawn Seafield-Stanley Road facilities a 1d transfer ticket was made available between Bonnington Toll and Foot of Leith Walk. This was available until February 1951, many years after transfers generally were withdrawn. Other fares on the Leith part of the system were now revised in line with the Edinburgh section, stages being extended and the 1½d, 2½d, 3½d and 4½d values discarded. Further transfer tickets were issued to cover cable through services temporarily withdrawn, and these were available where necessary until the conversion scheme was complete.

Other than one or two minor mishaps the electric cars replaced the old cable cars successfully, and the Liberton cable was stopped at 3.55pm. This event was celebrated by a banquet in the City Chambers, at which Councillor Goalen was able to remark that he 'was proud the first up-to-date tramcar in Edinburgh started from Leith!'. The old rivalry was far from dead.

* Part-day cars usually ran from about 7.0 to 9.0 am and then from about midday until about 6.30 pm, entailing a split shift for their crews. On Saturdays they continued to run all evening.

The third route 7 car also made its way through crowds, but was followed up Leith Walk by a less prepossessing former Leith car. (EOC)

During the next few nights alterations were made to the remaining cables. The main Princes Street cable was altered to run direct between Tollcross and Waverley without diverting to Haymarket, also eliminating the auxiliary cable at the West End, while the Murrayfield cable was extended from Haymarket to the West End. The Princes Street cable was now extended down Leith Street to Pilrig to replace the discarded Liberton cable. Cable services 2 and 4 were transferred from York Place to Leith Street and services 1, 6 and 9 now terminated at Waverley Steps. The York Place cable was thus out of use also and the Shrubhill power station was closed down completely. The Tollcross power station's Princes Street cable thus extend-

The scene in Clerk Street at the top of Rankeillor Street with the official car taken over by university students, 'incensed' by being omitted from the official party! Most were good humoured but scuffles broke out and some injuries ensued. Court appearance was the consequence for the ringleaders. (AWB Collection)

ed gave a means of getting cable cars to Shrubhill depot at night, and also continuing a through service between Leith Walk and the West End.

An unusual arrangement was adopted at Waverley Steps where most of the cable cars now reversed. A facing crossover was put in between the junctions facing North Bridge where cable cars coming up from Pilrig to Princes Street crossed, with the cable, to the 'wrong' line then re-gained the normal line along with the cable at the Waverley Steps crossover. The Grange cable may have also been shortened, at the top of Marchmont Road.

Residents on the former Northern routes were vociferous with complaints about the noise and vibration caused by the buses, which were generally unpopular, with no little justification. One claimed damages for ornaments being broken by the shaking. Mr Pilcher successfully fitted pneumatic tyres to one Leyland running on the Comely Bank route, and arrangements were made to extend this improvement to further buses. Meanwhile an 8 mph speed limit was applied in Inverleith Row where, due to the nature of the ground, the effects seem to have been particularly marked. But more satisfaction

For the return journey law and order prevailed with members of the constabulary taking a precarious seat on the roof of the tram car! By this time it has lost its route number plate. The Minto Street scene is observed with some amusement by the conductor of a passing SMT bus. (AWB Collection)

was found in the pressing on of the electrification of the Broughton Street – Goldenacre route. This was completed, with a new connection to the old Leith tracks in Ferry Road, opening on 28 August 1922. The new electric service was Salisbury Place to Granton – number 8. With the introduction of the Broughton Street electric service, the No 3 bus was curtailed at Canonmills, the portion of No 5 between West End and Stanley Road abandoned, and No 6 withdrawn. About this time the No 7 tram service was altered to run to Stanley Road via Junction Street, the No 11 taking the Pilrig Street route. On 24 August the Nether Liberton route was extended the short distance to Liberton Dams.

The scheme of conversion was now proceeding rapidly. Part of the Shrubhill depot was converted to an orthodox set of tracks though the old traverser was fitted with an electric motor and retained to give access to the body-building and paint shops on the south side. Redundant cable cars were speedily being rebuilt and fitted with electric trucks. Some did not get top covers but nearly all were provided with vestibuled platforms and balconies enclosing the stairs. Work also proceeded on poles and overhead equipment from Shandwick Place to Murrayfield and Gorgie.

Princes Street presented the greatest problem. Since the beginning of the year a fierce controversy raged. Mr Pilcher recommended new tracks on the gardens (south) side as the clearance between the cable tracks was insufficient to allow erection of centre poles. This did not find favour however and after several acrimonious meetings the Council decided that centre poles would be the best solution. To many this was sacrilege and, led by the Cockburn Association, many bodies opposed the application to the Ministry of Transport (whose approval was required for any use of centre poles). A 'Citizens Protection Committee' showed films of the conduit system in operation in London and

Shrubhill cable power station was very quickly closed down to allow for the building's conversion. Cable car access was maintained by extending one of the Tollcross cables. This allowed, for a few months, the sight of cable and electric cars operating together on Leith Walk. These two cars – both Brown Marshall build – show the transformation wrought by reconstruction. Little other than the saloon remained and the appearance became that of a thoroughly modern smart, uncluttered, electric tram. Electric car 159 is on service 12, Seafield to Liberton, the cable car running to Braids. The scene at the Elm Row junction with London Road records the distinctive Georgian architecture of Leopold Place. (EOC)

Thermit welding being undertaken on the old cable tracks in Princes Street. To avoid traffic interruption this – on the south side track only – was carried out at night. Since there was yet no available traction power, the generators of the Tilling-Stevens petrol-electric tower wagons were used. (EOC)

urged its adoption in Princes Street, while Basset-Lowke's model shop in Frederick Street had a model tram running round in their window with overhead wire on centre poles. A question was asked in Parliament. The Ministry of Transport held a public enquiry in the city on 29, 30 and 31 March 1922, at which many well-known personages gave evidence, those representing amenity or motoring interests being against centre poles, with others speaking for. On 10 April the Government announced in the House of Commons its acceptance of the enquiry Commission's recommendation, *viz* that centre poles be sanctioned. A special slender one-piece tapered pole with short bracket arms and scroll-work was designed, also carrying street-lighting lanterns, parallel with the tracks. Few could doubt that this was indeed an elegant solution. To effect the conversion was, however, no simple matter but Mr Pilcher devised a well thought out scheme. All overhead equipment was ready and anchored at Shandwick Place and Waverley, thus over Saturday night and Sunday morning, of 21-22 October 1922 the great change-over was undertaken.

As much work as possible was done in advance; the south track was bonded; holes for the new centre poles were excavated and the poles themselves, painted complete with bracket arms and fittings (except the street-lighting gear), were laid out along the street. Lengths of light tramway track of low grooved rails on flat steel plates were also assembled. Then on the chosen night, which fortunately proved dry, some 300 men watched by a large crowd of interested spectators, set to work even before the last Tollcross cable car passed at midnight. The task was formidable and Pilcher supervised personally. The old cable was shortened at the foot of Lothian Road, and the redundant machinery cleared out of the pits. The temporary rails were laid on the street surface clear of the old cable track, on the north side. These temporary rails had to lead back on to and off the old track past the islands, arranged by short ramp rails leading into the grooves of the ordinary rails (could the islands not have been removed in advance?). Meanwhile the thirty new centre poles were planted into their holes and concreted at twenty-minute intervals. The first two at the Mound and West End were cheered by the crowd, shortly after midnight. Then the trolley wires were run out, connected at each end and tensioned. On the same night the tracks below Dalry Road railway bridge were lowered to increase clearance. Food and refreshments were of course laid on for the well-organised workers. About 9.30am on Sunday morning the first electric cars were able to run out over the old cable track and on to Robertson Avenue on the Gorgie route. Returning eastwards along

The night of 21-22 October 1922 was chosen for the change-over, with all the new centre poles put into place, overhead strung, energised, and a temporary set of rails laid on the north side. This view, looking west from Hanover Street, is by necessity a time exposure which cannot do justice to the frenetic activity. It is, however, an historic record which has never before been reproduced. (EOC)

On the Sunday morning large crowds assembled to witness the first cars. Here 106 east-bound opposite South Charlotte Street takes cautiously to the temporary track, the driver watching from his platform and the conductor with the trolley rope in his hand. On the left can be seen two of the buses which were in reserve in case of difficulty. (EOC)

Princes Street they had to negotiate the temporary track. There were some hitches during the day until this settled down. The achievement received widespread and well-deserved praise, vying in the news with a contemporary political crisis.

The Tramways Department was now ahead of the Electricity Department. The Murrayfield feeder from Dewar Place substation and those from the new Robertson Avenue substation were incomplete, hence services initially provided along Princes Street were:

1   Liberton Dams to Haymarket
2   North Junction Street to Robertson Avenue
3   Waverley to Robertson Avenue
5   Abbeyhill to Shandwick Place
6   Churchhill via Grange Road to Haymarket
9   Goldenacre via Broughton Street to Shandwick Place
16 Stanley Road via Junction Street to Shandwick Place

The 13 and 14 Granton Circles were also extended to Shandwick Place, and service 12 Seafield and Liberton Dams was altered to run between Seafield and Haymarket. A part-day service, numbered 19, was run from Newington Station to Shandwick Place. Bus services were put on from Robertson Avenue to Gorgie, and Haymarket to Murrayfield. When 'juice' became available these ended and the trams extended, services 1 and 12 to Murrayfield and the 2 to Gorgie, the former on 3 December and the

Also photographed on Sunday 22 October was car 117, one of the first west-bound (unfortunately the clock on the NB Hotel cannot be distinguished to record the exact time). Leyland SG2140 is on a special service from Post Office to Haymarket operated for that day only. (EOC)

latter on 21 December. Braids, Craiglockhart, and Marchmont Road cable cars turned at the foot of Lothian Road.

Meantime the old north side track in Princes Street was torn up as quickly as possible and a new permanent track constructed the prescribed distance from the centre poles, the passenger islands being altered to accommodate this. The job was accomplished within a fortnight, and the temporary track removed. The space between the tracks was increased by just two feet. The temporary track was later used to form temporary crossovers for single-line working, during subsequent relaying work elsewhere on the system.

The Corporation still declined to provide a bus service from the city centre to Juniper Green, but when the SMT Co started its service to Balerno via Juniper Green from 15 July 1922, the Corporation, four days later, commenced a direct service from Waverley Bridge to Juniper Green via Slateford (fare 6d). Numbered 8, it ran at irregular intervals, the old route 8 from Craiglockhart tram terminus renumbered 6 and now terminating at Colinton. Also on 22 October, the Goldenacre to Tollcross buses were extended to Bruntsfield Place.

Before we leave 1922 it should be recorded that from 9 November bus service 5 was extended via King's Stables Road and Grassmarket to Surgeon's Hall. Results were disappointing on this seemingly useful 'short-cut' and it lasted only one month.

On 15 December 1922 the Edinburgh Corporation Order Confirmation Act 1922 was

Shrubhill works operated flat-out converting cable trams to electric operation. Much preparatory work was done, but the final transformation had to be done rapidly. In the heavy repair shop at the end of May 1922 car 159 is lifted (by hand operated jacks) to allow removal of cable bogies and their replacement by a new electric truck. In the background a former open-top car is being more radically reconstructed. (EOC)

authorised, with provision for a tramway down Easter Road, with triangular junctions at both ends, plus a long siding in Wheatfield Road for football cars to shift crowds from Tynecastle. Neither of these was constructed, though the latter materialised, in a different form, in 1924. A proposal for a line along George Street was rejected, as were powers to permit the Corporation to purchase the Musselburgh Company's tramway system.

The next conversion actioned was West End to Marchmont Road, and on 21 January

Sometimes the degree of reconstruction was so great as to make one wonder if it was, in fact, justified. Here a cable car of Brown-Marshall build is being converted, with new corner pillar and much of the saloon bulkhead to be replaced. After serving some twenty years as a cable car, it would probably give a further 15-20 years as an electric car. (EOC)

1923 service 6 was extended thus reverting to its cable route. A new service from Bernard Street to Marchmont Road via West End (18) was also commenced. At this time all other services turning temporarily at Shandwick Place (5, 9, 13, 14, 16, and 19) were extended to Tollcross. Only the Braids and Craiglockhart cables remained working from Tollcross.

The last half-mile of the Craiglockhart route was mostly interlaced track, and it was decided to remove this on electrification. Accordingly cable cars were withdrawn and replaced by a temporary bus service on 18 March 1923. On that date electric services 13 and 14 were extended to Braids, and services 15, 16, and 19 to Morningside Station, replacing the cable cars from Tollcross. At this time the 5 and 15 services exchanged numbers.

Tollcross power station closed and the redundant cable cars, less grippers, were towed to Shrubhill for reconstruction. Tollcross depot was now drastically altered. The old entrance facing Thornybauk was built up and the floor level lowered. The single track round Thornybauk was extended round West Tollcross to a trailing junction with the out-going Braids line. The facing connection at the Thornybauk end was removed and the line reconstructed as single. A new corner entrance to the depot was made nearer Tollcross and two fans of tracks provided inside; one set at right angles to the street, the other parallel to the street. The depot reopened on 3 February 1924, service 18 cars being first to use it, followed soon by services 15 and 10.

Electric service 9 from Goldenacre, and a new service from Waverley only, 10, were run to Craiglockhart Station from 15 April 1923, then extended to the old Craiglockhart

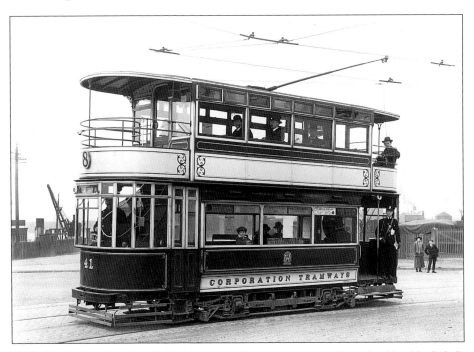

The finished product from Shrubhill looked very well, a credit to the workforce. Car 41, originally built by Brown-Marshall, but with top cover supplied by Craven, was placed in service on 21 October 1922. It is seen shortly thereafter at Granton Square, terminus of service 8 to Salisbury Place. The car still has the cable-style route number and does not yet have a 'stairhead' route colour light box. (EOC)

The scene as viewed from Seaview Terrace, Joppa in the Spring of 1923 when the tracks of the Edinburgh and Musselburgh tramways were joined to permit through operation from the Post Office to Port Seton – a run of some ten miles. (EOC)

terminus soon afterwards. The location became known as Happy Valley, after a small private amusement park there. At Ardmillan Terrace an east facing junction to the Slateford route was constructed and electric cars reintroduced on 29 April 1923 (service 4) from Waverley to Slateford. Bus service 2 was then withdrawn but it was revived 'part-day' from 17 December, now as service 4.

The worst effects of post-war prices had now passed; costs were reduced, and a revision of fares giving longer stages was introduced on 21 January 1923.

Widening of Corstorphine Road was put in hand, and the tramway extension authorised in 1916 constructed. West of Pinkhill the widening, to the north side, was considerable, and included a new entrance to the Zoo. A third track siding was provided on the incoming line here, with a crossover beyond. The next crossover was east of

Probably photographed on Saturday 23 June 1923 to record the changeover to electric cars on the final cable route to Joppa. On the final day as electric cars were introduced, the cable cars were correspondingly withdrawn to avoid any unseemly or rowdy displays. The 'Dick Kerr' cable cars were amongst the last to be converted. (EOC)

Station Road; the terminus was just east of Templeland Road. This extension was inspected by Colonel Pringle for the Ministry of Transport on 20 June 1923. Service 1 was extended to Station Road that day, and to the new terminus shortly afterwards. Bus service 9 was then withdrawn, the two double-deckers used transferring to route 5. Service 12 was extended to Corstorphine about October.

What was probably the last significant breakdown of the cable system occurred on 20 April when the Portobello cable stopped for 1½ hours during the morning. This was a Musselburgh Races day, but cars were running again in time for the race-going crowds.

Electrification of the Portobello route was also in hand, and on 20 May 1923 services 5 and 15 were extended from Abbeyhill to Piershill. By September service 4 cars were extended from Waverley via Leith Street and London Road to terminate at Piershill also. An agreement was made with the Musselburgh and District Electric Light and Traction Co Ltd for through running of Corporation and Company cars between Waterloo Place and Port Seton and the tracks and overhead were connected at Joppa.

On Saturday night 23 June 1923 the last cable car finally trundled into Portobello depot. The engines were stopped and cable traction in the city ceased. To avoid the scenes which had greeted the first electric cars, the new electric cars had been introduced gradually throughout the day, hence the occasion was almost unnoticed. The following day electric cars ran from Waterloo Place to Joppa, to Musselburgh Town Hall, or through to Port Seton, services 20, 21, and 22 respectively. Company cars shared in the latter service. During the last two or three days of cable operation, a few electric service 20 cars had been run between the cable cars and Musselburgh cars had made trial runs

The first through car on 24 June 1923 to Port Seton was refurbished Company car 15 – repainted in two shades of green and advertising 'Port Seton for Sea Breezes'. Corporation car 56 behind was converted in November of the previous year. Work on the track join-up is not quite yet complete. A shelter was provided for waiting passengers, a facility much enjoyed by courting couples. (EOC)

The last cable power station, at Portobello, was closed down on 23 June. This record photograph was probably taken the next day. (EOC)

to Waterloo Place. The Musselburgh Company's old single-deck cars were not allowed on the Edinburgh system but continued to provide a local service on their own tracks. Conductors of through cars carried both Corporation and Company tickets for use on the

The detritus of the former cable system was gathered as scrap, unwanted relics of a time-expired feat of Victorian engineering ingenuity. (EOC)

respective lines, plus a set of tickets covering through journeys, generally similar to the Musselburgh issue.

An Edinburgh electric car had been towed to Joppa for a trial over the line to Port Seton on 26 February, as a result of which some additional span wires were installed. Even so, the Musselburgh overhead layout precluded use of trolley ropes, so Edinburgh cars used beyond Joppa had the ropes removed and were provided with a hooked bamboo pole carried in clips on the side frame. A hook was provided at each end of the roof to hold the trolley as required. All cars allocated to Portobello depot were so fitted, and when additional cars were run on summer weekends, their trolley-ropes were tied round the boom, and the crew just hoped for the best. Shortly only ex-cable cars were used over the Musselburgh line, but later a number of ex-Leith cars were posted to Portobello depot, as the lack of headlights on the Port Seton service was a problem on the sparsely lit route. Post Office mail bags between Portobello and Edinburgh were carried by tram until after World War 2, and another familiar sight was Fisherrow fisherwomen, their creels travelling on the front platform.

An old horse-bus route was revived by a new half-hourly motor bus service from 18 January 1923, Mound to Blackford Hill via George IV Bridge, Causewayside, Argyle Place, Marchmont Crescent, and Kilgraston Road. This was numbered 12, with a white window board. From 4 June 1923 this was extended to Morningside Station. After Corstorphine service 9 ended, service 12 was renumbered 9. From 4 February 1924 the route was extended to the west end of Morningside Drive. Another old horse bus route was revived by a bus service numbered 2 from 1 November 1923 from Cameron Toll to Haymarket, via Preston Street, Clerk Street, Lauriston Place, Bread Street, and Morrison Street.

A further reduction of fares was effected on 28 October 1923 when the length of stages was considerably increased.

The Northern and Mound tram routes were the last to be electrified, much to the residents' disgust. The Comely Bank line was connected from Frederick Street eastwards into Princes Street. Being passed by the Ministry of Transport, service 24 from St Andrew Street to Comely Bank commenced on 18 November 1923, replacing bus service 4. The Hanover Street and Mound routes were both connected to the Princes Street tracks facing one another. At Tollcross the Mound route tracks were extended to cross the Marchmont route tracks (instead of joining them as before), and they then joined the Home Street line. Service 23 from Goldenacre to Tollcross via Hanover Street and the Mound commenced on 8 June 1924, replacing bus service 3. This was soon extended (part day) to Bruntsfield Place. For this and the Comely Bank route the Ministry of Transport stipulated that cars used must be fitted with mechanically operated track brakes. A trial was made in November 1922 and the first cars fitted were used on service 9 before the Comely Bank route opened. Drivers on these two Northern routes were considered to have a greater degree of responsibility and for many years were paid an extra ½d per hour wages. This differential was eventually abandoned. A number of specially strong cast steel bollards were placed on the pavement at the sharp curve on the Mound, designed to stop a car going over the edge in the event of derailment. Fortunately they were never called upon to perform for a tram, but skidding buses and other vehicles have been saved.

Conversion of the cable car system to electric traction and the integration of the Edinburgh and Leith tramway systems was now complete.

Chapter 3

CONSOLIDATION AND EXPANSION

On 1 June 1924 some changes were made to tram services. The junctions at Churchhill and Marchmont Road having been remade, service 6 became the one-time familiar Marchmont Circle, (Marchmont Road, Tollcross, Princes Street, Bridges, Marchmont Road – in either direction), while the 13 and 14 Granton Circles instead of proceeding to Braids, returned to the Post Office via Grange Road and the Bridges. Service 13 on the outer rails of the Granton Circle took the inner rails of the Churchhill Circle, thus forming a 'figure-eight' route, (Service 14 operated in the opposite direction). Service 11 became Stanley Road to Braids via Pilrig Street and Princes Street, and service 16 was extended from Morningside Station to Braids. Service 5 was extended from Salisbury Place (part-day) to Churchhill. On 2 June service 3 was extended (part day) to Gorgie, becoming all day from 1 July 1925. Service 17 now ran to Trinity Bridge but on Saturday afternoons until about 1928 it was replaced by un-numbered services between Liberton and Stanley Road via Pilrig Street, and from Restalrig Road to Salisbury Place. The extension up Liberton Brae to Liberton crossroads, authorised in the 1920 Order, had been completed and the number 1 service extended to the new terminus on 28 April 1924.

As the Musselburgh Company was short of double deck trams for the route up to Waterloo Place, they bought three old cars from Sheffield Corporation. One of these is seen reversing at the GPO terminus. Note that before the passenger loading islands were built in Waterloo Place, passengers queued on the footpath and then had to run the gauntlet of traffic – even then not inconsiderable – to board the tram. (AWB Collection)

A piece of ground was bought east of Westfield Road and a siding for football match cars laid there instead of in Wheatfield Road. This was eventually the site for a depot serving the west side of the city. To keep reversing cars off the 'main line', terminal sidings were formed in Belhaven Terrace at Morningside Station, and Northfield Broadway at Piershill. These were constructed under the general authority to provide passing places, sidings, contained in the original Acts, as were various Princes Street connections. Additional passenger islands were constructed in Princes Street and elsewhere, while neat small cast-iron poles carried stop signs where these were placed away from overhead or lighting standards.

These first five years of Corporation operation saw much expansion. All cable routes had been electrified and extensions constructed. Practically all cable cars had been converted, Shrubhill being fully occupied on this work, hence all new cars had been supplied by outside builders. A start was now made on new construction at Shrubhill. Bus services were firmly established, covering 35 route miles, the tramways extending to 36 route miles. Post-war housing schemes were under construction at Slateford Road, and Northfield, and the city's road traffic was increasing. Comparative figures of passengers carried are given in Appendix 4. In addition to the service number, tramcars showed a coloured light route identification at night.

Tram services operating in July 1924 were:

	Route	Lights	Window-board
1	Liberton to Corstorphine	Red/Blue	Red
2	North Junction Street to Gorgie	Blue/Blue	Blue
3	Waverley to Gorgie	Blue/White	Blue
4	Piershill to Slateford	White/Blue	Brown
5	Churchhill to Piershill	Red/Green	Green
6	Marchmont Circle	White/Red	White
7	Liberton Dams to Stanley Road	Red/Red	Red
8	Granton to Salisbury Place	Red/Yellow	Yellow
9	Goldenacre to Craiglockhart	Yellow/Yellow	Yellow
10	Waverley to Craiglockhart	White/Yellow	Yellow
11	Braids to Stanley Road	Red/White	White
12	Seafield to Corstorphine	Yellow/Blue	Red
13	Churchhill and Granton Circle	White/Green	Green
14	Churchhill and Granton Circle	Yellow/Green	Blue
15	Morningside to Piershill	Green/White	Green
16	Braids to Stanley Road	Green/Green	Green
17	Newington to Trinity Bridge	White/White	White
18	Marchmont to Bernard Street	Yellow/White	White
19	Newington to Morningside	White/White	White
20	Post Office to Joppa	Red/Red	Brown
21	Post office to Musselburgh Town Hall	Green/Green	Green
22	Post Office to Port Seton	Blue/Blue	Blue
23	Goldenacre to Tollcross	Green/Yellow	White
24	Waverley to Comely Bank	Red/Red	Green
-	Liberton and Stanley Road	Yellow/Red	White with red letters
-	Restalrig Road and Salisbury Place	White/White	White

For a considerable time the 'Northern' and Mound routes were operated by replacement buses, but there was never any intention that this was anything other than a temporary expedient. Here Leyland number 24, SG1651 – now on pneumatic tyres – turns from Princes Street into Frederick Street, displaying route number 4. (EOC)

Until the introduction of service 4, colours of the 14 were White/Blue. Most services ran at ten-minute frequency. Princes Street was used by no less than fifteen services.

Timetables, fare-tables, maps, and other aids to passengers were issued. A Rule Book was issued to staff in 1923. The strict disciplinary regulations of earlier times no longer applied, and the contents were more in the nature of instructions pertaining to electrical equipment and handling of motor buses. A staff magazine was produced quarterly from 1923, taking the title 'Speed' three years later. Its editor was Mr E. O. Catford

At this stage record has to be made of constructional details of the electric system. As

Believed to be a photograph of the Board of Trade inspection of the Tollcross to Mound route, when particular attention was paid to the final descent. At the Inspector's behest 'pawls' (or immovable posts) were erected to prevent a runaway car going over into the railway cutting below. Only when this was complete was public service commenced. The car is 'Dick Kerr' number 209. (EOC)

The ever-changing but always busy West End scene c.1924. The procession of converted cable trams is joined by unique former Leith car 265 with its distinctive flat dash. Car 10 en route to Gorgie on the southern track is running on the old cable track, complete with centre slot while the track to the left (north) has been reconstructed. (AWB Collection)

the cable tracks wore out they were re-laid with heavier rails of BS7 section, and the conduit and slot were then removed. This was a gradual process, and a short length remained at the end of Waterloo Place even after the electric service ceased there in 1954. When the roadway here was re-constructed this was lifted and re-set (albeit slightly out of position) as a permanent reminder of the cable system.

As has been mentioned, centre poles were used for the overhead equipment in Princes Street and Leith Walk. Generally elsewhere span-wire construction was used, with wall rosettes being used wherever possible (including some unlikely positions). There was however one side bracket arm pole at the short single-line outside the Theatre Royal. Poles used on the North Bridge were held in special base-sockets flanged to the bridge. An effort was made to minimise pull-offs, and the general overhead layout suffered somewhat in consequence. Small and medium poles were used equipped with tasteful finial, cross-arm and scrollwork. Copper trolley wire of round 4/0 section was used initially, but as it had a short life, cadmium copper alloy was introduced followed by a much harder bronze wire for the busiest parts.

Section insulators at the statutory half-mile intervals (or less according to the layout) were of the air-gap type and provided with pavement pillars from which four cables led up inside the pole and along the span wire. These pillar-boxes were equipped with four switches for the side-feed cables and two larger switches for incoming supply cables (though in many cases of course these were idle as the box was not a supply point). There was also a choke coil and lightning arrestor. Old tramway rails were sometimes buried and used to form negative feeders. On the overhead, facing 'frogs' were of the

Braids terminus with former cable car 184 on route 16 and ex Leith Corporation 246 running on route 13 to Granton. In mid 1924 the 13 and 14 terminus was removed from Braids and these routes thereafter took a circular route by Churchhill. The removal of the cable terminal pit and pulleys is underway, the scene observed by three young enthusiasts (?). (EOC)

'poker' type, a short movable tongue being directed to the turnout by the hanging 'poker' being lifted by the car's trolley-boom if it passed at an angle. This somewhat 'Heath Robinson' arrangement had to be precisely positioned, slightly ahead of the track points, so that the trolley-boom lifted the 'poker' neatly if the car had entered the turnout. To allow reversing back into depots *etc*, 'shunt frogs' were used, with a spring-controlled tongue that could be trailed through.

One of Edinburgh's many green 'lungs' – the Meadows – where the great International Exhibition of 1886 was held on the area to the left of this photograph. Car 7 on a working to the Post Office is followed by 98 on route 6, the Marchmont Circle, which ran its prescribed 'clockwork' circle without alteration for over thirty years. (EOC)

Because of several low bridges, trolley bases were of a special low pattern, and the tension exerted on the wire by the trolley varied from zero at roof level to about 25 or 28lb at normal height, then to zero when free in the air.

Automatic trolley reversers were fitted up at Liberton, Stanley Road, Gorgie, and Churchhill terminals. When the car reversed, the trolley was diverted back on to a 'Y' from which it then trailed in. They were found to be troublesome and all except that at Stanley Road were soon removed. This one remained in use until after the Second World War. More useful were the automatic point controllers provided at busier junctions except West End and St Andrew Street which were always manned by a points-boy with point 'poker', and at Register House, Mound/Hanover Street, and Frederick Street where electrically operated points were controlled by a boy from a switch-box on the footpath. All these automatic sets worked thus: if a driver wished to proceed straight ahead at the junction, he coasted while the trolley passed a 'skate' on the overhead; if he wished to diverge right or left he passed the 'skate' with power, using his handbrake to keep speed in check. 'Skates' used initially consisted of a complicated treadle arrangement which actuated a pair of fingers, one or other of which made contact feeding the requisite end of a solenoid in the ground connected to the point-rod. Another small solenoid mounted above the treadle was momentarily energised by the car's passage when drawing current. With many small exposed parts, these were inclined to give trouble, especially in winter. A simpler skate at Pilrig operated for the curve only, and a re-setting skate immediately beyond the curve ensured that the points were always set for the straight as the car approached.

Proposals for further extensions to the tramway system were advanced, and the

Corporation promoted the Edinburgh Corporation (Tramways *etc*) Confirmation Act 1924 (passed 1 August 1924). This authorised construction of the following tramways: Slateford terminus to Slateford village; Gorgie terminus via Chesser Avenue to join the foregoing; Bernard Street via Salamander Street to Seafield (with a triangular junction at Bernard Street); Craiglockhart terminus to Colinton; Melville Drive from Marchmont Road to Clerk Street; and George Street, which was envisaged as a useful relief to the growing volume of traffic on Princes Street. All were authorised, but the first three were never built, nor was an authorised connection from North Hanover Street eastwards to George Street. Consideration was also given to tramways in Fountainbridge, Dalkeith Road, and to Lochend; for extensions from Comely Bank to Cramond, and Braids to Hillend, but most were considered unjustified then. Braids-Hillend was revived some time later, and from 9 July 1924 a bus service was run, in summer, Wednesday, Saturday and Sunday afternoons 'weather permitting' from Braids car terminus to service the new Hillend Park on the east end of the Pentland Hills.

Construction of the Seafield to Kings Road line (authorised by the 1920 Act) was

under way, opening on 26 October 1924. Service 12 was extended to Kings Road, Portobello (described as Beach Portobello). The 'all-the-way' fare became 5d. Bus service 10 thereafter operated Bath Street, Portobello to Niddrie Cross Roads, later extended to Newcraighall. The original terminal stub at Seafield remained *in situ*. Other crossovers were at Craigentinny Avenue North and Kings Road.

Another track improvement was shortening the single line at Theatre Royal by extending the double track to south of York Place crossing. A double line connection was laid from York Place into Broughton Street, though this was not used for service traffic.

Something had to be done to service the grow-ing Lochend council

Car 78 takes the 'super elevated' curve leading from North St. Andrew Street round into York Place en route from Gorgie to North Junction Street. (EOC)

housing. From 26 October 1924 bus service 3 started, St David Street via York Place, Marionville Road, and Restalrig Road to Bernard Street (side board originally white, later yellow). It was normal to test the traffic levels with a bus service to determine if a tramway could be justified. Another new bus service, 12, white window board, started on 5 July 1925. This operated on a curious 60/30 minute time-table by one-man buses from Surgeon's Hall via Clerk Street, Newington, Lady Road, Craigmillar and Duddingston, to Portobello Town Hall. From 19 July 1925 early morning buses were run on Summer Sundays from Waterloo Place to Melville Street, Portobello for the benefit of bathers.

Passenger shelters were erected at various termini, including Port Seton. Portobello depot was now enlarged, by the conversion of the old engine-room (which was at a slightly lower level to the west of the main shed). Then, to serve the west services 2 and 3, a depot with three lyes, plus one outside, was built on the site of Westfield siding, known as Gorgie depot. It was opened on 12 August 1925, and later also operated services 1 and 4.

Early in 1925 work was commenced on the George Street bypass line, from Shandwick Place via Hope Street, George Street, and the north and south sides of St Andrew Square, with double track junctions at St Andrew Street. In George Street centre poles were used although span wires had been intended. Construction of the Melville Drive line was also in hand. This formed a triangular junction in Clerk Street. These two new routes opened on 19 July 1925, service 2 being diverted to cover George Street. A part-day service, 25, had been introduced between Newington Station and the Zoo on 4 August 1924 (later Restalrig Road and Zoo) and this was also diverted to run by George Street. The service colour, originally white, later became blue/yellow (white side board). Another service to use George Street was Comely Bank, its inward journey was diverted by George Street and the south side of St Andrew Square, thus avoiding reversal. The other services used the north side of St Andrew Square. The George Street route was much used for football match cars which ran round St Andrew Square on the 'outer' rail, loading on the south side for either Gorgie or Murrayfield. For the Melville Drive line a new service, 26 (colours green/red, and white window board), was added from Newington Station to West End, then by Princes Street and Bridges back to Newington Station, both ways round.

The Bonnington Terrace crossing on the old Leith system was redesigned about this time. Instead of each line becoming single over the crossing with single-line connections, double tracks were laid, including the two curves. Crossovers were provided at each side of both routes.

An innovation from 19 October 1925 was a bus service on two all-night routes. One bus ran hourly between the Foot of Leith Walk and Bruntsfield, and another between Salisbury Place and Ardmillan Terrace, meeting at Post Office. Fare to or from the Post Office was 4d; all the way 6d. It took some time for the public to appreciate this facility, but it became particularly popular with late dancers on Friday nights. The routes were suspended during the summer after 1 May 1926. Many more buses were now running on pneumatic tyres, and the results were such that it was agreed that these should become standard.

At this time the maximum speed authorised by the Ministry of Transport for the Edinburgh system was 16mph and it was thought this should be revised upwards. The maximum legal speed of motor buses was then still 12mph (no doubt frequently exceed-

The extension to Colinton Village ran on narrow tree lined roads and was built with a single track section, unusual for Edinburgh. The scene with the newly built line is captured here with car 33 near Redford Road. (EOC)

ed). A revision was sanctioned on 9 November 1925, providing for a maximum of 20mph on suitable stretches, with lesser figures for other specified lines. Only a few weeks earlier, on 17 October, a serious accident had occurred, but fortunately there were few such in the history of the tramway undertaking. On a Saturday afternoon with busy streets, a car coming down Ardmillan Terrace single line (apparently out of control), became derailed at the turnout on to the double line at the junction at the foot of the hill. Careering right across Gorgie Road it crashed into the wall of St Martin's Church, killing a boy and injuring six other people (two by jumping off the car).

Air-brakes operating on the car wheels instead of track-brakes were now being tried successfully, with the higher speeds planned. An experiment with a Fischer bow collector was tried on the Portobello route towards the end of 1925, a year of great development. As the overhead had to be adjusted to suit the path of the collector, the Portobello route (relatively straight) was used for the trial as the amount of work required was limited. However, if the complete system was to be modified – including the Princes Street centre poles – the cost would have been high. Cars 67 and 110 ran in service with the bow for only a few months.

Work had been proceeding on the Colinton extension, which opened on 21 March 1926, service 9 going to the new terminus, with service 10 extended to Craiglockhart Avenue. Near the terminus the track was laid over beside the south pavement at the beginning of Woodhall Road, with a short piece of single line past Inchdrewer House, where the ground could not be obtained for road widening. The interlaced former cable track between Lower Gilmore Place and Merchiston Park was relaid as double, the new outward track laid close to the pavement. The other similar section along Gilmore Place was however never doubled. With this extension bus service 6 from Craiglockhart ceased.

Doubling of the single line Slateford route was next undertaken, and again clearance between the incoming track and pavement was scanty east of Shandon Bridge. An interesting feature was a few yards of interlaced track, in order to provide room for a vehicle to park outside Messrs Lorimer & Clark's Caledonian brewery. On both these routes work started at the outer end and progressed inwards. The interlaced line in Strathearn Road was replaced by double line, but the Strathearn Place interlaced cable track was relaid as single. A proposal to form a kerbside loading loop at the foot of Lothian Road was turned down.

A Torchlight Tattoo at Dreghorn at the end of September 1926 attracted large crowds and a bus service (joint with SMT) was run from St Andrew Square to Redford Barracks at a 6d fare. Extra cars were run on the Colinton route but these were limited, as the ¼ sq.in feeder to Craiglockhart was unable to sustain the load, and the service was frequently interrupted. A ½ sq in feeder was subsequently laid to Craiglockhart Park (near the top of the hill) to ensure adequate power to the end of the route.

A new terminal siding was constructed in Merchiston Place for an extension of service 23, and a triangular junction formed at Churchhill. This enabled service 5 to be extended part-day, from 31 January 1927, to Morningside Station but with the forenoon and evening terminus remaining at Salisbury Place.

In April 1926 the town Council resolved to purchase the Industrial Hall in Annandale Street, built only a few years previously at a cost of £30,000, for its buses and motor vehicles. It was taken over in May 1926, bus use started on 10 July but lorries and other vehicles remained at Shrubhill. Henderson Row depot was vacated and became the

Police Traffic Department garage. This new large Central bus garage had disadvantages, particularly the main entrance and exit. These were not designed for vehicles and only single-deck buses could pass through, and even then with only a few inches clearance. These inconveniences persisted for several years. The 'pool' of motor cars which the Tramways Department maintained for the use of other Departments was located at Central Garage, and the Parcels Department transferred from St James' Square. A petrol tank with measuring pump mounted on a Vulcan lorry was used to refill buses at termini. Vehicles for expansion of bus services had hitherto been available from services replaced by trams, and no recent additions had been made to the fleet. Expansion now called for new buses and more modern types appeared. Included were four open-top double-deckers (which ran initially on solid tyres) used on service 5 together with the earlier two. These double-deckers carried a route board back and front, similar to the arrangement used in London. A similar scheme was applied to the old single-deck buses which received a board with the main points on the route alongside the front destination indicator. This was found inconvenient and soon ended.

1926 was the year of the General Strike, which started on Tuesday 4 May. Students and others manned cars and buses, and indeed enjoyed it. Many a tale of their experiences was later recounted. Fifty-four cars were run from Shrubhill that first day and all the buses were in use until about 6pm. Parts of Shrubhill workshops were transformed into a temporary dormitory for these volunteers, with pies and lemonade supplied. Those who essayed driving trams found it easy to learn. On 5 May cars or buses were run till 6 o'clock on most routes except in Leith. However, attacks on vehicles and crews increased in the afternoon and many cars and buses lost windows. Next day, Thursday, was similar and fewer cars ran. Trouble in the Canongate caused some buses to be with-

May 1926 and the General Strike saw the Heavy Repair Shop at Shrubhill turned into a dormitory for volunteer tram workers. Former Leith car 235 is in one corner, but of much greater significance to the temporary workforce are the beer barrels which line the back wall! (EOC)

drawn. However, on Friday and Saturday there was little trouble and more cars were run. No services ran on Sunday but 100 cars and all buses were out again on Monday, including some from Leith depot. Services were not attempted near the Docks. That day maintenance staff returned to work and the end of the strike was in sight. Many regular crews reported for work on Tuesday, Tollcross and Portobello depots opened and 150 cars ran, all services worked including Leith. The following day, 12 May, the strike was called off and full normal services resumed the next day.

New housing schemes were expanding and bus services were developed concurrently. Service 2 was extended from Haymarket to Ardmillan on 30 November 1925, and then on 12 August 1926 again extended via Balgreen Road, Saughtonhall Drive, and Murrayfield, back to Haymarket to continue its return. Those going the other way round the Saughtonhall loop carried service number 6. From 15 September 1927 these services were diverted from Lauriston Place and Lady Lawson Street to run via Forrest Road, Grassmarket, and West Port and later were extended to Craigmillar with a terminus at Mitchell Street. Service 4 was extended part-day to Longstone on 31 October 1926 and this became all day on 6 December. Service 5 was extended from Leith Docks via Charlotte Street (Leith), and Lochend Road to Sleigh Drive on 20 March 1927, and on 10 October at the other end from West End to Bread Street. On 10 October also, a new service, 14, with a brown window board, was inaugurated from the foot of Easter Road to Juniper Green, following most of the route of service 4. Another new part-day only service (13 with a green window board) started on 31 October 1927 from St David Street via Princes Street, Coates Crescent, Melville Street, Manor Place, Chester Street, Palmerston Place, Belford Road, and Ravelston Dykes to terminate at Murrayfield Road. Traffic was light and the one-man buses were used.

On the tramways, service 16 was diverted from Stanley Road to Granton Road Station from 11 July 1926. Service 9 was extended to Granton from 19 June 1927, while the 18 was extended from Bernard Street to a somewhat ambiguous 'Dock Gates' (the old North Leith LNER station). Service 25 was extended to Kings Road on Saturdays, and on Saturday evenings only extended also to Corstorphine terminus running via Princes Street.

Meantime further tramway extensions were proposed, and the Corporation's Provisional Act of 1927 authorised extensions from the Corstorphine terminus to 290 yards west of North Gyle farm; from Gorgie terminus to Saughton Road, (now Saughton Mains Street), including widening of the bridge over the Water of Leith; and from the Comely Bank terminus to a point just beyond Crewe Road. Part of the Corstorphine extension, as far as Drum Brae cross roads, was put in hand, opening on 5 April 1928.

In the summer of 1927 the Musselburgh company experienced severe competition from the new White Line bus service and on 1 August cut its fares to meet it. The new fares were: GPO to Hayweights 3d, to Levenhall 4d, to Prestonpans 5d, and to Port Seton 6d. Edinburgh accepted 2d as its share as far as Joppa. On 28 August there was a general reduction of fares on the Edinburgh system where 4d became the maximum fare, except for the complete Granton-Churchhill circle, which became 6d and some of the longer bus routes, (numbers 2, 4, 6 and 14) which retained a 5d fare.

The reduced fares did not help the Port Seton traffic, however, and the Musselburgh company decided to withdraw its cars and substitute buses. Consequently, on 1 March 1928, a supplementary agreement was concluded with the Corporation, whereby the Company resolved to lift the track beyond Levenhall, and cease to run cars. The

Company undertook to maintain the track and supply current as far as Levenhall, to where Edinburgh was to run its cars. Corporation cars had ceased to run beyond Levenhall from 26 November 1927. The arrangements with Post Office-Levenhall served by Corporation cars only came into effect on 26 February 1928 (service 21). Receipts from the Company territory were paid to the Company, less 8d per car mile. Protective fares were charged on the Company's new bus service. From 21 July 1928 the fare to Levenhall was raised to 5d, all bus operators charging one penny more. ('Through' tickets still in their old 'fareboard' layout were used, with presumably Musselburgh tickets locally.) Also at the beginning of 1928 the Department adopted the more embracing title of Transport Department, 'Tramways' and 'Motors' disappearing from vehicles.

The extension at Comely Bank was now in hand and this was brought into use on 19 July 1928. Services were still expanding. On the tramways a new part day service was started on 16 January 1928 from Pilrig to Tollcross via the Bridges and Melville Drive, but lasted only until 7 July. These reversed in Brougham Street, but did not carry a service number. Service 15 was extended to Kings Road on 26 February and service 10 to Colinton part day on 22 July 1928. An important amendment in fares was adopted on 16 May 1928 whereby the twopenny fare from the Post Office took the passenger to any car terminus except over the Musselburgh line beyond Joppa. The stages were also lengthened on the Cramond bus route, the only one on which 1½d stages still obtained, and the fare to Cramond became 4d.

Several amendments and extensions to bus routes were implemented in 1928. To serve new council housing developments, service 1 was extended from Ardmillan Terrace via Gorgie Road to Stenhouse on 30 April 1928. During visiting hours a bus was run from the Braids tram route to City Hospital. From 7 June service 13 was diverted from St David Street into Frederick Street from where it continued via Howe Street, Great King Street, London Street, Hope Crescent, Albert Street, Easter Road, St Clair Street, and Hawkhill Avenue to Lochend. One-man buses were retained. On 11 November 1928 service 12 was altered to run via Causewayside, Mayfield Road and Esslemont Road; while on 28 November service 5 was extended from Bread Street via Fountainbridge to Ardmillan Terrace, and on 16 December was extended from Lochend to St David Street. Service 13 was then extended from Lochend via Restalrig Road to Bernard Street. These latter extensions covered the former route of service 3, which was abandoned, apart from some rush-hour workings for a time.

It may be of interest that the city's first set of traffic lights was installed at the York Place-Broughton Street crossing on 21 March 1928. Others followed, and in several cases tram stops, which had been beyond the crossings, were re-sited on the approach side. Traffic halted for tram passengers would thus not obstruct cross traffic.

Chapter 4

UNDER NEW MANAGEMENT

In November 1928 Stuart Pilcher was appointed General Manager of the Manchester Corporation undertaking, and Edinburgh lost its manager – respected greatly by both staff and public. Mr F. A. Fitzpayne, the Deputy Manager (former manager of the Leith tramways) was confirmed as his successor on 10 January 1929. He soon proceeded to amend a number of car services: 17 extended to Granton on 8 May 1929; 8 extended to Newington Station, and 10 to Foot of Leith Walk on 2 June; 7 extended to Liberton on 17 June; 3 extended to Newington Station, and 19 abandoned on 14 July; 25 diverted from George Street to Princes Street on 1 July and extended (daily except Sundays) to Corstorphine on 15 July; 23 extended to Morningside Station on 28 July; 12 extended to Joppa (part day) on 1 September. Service 18 was diverted from Marchmont Road to run by Melville Drive to Newington Station on 17 November replacing service 26 which ceased. These lengthened routes retained the 4d maximum fare. Additional and longer circular tours were operated in the summer of 1929, and numbers 21 and 22 were allocated to the Hillend and City Hospital bus services respectively. Bus service 2 was diverted through the Prestonfield housing scheme.

A spectacular, but fortunately injury free, accident occurred on Saturday afternoon, 1 June 1929. The driver and conductor having left their car (349) for some minutes at

Car 367, seen when new on the left in this 1929 view of the West End, had just been placed in service, the first Edinburgh electric car with fully enclosed top deck. In this view it is evident that the south track has now been re-laid, the cable slot removed. (AWB Collection)

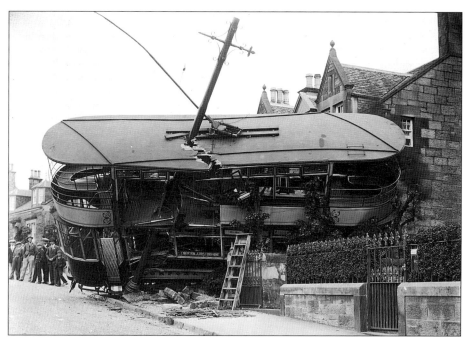

The accident on Liberton Brae on 1 June 1929 when car 349, left unattended at the terminus, ran away leaving the rails at the first bend. The overhead pole, in supporting the car, may have prevented injuries. (EOC)

Behind Shrubhill Works was a well-equipped permanent way department where track-work was prefabricated before being taken to site. The building was built for horse car storage and retained track into the 1950s. It was constructed using redundant tram rails as structural members. (EOC)

Liberton terminus, found on returning that it was moving off down the hill under its own momentum. The hand brake had not been on and the air-brake had leaked off. As it gathered speed, they were unable to catch up. At the bend it left the rails, ending up in a front garden leaning against a tramway pole which cut deep into its side and roof. Of the four elderly passengers, an old lady of 84 suffered only bruising, the others were completely unscathed. Indeed the couple on the lower deck (both over 70) just proceeded onwards on a later car! Also in June, track in Princes Street at Waverley Steps was straightened, eliminating the 'kink', a legacy of horse car days.

The tramway extension from Gorgie to a new Stenhouse terminus at Saughton Road (now Saughton Mains Street) was opened on 20 July 1930, prior to the Ministry of Transport's inspection five days later. A short extension at the Liberton terminus to keep waiting cars clear of the crossroads was also made. Several additional passenger loading 'islands' were built, and the west-going island at Princes Street was removed and replaced by others in Lothian Road and Shandwick Place. Some increases in maximum speeds were sanctioned and in July token dispensers were provided at Tollcross and Foot of Leith Walk.

A summer bus service, 23, from the Mound to the Castle started from 14 June 1930. The Sunday morning bus for Portobello Baths then took number 24. When the night services restarted in October, the Bruntsfield one was extended to Morningside Station (25) and the other service, extended to Robertson Avenue, became 26. Most tramway routes had a few early morning cars, but Comely Bank did not, so from 10 October 1927 an early morning bus was run (27). The Cramond bus was extended to Barnton on 24 December 1930, fare 5d, reduced to 4d from 1 July 1931.

At this time a universal penny fare was being debated. While this was not affordable, Mr Fitzpayne's report showed that 70% of tramway passengers paid 1d, but that only 1½% paid above 2d. A step forward came on 16 November 1931 when a 3d maximum tram fare (except Levenhall) was introduced. The child's fare, 1d, was now available up to age 14 instead of 12.

After the Musselburgh Company ceased tram operation, the position became unsatisfactory. No cars ran beyond Levenhall and the track, in poor condition, was not adequately maintained. Musselburgh Council asked the Ministry of Transport to make a closing order, but this was refused as the Edinburgh through running agreement was still in place. However a supplementary agreement of 7 March 1929 allowed the Corporation to exercise running powers but only as far as Levenhall (as it was in fact doing). The Musselburgh & District Electric Tramways (Cessor of Powers) Order 1929 was then issued, and the line beyond Levenhall officially abandoned, and subsequently lifted.

The Company still wanted rid of the rest of its tramway and in February 1930 asked the Corporation to buy it, together with its bus service to Port Seton, the replacement for its tramcars. To do this, Edinburgh would have had to obtain further Powers, with the SMT objecting to Corporation buses operating outwith the City in competition. Musselburgh Town Council however pressed Edinburgh to take over the remainder of the tramway. At the end of 1930 the Company arranged for the Corporation to undertake maintenance.

On 5 March 1931 Edinburgh Council resolved to acquire the Joppa to Levenhall track. A new agreement was made, whereby the Corporation would buy the Company tramway for £3000. The Company undertook to provide power outwith the City, and to charge protective fares on its bus service. This agreement was dated 7 May 1931, the

Corporation taking responsibility the following day. Stages to Levenhall were now included on Corporation tickets and the use of special tickets discontinued.

A new bus route (15) was instigated on 22 February 1931, from Eastfield to Juniper Green via Milton Road, Royal Park Terrace, High Street, George IV Bridge, Tollcross, and Colinton Road. The fare all the way was 6d, a new bright brown ticket being used.

Car service 10 now ran to Colinton all day and service 25 was extended to Joppa on Saturday afternoons. Some changes in car window boards took place; service 4 was provided with blue boards; service 25 with yellow boards and blue letters. From November 1930 service 2 carried a blue front board in the driver's window 'via George Street', while services 13 and 14 carried a white board lettered 'Granton & Churchhill Circular Drive'. A similar white board with red letters 'via Melville Drive' was provided for service 18 in September 1931, at which time new side window boards, yellow with green letters were provided for service 23.

The Road Traffic Act 1930 brought major changes for all transport operators. No longer could Edinburgh Council decide to run a bus service where or when it saw fit, or fix fares. Licensing of vehicles was no longer in its hands. Road service licences were forthcoming from the newly appointed Traffic Commissioners for existing services. Subsequent alterations required their approval, but there was seldom any difficulty. By April 1931, the 'public service vehicles', to give buses their new official appellation, were being examined for fitness under the new auspices, and appearing with new white enamelled oval licence plates. A few old

Redundant cable tracks remained in place for years, like those in Henderson Row outside the original cable car depot, still in place (albeit without points) a generation after the last tram passed. (Dr Hugh Nicol)

Ten cars of this design were supplied to the Corporation in 1932 by R. Y. Pickering. Number 257 is seen at the Braids terminus, the open fields on the west soon to be covered by Greenbank bungalows. (EOC)

buses and charabancs had only limited life left and soon disappeared. Coaches were used for a few years on service 13 and elsewhere, fitted (on the front only) with orthodox destination and service number blinds. These were not really suitable for 'stage carriage' work except where the traffic was light. In the summer of 1931 the Council adopted the style 'City and Royal Burgh of Edinburgh', and all vehicles henceforth bore this lettering.

The Edinburgh Corporation Order Confirmation Act 1932 was duly passed on 25 April, with the Musselburgh tramway system vested to the Corporation. The much needed reconstruction, estimated to cost £50,000, was started on 4 May and continued for two years. Double track was provided as far as the bend between 'Beulah' and Windsor Gardens, with crossovers at Eastfield, Hayweights, and High Street near the old depot entrance. The connection to the latter was removed. An extremely short piece of interlaced track was provided at the 'bottle-neck' at the Town Hall. For the last half-mile beyond Windsor Gardens single track sufficed, to the new terminus in Ravenshaugh Road opposite Hope Place. As before, there were three passing loops. The short length from the new terminus to the Musselburgh boundary was abandoned. All old overhead bracket arms were replaced by span wire construction and many new poles erected, most obtained second-hand from England. The Musselburgh Company continued to supply traction current as far as the Eastfield section insulators. Feeders in Musselburgh became the Transport Department's property while in Edinburgh they remained Electricity Department property. The Corporation now extended the 3d maximum fare to include Levenhall (2d to Eastfield) on 19 July 1932. A Saturday only service (22) colour blue,

Amidst a time of considerable experimentation in tramcar design, Shrubhill built the '£4000 tram'. Number 180 embodied several novel features and drew attention to itself in a bright red livery lined out in gold. Seen at Granton in 1932 on a trial trip with officials on board including F. A. Fitzpayne, H. L. Mittell and R. Shaw. The driver is motor inspector David Hampton. (EOC)

Twenty cars of this 'streamlined' style were supplied by contractors in September 1935, following three the previous year. Obviously some lessons were not learned as the first of the second batch got stuck under a railway bridge in the Lake District for two days (until smaller wheels were put on to the solid-tyred trailer). (EOC)

(blue side window boards) between Post Office and Musselburgh Town Hall commenced on 28 May 1932. By 21 January 1933, overhead reconstruction allowed use of normal trolley-ropes and bamboo poles were discarded.

The Corporation also took the opportunity in the 1932 Order to tidy up its transport legislation. All the Corporation's tramways Acts or parts relating to tramways, including those of Leith Corporation, and all the various old Companies' Acts, right back to 1871, were repealed. The existing tramways were described in a schedule plus unbuilt extensions authorised by the 1927 Order. Powers were included regarding bylaws, fares, luggage, parcels, freedom from licensing cars and crews, and to operate public service vehicles.

Reverting to service development, car service 10 was extended to Bernard Street on 9 July 1932, and the 18 cut back to Waverley (except rush hours, later permanently). Operation of services 11 and 25 were transferred to Leith and Gorgie depots respectively from 27 February 1932, use of Shrubhill as a depot then ceasing. Over the years there were changes in the depots from which some services operated, while some services were provided from more than one depot. Tram service 22 became daily from 4 November 1933. Time recorders were introduced at several places on car and bus routes in an endeavour to better regulate services. Traffic Regulators were still employed at Waterloo Place, North Bridge, West End, Haymarket, Tollcross, Pilrig, Foot of Leith Walk, and part-time at Morningside Station and Salisbury Place. Conductors didn't ring the bell to start until the Regulator blew his whistle.

On 2 October 1932 bus service 9 was extended from the Mound to Blackhall via Princes Street, West End, Orchard Brae, and Craigleith Road to a terminus at Telford Road. Services 2 and 6 were extended to Harewood Drive on 15 January 1933, and these together with 7 diverted from Nicholson Street to Pleasance, and St Leonard's Street from 9 July 1933, the 7 terminus being also altered to Davie Street. Then on 3 September 1933 bus service 1 was diverted from Gorgie Road via Westfield Road, Balgreen Road, and Stevenson Drive to Saughton Road to serve the growing housing area. To cater for pupils of Daniel Stewart's College from Corstorphine a useful bus was run to the College each morning. This was numbered 28, but there was no return service! Another hospital bus service started on 5 August 1933 from Granton Road to Pilton Hospital (29).

In 1933 single-track working was used when each side of the North Bridge was closed for several weeks to allow repairs to the bridge. Crossovers were laid in and work started in March. To reduce congestion by waiting cars at Post Office, from 24 April services 4 and 10 were diverted via York Place. Operations transferred to the west side in August, the crossovers being relaid. Work was completed in November. Service 10 then reverted to its former route, but 4 continued to use York Place. White front window boards lettered in red 'via Pilrig Street' were provided for 11, while 13 and 14 got similar new boards, green lettered 'Churchhill via Princes Street' and 'Granton via Pilrig & Goldenacre', and red lettered 'Churchhill via Bridges & Grange' and 'Granton via Princes Street & Bernard Street' respectively. Red letters appeared on 8's side window boards. A series of advertisements exhorting 'Travel by Tram' were at this time displayed inside the cars. The Zoo was a favourite theme and the first enjoined one to see 'A for Antelope', with eventually the whole alphabet covered. (Use of the word 'Tram' was alliterative: it was a 'car' in Edinburgh usage.)

A trial with a pantograph overhead power collector was undertaken in 1933. Again the Portobello route was used and side runners were fitted to poker frogs to prevent the pan-

In 1934 appeared car 69 – first of the final standard Shrubhill design, of which a total of eighty-four were built (until 1950) although there were minor variations. Seen at Liberton Dams this scene shows the first livery which was soon refined into the well-remembered 'standard' style. (EOC)

tograph fouling. Such makeshift arrangements were troublesome and car 73 carried the pantograph only from April until November.

An innovation was the first covered top double-deck bus, which went into service between Surgeon's Hall and Craigmillar on 3 July 1933. It was to be some time until the double-deckers became part of policy, although SMT had several years' experience of them.

Construction of a further extension of the Corstorphine route from Drum Brae to North Gyle Farm started in November 1933. A trial run was made on 9 May 1934, but it was not opened for traffic till 1 July, with all three services then extended. This extension was found to be particularly useful when International Rugby Matches were held at Murrayfield. Hitherto on these occasions cars had been stored on the incoming line east of Drum Brae, plus four on the Zoo loop, to run in to shift the crowds. This had involved turning back service cars at Corstorphine Station Road crossover, and running a bus between there and Drum Brae. Now the service could continue to Drum Brae and only the much quieter length beyond was covered by the bus.

Corstorphine Road east of Saughtonhall Drive was widened, on the south side, and a new outgoing track was laid, the old outgoing track became the new incoming line. The old track was slewed over at the east end to connect with the new, which were now centrally situated and in line with those west of Saughtonhall Drive, removing a 'double' bend there. This work occupied September to December 1934. The number of passenger 'islands' was still gradually being increased and two were provided in Musselburgh, at Hayweights and the Town Hall. The last remaining old cable tracks, in Morrison

Street and Hamilton Place, were removed in 1934, and several old cable junction and other pits were filled in.

Bus services 2 and 6 were altered on 16 September 1934, and instead of making the loop at Saughtonhall, both services now proceeded via Whitson Road to Stenhouse. At the other end the terminus was extended from Harewood Drive to Hay Drive.

Some new bus services started on 7 April 1935, St David Street to Craigentinny Avenue via Lochend (3); Willowbrae and Ardmillan, via Willowbrae Road, Royal Park Terrace, High Street, and thence the number 1 route (16); and West End and Pilton (19). The latter started from Randolph Place, proceeding via Orchard Brae and Crewe Road. Window boards were respectively, black with yellow letters, yellow with red, and white with red. In each case the service number was included at the left hand end, which commenced when boards were provided for service 9 two months earlier. Authority was obtained for tramway extensions in the Corporation's 1934 Provisional Order (approved in February 1935). These were: Braids to Hillend; Granton Road to Crewe Toll; and Liberton to Kaimes. On 4 April 1935 the Council decided to proceed with the extension from the Braids as far as Fairmilehead, and work soon commenced on this, together with a re-alignment of the existing track towards the centre of the widened roadway approaching the Braids terminus.

Chapter 5

ROBERT McLEOD IN CHARGE

Mr Fitzpayne died in harness on 3 March 1935. Of gentlemanly demeanour he had pursued a progressive policy, particularly in the engineering field. Robert McLeod, former traffic superintendent, who came from Aberdeen with Mr Pilcher, was appointed to succeed Mr Fitzpayne.

A touch of gaiety was added for a Royal visit on 11 May 1935. All cars flew a small coloured pennant on the trolley rope, a practice followed on subsequent festive occasions.

On 4 August 1935 car service 18 was extended to Liberton Dams, while a new service 19, started on 7 October, Seafield Place to Tollcross (Brougham Street) via Bridges and Melville Drive. This was part-day initially, but became all day from 3 November. On 6 April 1936 it was extended to Craigentinny Avenue, then to Kings Road (weekends only). The service colour was green over red and the side boards were green with red lettering. On 10 November 1935 car service 2 was extended to Granton and service 17 cut back to Trinity Bridge.

Bus services 3 and 5 were slightly altered from 15 December, now starting from the

Decorated cars were a frequent feature of the Corporation tramway. In July 1934 car 50 was decorated with 7,500 blooms for the visit of King George V and Queen Mary. EOC was not happy with this view in Pilrig Street, noting that the final decoration was only completed in time for the event then dismantled the following day, so he could not get the car posed as he wished. (EOC)

'Telephone Week' of October 1934 saw car 58 decorated and EOC took various shots – and was particularly happy with the effect achieved in St Andrew Square in the rain. (EOC)

south side of St Andrew Square. Bus service 13 became all day from 13 January 1936.

Modern covered-top double-deck buses began to appear towards the end of 1935, on service 2 at first. Low bridges precluded their use on most other routes. Carrick Knowe was now being developed, and although the widening of Saughton Road had only just begun, bus service 1 was extended through this area to High Street Corstorphine on 2 February 1936. Also on 2 February the maximum bus fare was reduced to 4d and workmen's fares were made available on buses as on cars, satisfying a grievance felt in areas not served by trams.

1 June 1936 saw a change in bus stances with SMT moving from Waverley Bridge to St Andrew Square, while Corporation services 11 and 23 moved from the Mound to Waverley Bridge (via Mound and Market Street inwards) where service 8 already terminated. Service 7 was also extended to Waverley Bridge from Surgeon's Hall. Traffic arrangement at the West End were altered on the same date. Access between Princes Street/Shandwick Place and Queensferry Street/Hope Street was ended. Trams continued to use the tracks linking Hope Street and Shandwick Place, while buses operating between Princes Street and Queensferry Street used South Charlotte Street, Charlotte Square (South) and Hope Street in both directions..

To bring the Corstorphine route tracks into the centre of a new traffic roundabout at Haymarket, the junction was re-aligned. As the overhead had to be altered concurrently, the work was carried out overnight 9-10 May 1936. Subsequently new 'islands' were provided on both routes. On 4 April the re-alignment at Braids was brought into use, followed on the 19th by the extension up to Fairmilehead, service 11 being extended, plus services 15 and 16 (Saturdays and Sundays only). Front window boards were white with red letters. The bus to Hillend Park was cut to Fairmilehead. Service 16 was extended at its other terminus, to Granton, from 26 July, and a completely new service, 27, from

For the May 1937 Coronation the Corporation prepared car 40 as a gold painted crown. Seen here on the Mound, looking over to the Scott Monument, the car toured the system for two weeks before being scrapped. (EOC)

Granton Road Station (via Hanover Street and Mound) to Craiglockhart Avenue was introduced on 6 September. Light colours were yellow over red, and side window boards were red with yellow letters. New white front window boards lettered in black 'via Tollcross & Melville Drive' were provided for service 18 that summer.

An interesting summer only car service was provided on Wednesday, Saturday and Sunday afternoons, from 12 July 1936 until 19 December that year – running from Granton Road Station via Ferry Road, Junction Street, then across the hitherto unused line at the Foot of Leith Walk to Duke Street, Seafield, and Kings Road. It was numbered 26, lights white/white, and used pink side window boards lettered in black. It operated during the three subsequent summers also, but was not revived after the war. Cars on various routes going to Kings Road or beyond were now provided with front window boards, black letters on white, 'To and from Bathing Pool Portobello'.

From 9 November 1936 service 25 became Craigentinny Avenue to Drum Brae (side window boards yellow with blue letters). The service still ran to Joppa on Saturday afternoons. Up to this time the first early morning journeys on the Comely Bank route had been run by buses showing 27, but now service 24 cars took over.

The final extension of the Corstorphine route, to Maybury Road was opened on 14 February 1937, services 1 and 12 being extended. The crossover at North Gyle was soon removed.

A major extension to Leith depot was undertaken in 1937, increasing capacity to 150 cars. This included extending the shed front, and widening to include the old workshop to the south side. Entrances were provided each side of the new office block fronting Leith Walk thus forming a loop round the back of the office, with the depot lyes fanning off. If necessary, cars could be reversed by going in one entrance and round the loop, hence the crossover in Leith Walk was removed. Another block with recreation room, offices, and stores, was built to the right of the shed. While building work was under way, the old sand house and stores were out of commission. Bagged sand was supplied from Shrubhill, sent down in car 40 which was stripped of its seats and used thus until March 1937. Car 82 served as a temporary store, at the back of the depot.

About this time improvements to the power supply were made by the Electricity Dept who opened a new mercury-arc rectifier substation at Turnhouse Road to supply the Corstorphine route west of Belmont Crescent. This was used during the night to feed back through the old Pinkhill feeder to Robertson Avenue substation, thence Gorgie depot, to avoid running the old rotary machines all night at the latter substation. Another rectifier at Wardie substation was used similarly at night to supply Leith depot. Both substations were remotely controlled from their parent substation. The Leith Walk feeder was extended into Leith depot where a new high-speed circuit-breaker was provided. To meet the additional Lothian Road traffic, an additional feeder was laid to a new pillar at Lothian House. A less successful scheme followed a plan to load up new rectifier equipment in Causewayside substation, by laying a new feeder to Greenhill Gardens, and supplying Bruntsfield and Churchhill from the old rotary machines at Morningside substation. Such a long feed gave rise to excessive voltage difference between adjoining substations, hence trouble at the section-insulators. There were also problems with the return currents in the rails, which were wont to take strange courses – even in normal circumstances. An improvement in reliability of side-feed cables from pavement boxes to the overhead was achieved by routing these through a separate swan-necked pipe bracketed to the pole, straight out of the top of the box. This was done as and when renewal was required. An improved design of automatic point controller was installed at all junctions in regular use (other than Princes Street). In this the trolley bridged a skate insulated from the trolley-wire, there being a path between the latter and one side of the skate through a relay contactor which operated in series with the car drawing power. Otherwise the skate being bridged completed a circuit from the other side of it through a second relay contactor operating on voltage, the first contactor not operating in these conditions. These relay contactors completed circuits to the points solenoids accordingly, and were housed in a pole-mounted box, hence without exposed moving parts.

The 1936 Provisional Order included powers to extend the tramway from Stenhouse to the City boundary. Extensive council house construction was in progress south of Calder Road, which required widening. It was suggested that this extension could be laid on its own right of way to the north of the road, but this did not find favour. There seemed a reluctance to proceed with the road widening, but in order to provide street lighting as normal on tram standards, their positions were plotted along the south side of the road. Those which the Lighting Dept required were erected in 1937 ahead of the proposed tramway extension. In the event this tramway never was constructed and standards served the Lighting Department only.

Bus service 9 was extended to Greenbank Row, and bus service 3 to Portobello Town Hall on 3 January 1937. To serve Sighthill, bus service 4 was extended from Longstone by Calder Road to Sighthill Avenue on 26 September 1937. Then on 3 October, service 5 was extended from Ardmillan Terrace to Stenhouse. At the same time service 16 was extended from Willowbrae to Portobello Town Hall via Duddingston Road and at its other end, from Ardmillan Terrace via Stevenson Drive and Calder Road to Sighthill Avenue on 30 January 1938.

Car service 17 was again extended to Granton on 15 November 1937 though it had been so extended on Saturdays a few months earlier, while car service 27 was extended to Firrhill from 6 February 1938 to serve new housing nearby at Colinton Mains. This district benefited further on 14 August when the Hillend to Fairmilehead bus service was extended via Oxgangs Road and Colinton Mains Drive to Firrhill. At that time the traffic was mainly from Colinton Mains to the cars at Firrhill, and transfer fares were available between Colinton Mains and Tollcross. (When issuing tickets stage 99 was used on ticket machines.) On 31 October 1938 car service 25 was extended to Kings Road daily.

Revised Regulations and Byelaws for the tramway system were made by the Minister of Transport in August 1938, including increased speeds of up to 25mph on suitable stretches. 'Compulsory stops' were considerably reduced; retaining – on the descending journeys – Broughton Street at Forth Street, North St Andrew Street, North Hanover Street at George Street, South Hanover Street at Princes Street, North Frederick Street at George Street, South Frederick Street at Princes Street (not in normal use), Howe Street at South-East Circus Place, Royal Circus at North-West Circus Place, Bank Street at North Bank Street, Pitt Street at Fettes Row, and Liberton Brae at Alnwickhill Road.

To serve the increasing traffic to Portobello Bathing Pool on Saturdays and Sundays, an unnumbered tram service was run during the summer of 1939 from Stenhouse to Bath Street via London Road. Service 5 was also extended to Kings Road. At this time yellow front window boards, lettered in black 'For Colinton Mains' were used on services 9, 10, and 27, with similar boards 'via Mound' for service 23.

It will be clear that bus services were increasing in importance. The all-night bus service was extended to Balgreen Road from 17 October. Indeed some extensions were having an affect on the revenue of adjacent tramway routes; but while additional plant was installed at Central Garage and more accommodation for bus body repairs, the tramway development policy held good.

On 6 January 1938 the Council decided to build the tramway along Ferry Road to Crewe Toll (authorised by the 1934 Order) in connection with road widening. No rails had been laid, but the road widening was nearly finished (except Granton Road to Arboretum Road) when, on 2 March 1939 the Public Utilities Committee recommended reversal of the previous decision. This was rejected, but on 6 April the Committee suggested that, as trams could not serve the housing schemes beyond the low railway bridges west of Crewe Toll, the extension should not be built and a bus service run instead from Drylaw Mains via Pilton, East Trinity Road and Ferry Road, to Dock Place. The Council adhered to its decision and construction commenced. Following the road widening, work proceeded from Crewe Toll. To facilitate rail welding, overhead poles were erected and one wire strung along on temporary brackets, a second wire hung below for the return current. A temporary feeder connection was made to the existing overhead line on the curve into Granton Road. Most poles were erected, one track laid to East Fettes Avenue, and the other for a short distance complete with crossover, when that fateful day, 3 September 1939, fell. Work was suspended on outbreak of War, never to restart. (Although this did nearly happen – as will be described later.)

Chapter 6

WARTIME OPERATIONS

Blackout conditions were imposed from Friday 1 September, and there was a great hustle to get office windows and depot roofs darkened in the shortest possible time. Signal lamps for single line sections were screened. Buses had to run with sidelights only, until improvised screens allowing a small glimmer from headlights were approved, followed later by standard slotted metal masks designed by the Ministry of Home Security. Cardboard shields were fitted round some of the interior lights on buses, and the remainder removed.

The tramway cars fared rather better at first. Tramcar bumpers and steps were painted white, and the crews continued to wear their summer white-topped caps all the year round. Lamps were removed from some circuits and blue lamps used elsewhere. Blue lamps were much required at this time and for a week or so large numbers disappeared every night until it was eventually realised that traction lamps had no domestic use.

After withdrawal from passenger service in 1939 car 221 was decorated to promote several events. An RAF exhibition in Waverley Market was first with the car in 'silver' paint. A year later it promoted 'Savings Week' – by then painted gold. (EOC)

The Shrubhill decontamination squad at the ready, 12 May, 1939. DLGH is second from the right. (EOC)

Destination screen boxes were painted with a blue lacquer. Headlights on the newer cars were dimmed, with brake-stop lights and platform lights removed. By running on their defined routes cars managed well, though inevitably there were incidents. The dim blue light from the destination screen aided cars without headlights, but when a 'yellow warning' was in force all these lights were off, and it became difficult creeping along in total darkness. The 'blue phase' did not last long, and, in November 1939, 200-volt carbon filament lamps with cardboard shades were fitted to most older cars, and for cars with long-series lighting circuits, these were connected into one circuit so that using ordinary lamps gave reduced illumination.

Contrary to rumour, the Transport Department was quite well off in its stock of material and maintenance and painting continued normally, though with some staff reduction. The blackout halted any night outside work that could not be undertaken by pocket torch! Overhead linesmen were supplied with caps with a shaded lamp operated by dry batteries strapped to the belt. This enabled localised work to be undertaken.

In addition to general ARP measures, a number of staff were trained in decontamination duties. A vehicle cleansing station was built beside the rear of Gorgie depot and track laid in, hence both cars and buses could be accommodated. No one knew what to expect but most feared the worst. A salvage wagon was lacking, so an old AEC bus (SC3430) was partially stripped and equipped with a crane, early in 1940. An unfortunate decision was to cancel enquiries for new buses. Soon many of the older buses were unserviceable but by then replacements were unobtainable.

From November 1939 bus services were reduced, to save fuel, and an 'Emergency' timetable was issued with earlier times for last buses. Last car times were also a little earlier, now about 11 o'clock. The Corstorphine-Stewarts College bus ceased.

Disquiet over older cars running without headlights led to these cars being fitted with a cylindrical lamp with red and white spectacles. A similar shield was also fitted to head-lights of newer cars between February and June 1940. A white band was also painted round the bottom of all cars.

Before the war some renewals of trolley wire had used a grooved wire known as 'Portsmouth' section, attached to section insulators by detachable end pieces into which the top half of the wire fitted. This gave a smoother run-on on to section insulators so a decision was made to standardise on this wire. At crossovers normally only used in one direction (*eg* the Zoo, Newington Station, *etc*), the shunt frog was removed from the out-going wire and the crossover wire led alongside it for a short distance and terminated separately. All these measures helped to reduce arcing, a source of complaint in black-out conditions. If drivers shut off current when passing section insulators *etc*, arcing reduced, so to assist location in the dark, white glazed tiles were let into the setts between the tracks as markers. These were also used at automatic point skates, and, out-side the rails, as stopping marks at passenger islands. Drivers did not always comply hence some arcing continued. Many suggestions were proposed for elimination, includ-ing use of bow collectors, but experience elsewhere showed these to be even worse; it was even proposed that only buses be used after dark.

Introduction of grooved wire was coupled with use of carbon-shoe collectors instead of trolley-wheels. Experiments were made with a specially made, more robust shoe than those on the market, to see if this would have a reasonable life. This was tried on 23 November 1939 on car 22 to Levenhall. An improved production design was then, from 9 October 1940, fitted to cars on services 21 and 22. After further modification, their use was made universal, completed by April 1942. The new design was registered as the 'Edinburgh' design number 839503. Local requirements were produced in the Shrubhill workshops and it was successfully marketed for trolleybuses. These shoes were much more economical than the old wheels, and besides reducing arcing had the advantage of being almost silent. (The noise of trolley-wheels was not realised until they had been superseded.) One difficulty that remained was locating the wire at the terminus in the dark. During the winter of 1940-1 a device was produced to assist in this operation. The idea originated in America where streetcar overheads crossed railway tracks. If the trol-ley became dewired a car would not stall in front of an oncoming train. A metal plate 18 inches wide and five feet long was fitted just below the wire, with a 2 inch angle along its edges tapered to lead the trolley into the middle, and thus on to the wire. The first trial

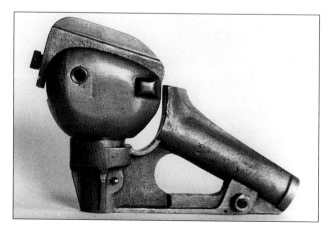

The registered 'Edinburgh' style trolley head introduced from 1940 gave imporved operation in wartime condi-tions and was successfully marketed for trolley bus oper-ation. (DLGH)

was at Liberton terminus. It proved a boon and all termini were so equipped, except Stanley Road where the old reverser remained. Later, an improved version was designed with a more gradual taper, and two grooves pressed into the plate. These guided the place at the running-on end. This could be used at crossovers such as Earl Grey Street, and worked satisfactorily, provided the car travelled slowly.

Renewal of trolley wire was prevented during the blackout and a method of operation in daylight without interrupting the service was devised. The wire to be renewed was isolated by the section-box switches, and cars were stopped with trolley transferred to the wire above the other line. They proceeded on, stopping to remove the trolley only if they met a car coming the opposite way. If cars caught up on the wagon with the drum of new wire, it would just draw aside to let them pass. With little traffic about in a forenoon the scheme worked well. It did not work in busier, narrow streets, nor with centre poles, except where cars could coast downhill with trolley held down (as on Leith walk). Renewals at other places took place on clear moonlight nights.

There was never any shortage of wire, and overhead fittings were produced at

After completion of bomb damage repairs to the track at North Junction Street (Portland Place) in July 1940, car 184 on service 17 makes its way cautiously over the open track. Commercial Street stretches in the distance. (EOC)

The busy east end of Princes Street with Waterloo Place and Nelson's Monument on Calton Hill beyond,
belying the date of the photograph as mid-1941. Very much business as usual, with only the wartime
white paint to indicate any change. (DLGH)

Shrubhill in adequate quantity, so that it was possible to incorporate the re-alignment of
all curves for tangent running and also reconstruct all junctions. An improved facing frog
was devised, based on the shunt frog, with the tongue closing for the curve when the trolley-boom lifted the poker. A trolley could pass backwards through it if necessary.
Drivers found they could negotiate curves and junctions at normal speed, confident that
the trolley was now unlikely to come off. The number of de-wirements was reduced, and
of those which occurred most were attributed to the use of trolley ropes which were
liable to get caught. These however, could not be dispensed with in the blackout. The
breakdown squad found a difference too. Before the war there were usually eight or nine
calls to the overhead equipment per day. By the end of the war there were often none.

The permanent way presented problems too. It was found possible to lay new rails during the day without delaying the service. The ground was prepared in advance and the
P.W. gangs got so adept at cutting out the old and slipping in the new (with temporary
bolts and packing) that two minutes were all that was required. Then more complicated
work was attempted. Junction work was carefully prepared beforehand, and the pieces
similarly fitted in, piecemeal, between cars. Even the busiest junctions such as the
Mound and Post Office were renewed in this way during daytime without seriously
delaying the service. The supply of rails was not good, however, and renewals could not
be done until absolutely necessary, even though in some cases the inside flange was
completely away. Use of the track brake by drivers was discouraged, and in some places
the position of stopping places was moved so that heavier wear on rails was transferred
to a less worn part. A remarkably high standard was maintained throughout the war period. Rails were renewed at the top of Leith Street in July 1940 and service 10 temporarily diverted via York Place, other cars for Princes Street occasionally going that way too
at times of pressure.

All services from Levenhall to Kings Road and Seafield, also Bernard Street and the length of Ferry Road stopped for the afternoon of 23 February 1940 to allow passage of a shot-down German aircraft, on its wheels, from East Lothian to Turnhouse.

Returning to that hot June of 1940 when everyone anticipated invasion, roofs of all cars and buses were painted a grey/brown colour. Road blocks were set up in several places, and on 8 June concrete blocks were placed across the road at Musselburgh bridge, leaving only a single track space, on the incoming side. Service 22 now terminated at Hayweights, with single-line working adopted for service 21 from Hayweights to the Town Hall, a pilotman accompanying the cars to and fro. This block was removed about the end of July and normal services resumed.

One of Edinburgh's few wartime 'incidents' occurred about 7.30pm on 18 July 1940, when a 'hit-and-run' raider attacked Leith Docks. One bomb fell on the junction at Portland Place leaving a large crater. The point blades were intact on the edge, the rest had disappeared while all the overhead was down. The surrounding buildings were pock-marked by shrapnel, but car 365 standing close by picking up passengers for town, suffered minimal damage. For a few days cars ran to either side of the obstruction, while the crater was filled and rails supported across it, connecting Commercial Street to Granton. This overhead line was also re-connected and these services restored on the afternoon of 22 July. By mid-day, five days later, repairs were complete, the junction rebuilt from stock materials and service 2 was also restored.

In July 25 of the latest single-deck buses were requisitioned by the War Dept. Then in October the coaches were taken over for ambulance and fire service duties. Many of the old vehicles that had been laid aside had then to be made to run again, several with second-hand engines.

A fare increase followed rising costs. The first proposal was that the 1d fare be increased to 1½d, but with a short 1d stage in each direction from Post Office, West End or Mound. In March 1940 the Council approved this scheme but restricted the 1d stage to one only, *viz* Post Office to West End. The Regional Transport Commissioner refused to allow this scheme, and required the Corporation to prepare a better scheme. The result was the dividing of the whole system, car and bus, into stages of approximately half a mile. Two stages were given for 1d, three for 1½d, five for 2d on cars (four on buses), seven for 2½d, and 3d maximum as before. Where buses followed tram routes no 1d or 1½d fares were given. SMT examined its fares at this time and objected to the Corporation's 3d fare to Juniper Green which it considered too low. The Commissioner fixed the fare to Juniper Green at 3½d, using a pre-printed ticket as no more values could be arranged on the TIMs. The ticket, (pale green) was cancelled by tearing out a small piece. These fares came into operation on 4 August 1940.

Lighting was still to come in for more attention however. In September 1940 small battery lamps were fixed above the car bumpers so that a light could be shown if cars became stranded without power in the blackout. Of course the batteries didn't last and were replaced by small candle lanterns. New destination screen and route number screens had thinner characters so that less light was emitted. In November 1940 a detachable hood was provided for the headlamps of older cars, then in April 1943 this type of hood was also fitted to the headlights of newer cars. ARP signs were put up to warn traffic of cars swinging on to the passing loops at Levenhall.

Lighting was now (in the circumstance) satisfactory, and remained in this form until towards the end of the War. Nevertheless car drivers could lose their sense of location,

Car 57 displays wartime modifications – a white line applied at fender level, black fabric over the lower saloon windows and headlamps covered to show only the meanest glimmer of light. Photographed on 3 May 1941. (DLGH)

and not infrequently a car would shoot off the end of the rails at a terminus. (Yes, the driver knew he went over a crossover but 'thought that was only Drum Brae'!) Conductors too, had difficulties, making up their waybills in the dim light; plus the unscrupulous passenger who passed off a spurious coin in the dark. In November 1940 three cars had a white anti-blast fabric stuck to the inside of most windows. The next month a further three cars had black fabric on the outside of lower saloon windows, with transparent strips stuck to platform windows. From January 1941 all cars were fitted with non-splintering glass to the platform and lower saloon bulkhead windows, plus black fabric to the outside of lower saloon windows. Buses were treated similarly.

The welding car (No 2) was now disused, and in December 1940 it was proposed to re-build it as a tower wagon so that track (such as prevailed after the Portland Place 'incident') could be negotiated. Fortunately this need did not arise.

The air-raid warning system was altered in December 1940, when the Ministry of Home Security decided that work should continue through 'alerts' until an 'imminent danger' signal was given by telephone to large industrial establishments. This signal was given when raiders were only a few miles away, but as it was not given publicly, cars and buses were expected to continue to run until things started happening. Aberdeen, right on the misty coast, had suffered much from 'hit-and-run' raiders, and a useful scheme was devised. Cars' lights would be switched on during an 'alert' and when the 'ID' message was received the substation attendant opened traction circuit breakers twice for three seconds, with one second between. The crew watched the lights, and took immediate shelter with the passengers if they received the signal. A longer interruption of supply was the 'ID' clear signal and should be seen from the shelter entrance. Bus crews knew to follow the car crews' actions. Edinburgh adopted this scheme from 18 January 1941, but at the end of that year the Ministry of Home Security vetoed it. They decreed that the 'ID' signal was not public knowledge, hence tramway men were in a privileged position compared to other transport workers!

From January 1941 firewatchers were provided for Shrubhill and Head Office. The nights of 13 and 14 March had 'alerts' all night while the raiders were on their way to and from Clydebank. In Edinburgh cars stopped where they were, remaining there until the morning when the early shift crews started. Most bus drivers got tired of waiting and took their vehicles back to the garage. Only a few incendiary bombs fell on Edinburgh. Some landed in front of a car in Montrose Terrace, but the driver quickly reversed out of danger. Throughout the war, Edinburgh escaped remarkably lightly. By the spring of 1941 the ARP organisations were becoming centralised, and a Transport Dept control room was set up at Central Garage, manned overnight by a rota of officials with authority to initiate any action necessary (if the appropriate officials could not be contacted).

The winter of 1940-1 was very hard, with much snow. The limitations of the very old salt cars for snowplough duties became apparent. Early in 1941 arrangements were made to fix ploughs to some of the oldest passenger cars, though not much use was made of these.

Conductresses were taken on from the end of May 1941, first on single-deck buses, but soon spreading to all car and bus services. Many served extremely well, and some remained on the job long after the war. Others (and some men too) impressed under direction of labour, were less willing. There was a high turnover of platform staff and discipline suffered. Early in 1941 some double-deck buses were lent to London. It now appears it was staff, not vehicles that London required, but it was considered that the sight of these borrowed buses in London would boost morale. They were returned in September and subsequently carried small plates recording their war service. Most of the older Daimler single-deckers had their seats fixed longitudinally down both sides. allow-

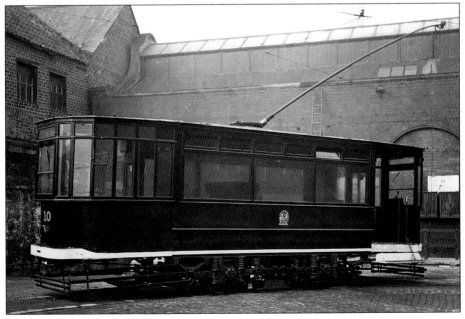

Even works cars had the white strip applied. This is number 10 (later 3) photographed on 13 November 1941. (DLGH)

ing more standing passengers. In this Ministry of War Transport scheme, up to 30 standees were permitted, but the idea was not popular, and no further such alterations were made. Further cuts in bus services were effected in April 1941, the last buses from the central points now being about 10.30pm. This nevertheless compared well with cities further south.

In December 1941 the Ministry of War Transport provided a few new buses. Most makes were new to Edinburgh, some double-deck and some single-deck, but everything was welcome, even some of the Ministry's standard utility Bedford buses. In May 1942 the army returned the buses they had requisitioned and after repainting they were restored to service. The utility Bedfords ran as supplied in dark brown at first, but later these, and some of the new double-deckers, were painted grey, even fully lined out. The only standard vehicle to receive a grey livery was single-deck bus A51. Otherwise the Department continued, on a slightly reduced scale, its regular vehicle repainting programme.

To aid fares collection, small red metal boxes appeared on the vehicles into which the passenger was invited to drop uncollected fare money before alighting. While these were fairly successful, the cost of emptying them proved uneconomic! Another scheme was use of the male office staff as auxiliary conductors on journeys from and to work. A white linen arm band was issued. The scheme was extended, with volunteers accepted from the public generally. A card of authority and a navy-blue armlet were issued, for use during morning and evening rush hours, and the volunteers were not required to pay their own fare. The scheme was subject to much abuse, as some made a practice of always travelling in this capacity whether or not their services were needed. The scheme was terminated on 27 July 1946.

The Ministry of War Transport, in June 1942, asked that the number of stopping places be reduced to save fuel and wear and tear. About 120 tram stops were removed completely whilst others were moved beyond the top of hills to reduce the re-starting effort. For buses this actually meant many new stopping-place poles, as rural bus stops were not usually defined. Buses would stop where hailed, though regular passengers used regular places. Stops sometimes applied to both directions with no indication on the other side of the street. Cast-iron poles were no longer available so a plain steel tube was used instead.

One bus was spared to start a new service on 14 September 1942. This ran alternate trips from Pennywell Road to Comely Bank car terminus, and to the Granton tram route at the top of Granton Road (both workings used No 18). There was considerable use of the latter route to Ferranti's works, and with no more fuel available the Ministry of War Transport wanted the Corporation to complete the tramway to Crewe Toll, even if just one track was laid for a shuttle service. The Corporation was unwilling and eventually persuaded the Ministry to drop the idea. However when the curve at the top of Granton Road was renewed, the new junction, already in store, was laid in. Last car times were made earlier from 1 November and buses followed suit, three weeks later. A further reduction in bus frequencies followed from 1 March 1943.

The next 'headache' was an instruction that some buses must be adapted to use producer-gas as fuel. Considerable experimental work had been done on petrol engines, but other than some old vehicles, Edinburgh now used only diesels which were more difficult to convert. Standard two-wheel trailers were supplied by the Ministry, some of the latest single-deckers fitted with tow gear, and experiments proceeded with nine buses,

Braids terminus, probably in 1945, with car 91 still in wartime guise. The white 'skirt' line has gone but the brown roof and headlamp restriction remain. Note the 'pan' on the overhead for ease of locating the trolley. (DLGH)

including A71, A86 and A88. A fair measure of success was achieved. By about April 1943 they were on the Barnton route, but the difficulties, lack of pulling-power, use of trailers, and troubles with the gas plants, made Edinburgh just as keen as every other operator to drop the scheme as soon as the Ministry permitted. The last 'gas' run was on 7 October 1944.

A new tram service between Piershill and Drum Brae via London Road and Leith Street started on 19 April 1943 (26) and when route lights were restored after the war, became blue over red. Side window boards were white, but paper bills were used at first. The indication 'Drum Brae South' came into use for the first time. Some of the part-day extra cars and crews from services 1 and 5 were used for the new service. From 16 September service 16 was extended daily to Fairmilehead, while part-day extras on service 11 ran only to Braids, displaying no service number until June 1946, when No 28 was allocated. Route colours, later, were blue over green. New side window boards, yellow with blue letters, were provided in December 1944 for tram services 14 and 25.

Bus service 9 was extended to Davidson's Mains on 14 November 1943. In April 1944 the use of double-deck buses was extended to service 13 which was now serving Scottish Command HQ. 'Holidays at Home' brought increased traffic and in August 1944 car service 4 was extended to Kings Road, and car service 15 to Fairmilehead. By the end of the year the situation was a little easier and some strengthening of services became possible, and the Ministry of Home Security allowed some relaxation of the blackout.

VE day on Tuesday 8 May 1945 saw Princes Street packed with humanity, but despite the crowds services kept moving. Normal vehicle lighting was quickly restored and white bumper paint was removed as vehicles went through the workshops. Masks were removed from the headlights, the older cars now having an orthodox headlamp for the first time. Brake stop lights were also restored. Route colours were not restored to cars until 31 October 1946, and it was some time before crews got used to adjusting them (and most people had forgotten them anyway). Soon those few buses which had worn the grey livery were appearing in standard colours, and the wooden seats and other makeshift features of the utility buses gave way to normal equipment. The bus fleet was augmented with new vehicles.

Although difficulties remained, the war was over and the Transport Department had come through remarkably well. The tramcar and bus fleet had been maintained to virtually normal standards. Permanent way had also been reasonably maintained and was still sound, while the overhead equipment was also in good shape. Junction renewal was still being done in daytime, but on 23 August 1945 there was an unfortunate slight 'misfit' at the east end of George Street and for some hours incoming service 24 had to proceed by Frederick Street and Princes Street. To assist in loading and despatching the frequent (2½ minute service) cars from Waterloo Place a second crossover was provided at this time. A change was also made at London Road junction; the passenger island on the down line junction, at which London Road cars did not stop, was removed and replaced by one opposite Gayfield Square. (There was already one in London Road.)

In 1944 the manager had submitted a report on Post War Reconstruction, which in the long term was dependent upon the overall development plan for the city. In the short term he proposed completion of the car renewal programme, replacement of old buses with some 20 new ones, and completion of arrears of track renewal. The main need highlighted was the provision of new depots and a new head office. New depots were proposed at Stenhouse or Sighthill, Craigmillar, Granton and Portobello; with extensive rebuilding at Shrubhill.

A part-day car service between North Junction Street and Stenhouse via George Street introduced in October 1946 was numbered 22 (blue/blue colours and blue side window boards), the previous part-day service to Musselburgh having been withdrawn. Additional rolling stock was urgently required so eleven second hand cars were bought from Manchester Corporation, the first arriving in November 1946.

A bus service was run from Corstorphine car terminus to Turnhouse for an air display on 15 September 1945, becoming a regular procedure. Bus service alterations were made from 21 October 1945. Service 4 terminated at Holyrood; service 16 at Ardmillan Terrace, while service 5 was extended to Sighthill to compensate. Part day service 5 buses turned at Ardmillan Terrace as before but were numbered 25. Bus service 18 now ran Goldenacre to Drylaw Mains, its alternate journeys to Comely Bank now replaced by a new service, 17, Randolph Place and Muirhouse.

Tours restarted, on a limited scale, at Easter 1946. All-night bus services resumed in the winter in 1946, now numbered 28 and 29.

Bus services 4 and 5 were extended to Calder Crescent in February 1947 as housing extended ever westwards. The Mound to the Castle summer bus service recommenced on 2 August 1947, and a special service operated under contract to British European

War time scene outside Central Garage on 13 July 1943. To the left is grey-liveried Daimler (A51), on the right a wartime Bristol. Despite the wartime concession to white extremities, the livery was still comprehensively lined out. Between the buses can be seen two producer-gas trailers. (DLGH)

Airways from its George Street office to Turnhouse. For the winter of 1947-48 all-night bus services were recast, an hourly service being run on five routes:

1   Foot of Leith Walk to Firrhill via Princes Street.
2   Bath Street to Morningside Station via Princes Street.
3   Bonnington Terrace to Corstorphine, Manse Road via Princes Street.
4   Craigmillar to Crewe Road North via Princes Street.
5   Waverley to Sighthill.

A uniform fare of 6d applied, with ordinary fares charged after 3.20am for early workers. The terminal stances were shown by black plates lettered in white. These were popular and thereafter continued all the year. From June 1947 tram service 18 was extended to Liberton terminus during part of the evening.

New passenger islands were erected on the incoming side at Waverley Steps and at the foot of North Bridge, and the stopping place for cars proceeding to Leith Street at the Register removed, so that passengers had to guess from which direction the first car would come, then move to the appropriate stop.

Accommodation had to be found for the expanding bus fleet, at a time when building was severely restricted. Vehicles were being parked overnight in Central Garage Forecourt. A plot of ground off McDonald Road was taken for an open-air bus park, with a heating system provided for radiators. Bus service 17 was now extended to Granton Square and service 18 to Davidson's Mains. At about this date the West End terminus of bus service 19 was removed from Randolph Place to Melville Street. From July 1949 a summer Saturday and Sunday afternoon bus service was added between Parkhead Drive,

Sighthill, and Cramond, via Corstorphine High Street, Drum Brae and Barnton. It was numbered 20 and a flat fare of 3d was charged. Bus service 18 was also extended at weekends to Silverknowes Promenade to which an access road had been recently completed.

The manager, Robert McLeod, died in September 1948, and was succeeded by his deputy W. M. Little. The latter had previously served in the undertaking until 1941 and after a period as manager at St. Helens then Reading, returned to his native city as deputy manager in 1946. His appointment was popular – but so far as the public were concerned this was short-lived. (There must, however, be few transport managers who do not have to suffer a disgruntled public.) His report for year ending 28 May 1949 showed losses in both tram and bus accounts hence, unusually, no contributions could be made towards renewal or reserve funds.

The passenger island at Hayweights (Musselburgh) was being run into so frequently that it was moved round to Bridge Street. An alteration to car services was by extension of services 7, 11, and 28 from Stanley Road down to the foot of Craighall Road (destination screens still showing Stanley Road). This commenced on 17 October 1949 and provided a service on Craighall Road after more than thirty years. A crossover wire was erected at the new terminus and the old trolley reverser at Stanley Road removed.

Chapter 7

POSTWAR CHANGES
AND DECLINE OF THE TRAM

To meet rapid housing development two new bus services started on 24 October 1949. 24 from St Andrew Square to Bingham Road, and 25 shuttle from Liberton car terminus to Burdiehouse. Mr Little next proposed to abandon the poor paying tram service 18, replacing it with a bus service from Burdiehouse to Davidson's Mains via Newington, Melville Drive, and Queensferry Road. This took service number 18, starting on 26 March 1950. Shuttle 25 from Liberton terminus was withdrawn, and existing service 18 was renumbered 28. Soon Davidson's Mains bus terminus was moved to Quality Street and a turning circle cut through the grass at the cross roads. From 7 May 1950 bus service 13 ceased to meander through the streets and crescents of the west end, being diverted via Atholl Place and Palmerston Place. A passenger island was provided at Waterloo Place, the original west-most cross-over being removed. Other cross-overs were removed at the top of Broughton Street and at the east end of George Street.

It was clear something would have to be done about revenue, and a fares revision was discussed by the council, hence on 4 February 1951 fares were increased. The 1d fare disappeared; 1½d, 2½d and 3d fares covering three, five, or over five stages on all ser-

Car 49 was newly built, used for a tram enthusiasts tour on its first run on 15 August 1950. The detail of the livery is now in its final, but still well detailed, state (before contamination by advertisements). Seen on the south side of St Andrew Square – this track used only by football and rugby specials, not by any regular routes. (RB Parr)

vices (to Juniper Green remained 3½d). Too much time had been lost however, and with deficits increasing a further increase was already required. This was implemented on 2 December 1951, the maximum becoming 5d.

Abandonment of the tramway system was by now being mooted, and in June 1950 the manager put forward a report recommending that 25% of the rolling-stock, and a like amount of the existing system be scrapped, and replaced by motor buses. The Transport sub-committee (of which Councillor Harkness was convener), and the Civic Amenities committee endorsed this, but the full council remitted it back at the end of July. In September the committee returned the same recommendation, and a special meeting of the council followed on 12 October. It was now clear that Mr Little envisaged a quick end to the tramway system, though a section of the council seemed loath to commit the city to such a drastic change. On 2 November the committee's recommendation was approved, by 41 votes to 17. After a spate of newspaper correspondence there followed a lull till the following autumn, when the replacement proposals were brought up.

Meantime, some older cars were scrapped, but track maintenance deteriorated rapidly. Some junctions, *e.g.* Theatre Royal and Leith Depot, were repaved in concrete but this was not satisfactory. The facing junction at Waterloo Place, never in ordinary use, was removed in October 1950. That at the top of Granton Road for the Crewe Toll extension was also removed (for the second time) without ever being used, at the end of 1950. The poles to Crewe Toll were removed in March 1951, the rails in October 1953. The junction in Great Junction Street leading to Duke Street was lifted in January 1951, and crossovers in London Road and at Corstorphine Station Road removed later that year.

Resurfacing of Princes Street was planned, and as complete abandonment of the tramway system was not agreed, tracks between Castle Street and West End were relaid in concrete, with an asphalt surface. Passenger islands in Princes Street were resited and enlarged in the summer of 1951. Automatic point controllers were provided at Hanover Street and Mound junctions, while that at Frederick Street was set for the Comely Bank cars by drivers operating a switch on the adjacent centre-pole, in each case reset for the main line by an overhead skate. The Post Office junctions continued to be operated from the pavement box, now enclosed in a kiosk. As the Electricity Board intimated that it intended to cease DC traction supply in Portobello, the Transport Department installed a mercury-arc rectifier at Portobello depot, brought into use on 4 March 1951.

Staffing shortages on Saturdays and Sundays led to the Corporation having surplus buses, which SMT was glad to hire in the busy summers of 1951 and 1952. Still more bus accommodation was required, and another open-air bus park was created adjoining Gorgie depot with a basic workshop. This was brought into use on 3 June 1951 and buses on services 1, 2, 4, 5, 18, and 21 were garaged there. (The rails outside at the rear were removed.)

On 18 September 1951 the routes proposed for withdrawal under the 25% scheme were announced; Comely Bank, Slateford, and Stenhouse. There followed another spate of press 'correspondence' and much argument in the council and elsewhere but it was nevertheless approved, on 27 September. Meantime changes in bus services continued with service 18 shortened at Blackhall from 30 December 1951. More comprehensive alterations applied from 17 February 1952. Service 2 was extended to Newcraighall, the double-deckers turning just short of the village as they could not go under the railway bridge, and service 7 was withdrawn. Service 2 was diverted from Whitson Road to operate via Stevenson Drive and was extended from Stenhouse to the Broomhouse hous-

Part of the Crewe Toll line was built, and overhead was strung but never used. The unused track is seen being lifted on 27 September 1953 – looking east from the proposed terminus. (G Fairley)

ing scheme. A further extension to Bankhead Broadway ran at factory hours to serve Sighthill Industrial Estate. At this time also a regular short working (2A) was introduced between Broomhouse and Hay Drive. Service 5 was re-routed via Gorgie Road (instead of Stevenson Drive) to the Sighthill terminus. In evenings and on Saturday afternoons and Sundays this service cut direct from Junction Street to Lochend Road eliminating the section via Bernard Street. It was also proposed to withdraw service 6, a move which Councillor Harkness found difficulty in explaining since the part of the route between the Saughtonhall area and Haymarket via Roseburn, run only at 'rush' hours was well patronised and Saughtonhall would have been left without any service. The residents argued their case before the Traffic Commissioners, and kept their service. Bus service 6 was thus cut back from Stenhouse terminus to Saughtonhall Drive at Balgreen Road. Buses no longer operated along Whitson Road. Following demolition of the old railway bridge at Davidson's Mains double-deck buses were introduced to service 11 from 31 March 1952, but the service was reduced to twenty minutes frequency. Some journeys on service 21 were diverted to the Princess Margaret Rose hospital on Saturday and Sunday afternoons from 12 April 1952.

The revenue situation was now becoming ever more difficult and a contract was let to use the upper side panels of cars and buses for advertising which brought in several thousand pounds a year. Buses were now used on occasions to augment tramway services, should there be a shortage of cars, or a breakdown. Electric heaters were removed from the cars (after all, the buses did not have such amenities!). Passenger islands at Waverley Bridge were removed in January 1952.

By the end of 1951 many citizens were getting very interested in the future of their transport system and at ward meetings the convener or other councillors were invariably left in no doubt as to the desire to retain the trams. The council was still divided and unfortunately the question became largely a political one. Certain of the so-called

The first phase of abandonment included the routes using George Street. Car 155 was photographed on 8 August 1952 negotiating the West End traffic in Hope Street with Charlotte Square behind. (RJS Wiseman)

Progressive councillors became propagandists for scrapping the trams. On the other hand a few of the better informed refused to agree right to the end. Some arguments put forward by the scrapping propagandists were quite fanciful. Figures, 'facts', and costs were quoted in confusion. The corporation was asked to accept a loan of a modern tram-car to let the public see what could be done. An independent inquiry was sought – and a plebiscite – but these reasonable requests were all refused. At the 1952 elections, the Dalry ward was fought on the transport issue and the tram-scrapping councillor lost his seat.

Much of the track had been allowed to deteriorate to a deplorable condition and the council sought to borrow £250,000 for renewals. This was refused, as nearly half the work should have been provided for from revenue. They were however prepared to sanction £150,000 for certain lengths that Brigadier Langley came to inspect.

The first tramway route to be withdrawn was Comely Bank, replaced by a service of new single-deck buses on 1 June 1952, starting from South St David Street (service 29). The terminus at Comely Bank was extended via Craigleith Road to Craigleith Hill Crescent. The track junction at Frederick Street was taken out immediately. The single-deck buses did not continue for long, being replaced by double-deckers on 7 July.

It was now evident that the ruling body in the council was determined to get rid of the trams, hence any criticism was greatly resented. A prominent member said they should ignore newspaper comment. And so, on 15 July, recommendation to scrap the tramways entirely was made public. The controversy now grew fiercer than ever, both inside and outside the council. The matter was finally laid before the council on 25 September 1952; the decision to scrap the remaining system within three years or as soon thereafter as possible, was carried by 31 votes to 21. But before the minutes were confirmed a public meeting was held in the Central Halls on 3 November. Some 400 persons attended and unanimously resolved that the council rescind its decision. Councillor Harkess was present but did not oppose the motion! Of course the council paid no attention to this or

Crowds travelling to Musselburgh races were catered for by trams drafted from all depots. Number 256 was from Leith, rather than the usual Portobello cars which served the Levenhall 21 route. It is turning short of the terminus on a race day, 12 April 1954. (G Fairley)

to any of the protests received from many local organisations. An awkward question which the Edinburgh and District Trades Council had raised with the Town Clerk made no difference. The E&DTC asked how figures quoted to the Traffic Commissioners by the Chamberlain in support of applications for fares increases, and also used in preparing 'the case' for motor buses, differed greatly from those in the official account. The City Chamberlain had stated that from May 1945 to May 1951 the trams lost £452,240 and the buses lost £84,053, while the accounts showed the former to have in fact a surplus of £70,218 and the latter to have lost £757,804. In an amazing response, the Chamberlain stated 'both sets of figures were quite correct' (!) and admitted that in the figures he had deducted £615,836 from the tramways surplus and paid in income tax, while £720,000 spent on purchasing new buses was 'not included' in the bus deficit! Councillor Harkess (convener of the Transport committee) resigned in April 1953, and when his successor in office came to seek re-election in Craigentinny ward in May 1955, the electors expressed their continuing dissatisfaction by electing his opponent.

During this time finances were going from bad to worse, and another fares increase was called for, requiring a Ministry of Transport Order, since the statutory maximum was now exceeded. This took effect from 7 December 1952, with the minimum fare now 2d. Early morning return tickets were now 6d.

It was alleged the 25 and 26 tram terminus west of Drum Brae constituted a traffic hazard and to obviate this the former service was extended to Corstorphine while the latter was shorted at the Zoo, from 24 August 1952. A week earlier double-deckers had been introduced on bus service 12 consequent on a lowering at the Lady Road railway bridge, plus single line traffic with signals through the skew arch at Portobello station. Crossovers were removed at Iona Street and in Ferry Road at Goldenacre and east of Bonnington Terrace, but a crossover wire was erected at Saughtonhall Drive for 'rush-hour' cars.

On 14 December 1952 tram service 2 between Stenhouse and Granton via George

Terminus for cars to Joppa, Musselburgh and Levenhall was Waterloo Place. A 2½ minute service was given at peak times. Car 409 was purchased from Manchester Corporation in 1949, and is seen on 7 September 1953. Flags are flying from the trolley rope – a feature during the Festival period and also for Royal visits. (AD Packer)

Street, and also the part route service 22, were replaced by a double-deck bus service also numbered 22. The buses could not run direct between Hope Street and Shandwick Place as the trams had done, but instead proceeded via Queensferry Street, Melville Street and Manor Place. They also departed from the tram route by using North St David

Car 65 was a Portobello depot-based tram, found frequently on route 21 and seen on the Esk bridge at Musselburgh (originally single track until the bridge was widened) followed by an SMT AEC single deck bus. (RJS Wiseman)

Terminus view at Fairmilehead illustrating the diversity of the Edinburgh trams – it was said that each tram had its individual characteristics and could be recognised, if not by sight then certainly by sound. Car 180 on the crossover is working an enthusiasts' special, while Pickering 252, a 'standard', Hurst Nelson streamlined 14 and a 'wooden standard', wait. (G Fairley)

Street northbound. It was not until March 1953 that removal of overhead equipment on the George Street and Comely Bank routes commenced, with rail lifting on the latter.

Bus services 4 and 5 were reorganised on 1 March 1953 and re-numbered 34 and 35. From Sighthill terminus the 34 followed the old 5 route through Gorgie, Fountainbridge, West End, Stockbridge, Leith and Lochend to London Road then continued via Leith Street and Post Office to Tron Church where it took up the old 4 route via Fountainbridge, Slateford, and Longstone back to Sighthill. Service 35 followed this long circuit in the opposite direction.

The Stenhouse tram route closed down on 28 March 1953 with service 3 to Newington station replaced the following day by a double-deck bus service of the same number, extended from Newington to Greenend. At the same time the route was also covered by another bus service (33) which continued from Newington via Lady Road to the Inch housing scheme. Existing bus service 3 was renumbered 43. Passenger islands in Dalry Road at Haymarket were removed a few days before tram service 3 was withdrawn. Tram track to Gorgie depot continued in use until service 4 was withdrawn on 2 May 1953. Double-deck bus service 4 which replaced it the following day was extended at one end from Northfield Broadway to Bingham Road (service 24 being withdrawn) and at the other end to Oxgangs Terrace via Craiglockhart Avenue. St Andrew Street was used from York Place only, the other direction using St David Street as was now the usual practice. Pits in Gorgie depot were filled and the premises converted for buses with service 1 trams re-allocated to Tollcross depot. Removal of overhead and track quickly commenced. With this reduction in service one of each 'twin' passenger island on Princes Street south side was removed, while all north side islands were replaced by single, temporary, wooden ones which were removed for a state visit in June 1953. These were in turn soon replaced by permanent islands.

At some busy termini trams reversed at short terminal stubs off the main route. At Morningside Station car 78 on route 23 waits its allotted time on 24 May 1953. (RJS Wiseman)

Sixty redundant trams were sold to J N Connell Ltd of Coatbridge for £90 each as scrap. They were driven to Corstorphine terminus on to Connell's special low-loading lorry.

The original 25% reduction of the tramway system was now accomplished but com-

Cars outside Tollcross Depot waiting to enter the depot after rush hour service. (RF Mack)

plete abandonment was now authorised and plans to achieve this were proceeding with undue haste. Delivery of new buses, plus re-training of tram drivers, restricted progress however, hence there followed a lull before the next conversion. Tram alterations from 31 January 1954 were as follows: service 10 was diverted via Junction Street and Ferry Road to Granton, while service 16 was diverted from this route to Bernard Street in place of service 10, but part-day only. Service 20 was operated during 'rush-hours' only and service 27 was withdrawn in the evenings and on Sundays. Service 15 was shortened at the Braids and service 28 withdrawn. Complaints from Fairmilehead however succeeded in reversing the 15 and 28 cuts from 10 May. Bus service 4 was also extended from Oxgangs Terrace to Fairmilehead on 7 March 1954, service 21 being withdrawn. Additional garage accommodation was acquired in January 1954 by purchase of ground in East London Street adjoining Central Garage.

The next tram conversion was number 1, Corstorphine and Liberton, replaced by buses on 28 March 1954. These carried route number 31, and were extended from Liberton via Lasswade Road to Captain's Road pending completion of road access into Hyvot's Bank housing scheme, which was achieved on 8 May. A temporary shuttle bus (25) had covered the section beyond the tram terminus since 25 January 1954. As now became the norm, the bus service had considerably fewer stops than the trams. The remaining Corstorphine trams (12, 25, and 26) were replaced on 11 July 1954. These all terminated in Meadow Place Road at Drum Brae crossroads which they approached via Featherhall Crescent North returning by the main road. Only the new 25 followed the same route east of Princes Street, while it used St David Street going eastwards. Service 12 left the old route at Fillyside Road and ran by Craigentinny Avenue to Inchview Terrace on Portobello Road, thence to Portobello Town Hall. Service 26 ran via Regent Road to Piershill, then on to a new terminus at Restalrig Avenue. Previous bus service 12 was now renumbered 42.

During the following week scrap trams still ran over the line to Connell's lorry at the Maybury as before, but the next weekend the overhead was cut down between Wester Coates and Belmont, as urgent roadway reconstruction and track removal between Roseburn and Saughtonhall had to be started. This entailed traffic diversions through residential streets, an unsatisfactory practice which became very prevalent. Messrs Connell thereafter loaded in North Junction Street where track and overhead were still *in situ* though carrying no tram service.

In the summer of 1954 bus service 4 was extended to Hillend Park on Saturdays and Sundays. Tram service 27 was shortened to Craiglockhart Station on 6 June 1954, 'POL-WARTH' being shown on the screens, but was extended to Happy Valley on 17 October 1954 (showing 'CRAIGLOCKHART'). Bus services 9 and 11 were diverted from South Charlotte Street to Castle Street and George Street on their way to and from Charlotte Square from 9 August 1954. An overview of traffic requirements, particularly on occasions such as football match days, became possible with radio communication between a Head Office control room and patrol vans, breakdown lorry and tower-wagon.

The time was now approaching when the Musselburgh tram service would be withdrawn, and as this was outwith the city (beyond which the Corporation had no power to run buses) a matter of policy had to be decided. Any application for powers would be opposed by Scottish Omnibuses Ltd, the former Scottish Motor Traction Company, and a new agreement was now necessary in view of the expansion of the city (although not in the direction of Musselburgh). The new agreement stated the Company 'will not operate any route wholly within the city boundaries and the Corporation will not operate any route outwith …' The protective fare structure was modified as follows: on Corporation fares up to 4d the Company to charge 1½d more, and on 5d fares 1d more. Fares over 5d were to be equal. The agreement was completed on 1 July 1954 but did not take full effect until dates as later noted. The spheres of operation were logical, and meant that the Corporation could now operate to Gilmerton, at the expense of Musselburgh, whose residents expressed disappointment. The new fare arrangements were clearly advantageous to the Company and to suburban passengers.

Tram service 15 between Fairmilehead and Kings Road via London Road was replaced on 19 September 1954 by buses following the same route (eastwards via St David Street), to a new terminus at Morton Street, Joppa. Old bus service 15 became 45. Then tram service 5 (Morningside Station to Piershill) was replaced by buses with the route extended slightly at Piershill to Restalrig Avenue from 31 October 1954. Next trams between Waterloo Place and Levenhall (20 and 21) were abandoned without any Corporation replacement after the last car on 13 November 1954. The Portobello route season tickets also disappeared. From the following day bus service 26 was extended from Piershill to a new terminus at Seaview Terrace, (described as 'Eastfield'), thus covering the whole tram route from Waterloo Place and now operated all day, each day. On this date service 25 was extended from Kings Road to Eastfield, and service 12 from Portobello Town Hall to Niddrie Road at Mountcastle Drive South. Portobello to Musselburgh was catered for by a new Scottish Omnibuses route from St. Andrew Square traversing Portobello but on which the new protective fare agreement applied. Over most other routes the agreement did not come into effect until 5 December when further re-arrangement of Corporation services took place, and in Corstorphine, not until 9 December.

A rearrangement of services from 5 December 1954 included withdrawal of bus services 8, 14, 16, and 45 all operated by single-deckers by reason of low railway bridges.

Trams were much used for 'special' operations, Sunday School outings, or, as here, to take Heriot's schoolboys from Lauriston to Goldenacre sports ground for games practice. The long queue of waiting scholars is closely observed by the Traffic Inspector in his Trojan van. (G Fairley)

'Journeys end' for the young sportsmen was at Goldenacre, where car 173 on route 23 pauses at Warriston Gardens stop. The Leyland is on the tram replacement service 8 – these buses have been referred to as 'monstrous masses of shivering tin'. (RF Mack)

At Slateford the road was lowered, hence double-deckers could be used on a new service. This (numbered 44) ran from Eastfield via Milton Road and London Road to Princes Street then by the old service 8 route to Juniper Green. Other new services were still single-deck operated between Portobello Town Hall and Juniper Green via Duddingston Road, Abbeymount, Canongate, and High Street, whence those numbered 45 followed the original route of that number (via Tollcross and Colinton Road) while those numbered 46 followed the old 14 route (via Fountainbridge and Slateford). The 45 timetable was arranged to connect with the Scottish Omnibuses Balerno via Slateford service hence the latter's Balerno via Colinton service was much reduced. At the same date the 33 was extended to Fernieside Drive ('LITTLE FRANCE') at one end and to Saughton Road at the other. From 9 January 1955 bus service 3 was extended to Saughton Road and at the other end to Moredun Park Grove, while a week later service 9 was extended to Silverknowes Roundabout.

As soon as the Portobello trams were withdrawn, the overhead in Waterloo Place and Regent Road was cut down, while the Leith Walk/London Road junction had already been lifted. When the remaining cars in Portobello depot were to be removed it was discovered that their route via Seafield was severed, with track having been removed for road repairs. The cars had to be towed away via Regent Road, by motor lorry. The old Portobello depot was not converted for bus use as the site was quite restricted.

Fares were raised yet again on 17 October 1954 with now only two stages for 2d. The early morning 6d return was also withdrawn, but to assist the outlying housing schemes, the maximum fare was reduced to 4d. After less than two months another wage award upset calculations, and from 27 February 1955, threepence covered four stages instead of six.

Operation of so many buses in busy city centre streets now created difficulties, and it

Trams on busy Lothian Road – where the Western Approach road now disgorges its never ending stream of traffic through the architectural jungle which has grown on the former Caley station goods yard. (AWB Collection)

became necessary to spread out the stopping places so that different groups of services stopped at different points. These were generally sited well away from intersections of side streets, hence were less convenient than the former tram stopping places. The benefit of the virtually reserved tram space in the centre of Princes Street was thus lost.

The next tram abandonment was on 3 April 1955 when service 8 gave way to buses, also numbered 8, with the route extended beyond Granton into Muirhouse, and at the other end to Gilmerton Station Road providing the first Corporation service through the old village. On 7 August 1955 service 27 followed, the replacing bus (also 27) extended to Oxgangs Terrace and Crewe Toll. A small bus lay-bye terminus was formed immediately east of the low Ferry Road 'double bridges' which had insufficient headroom for double-deckers (though this didn't preclude drivers from 'having a go' on several occasions!)

The next tram closures were the Colinton routes (9 and 10) to buses on 23 October 1955. These were both extended at Colinton, service 9 to Bonaly Road and service 10 to Westgarth Avenue. On 25 December the latter was altered to proceed to the terminus outwards via Redford Drive, while the former was further extended to Torphin Road from 29 January 1956. (Former buses 9 and 10 were re-numbered 39 and 40.) Concurrently with the Colinton conversion bus service 19 was altered to become a circular route, extended from its previous Melville Street to Pilton route by way of Wardie Crescent, Granton Road, Canonmills, Broughton Street, York Place, George Street, and Queensferry Street. On 19 June 1955 service 26 had been extended to Drum Brae Drive, (described as 'Clermiston') from April 1956. Service 22 was extended on 17 July 1955 from Granton via Muirhouse, Pennywell Road, Groathill Road and Telford Road to the 18 terminus at Whitehall Garage Blackhall. From this date also, a new double deck bus service (47) was inaugurated from Randolph Place to Drylaw Circus via Orchard Brae, Blackhall, Telford Road, and Groathill Road. From 4 December this ran via Crewe Toll, Telford Road and Groathill Road North, and was extended to Muirhouse.

Foot of Leith Walk, with passing car 239 observed by large numbers of men at a favourite gathering place. (AWB Collection)

Foot of North Bridge just after replacement of car service 3 by the like numbered bus service. JWS 582 was rebuilt for the tram conversion programme from a London Transport vehicle. (Large numbers of these were parked off London Street for some time before reconstruction.) Car 172 is on route 1, running to Corstophine. (G Fairley)

Two 'express' services were run to the Royal Highland Show held in June 1955 near Maybury (before the show settled into its permanent home at Ingliston). One (49) ran from Waverley Bridge via Frederick Street, Comely Bank, Blackhall, Barnton, and Maybury Road; the other (50) from Atholl Crescent direct, via Corstorphine Road. Double-decker buses were used. The Corporation took over the service to Turnhouse Airport under its own licence from the beginning of 1956, ending running under contract to BEA. Night bus services were augmented, a new route (6) from Gilmerton to Blackhall commencing from 5 December 1955 (it had been operated during the 1955 Edinburgh Festival, over a longer route to Groathill Road North). Night service 1 was extended to Oxgangs Terrace, and later, on 26 December 1955, night service 4 was extended to Hay Drive.

As the converted Gorgie depot was incapable of extension, a site for a new garage was acquired at Longstone. This was brought into use on 23 October 1955 and in 1957 Gorgie was sold.

The sixth increase in fares in less than five years took effect on 29 January 1956 when the 5d fare was reintroduced, the child's fare becoming 2d.

The final year of tramway operation had arrived, the situation then being – Fairmilehead, Liberton, Grange, Marchmont, Melville Drive, Mound, Hanover Street, the Granton Circle, Seafield, Junction Street, Ferry Road, Stanley Road were all still served by trams 6, 7, 11, 13, 14, 16, 17, 19, 23 and 28. Track and overhead had now been

Earl Grey Street traffic was held up as one of the reasons why Edinburgh should rid itself of its obstructive trams (what was not made apparent was that the replacement would be more obtrusive, more polluting and – even after deregulation – grossly inadequate). Note the track leading off into West Tollcross and the adjacent depot. All the buildings on the right have been demolished, the site laid bare for years. (AWB Collection)

Princes Street, east end, again illustrating the variety of the Edinburgh tramcar – here no two trams are identical. From the left 180, 18, 59 and 260 – overlooked by 'Edinburgh's Disgrace' on Calton Hill – plus Nelson's monument. (AWB Collection)

quickly removed from George Street, Charlotte Square, Hope Street, and Shandwick Place out to Corstorphine, Stenhouse, and Slateford; also Comely Bank, London Road, Craigentinny Avenue to Kings Road, and most of the Waterloo Place to Joppa section. Gorgie and Portobello depots were closed and substations at Robertson Avenue, Turnhouse Road, Pennywell, Portobello, and Musselburgh no longer supplied traction current. On most main roads complete reconstruction was undertaken, the cost now assuming alarming proportions. Princes Street (except for the portion between Charlotte Street and Castle Street resurfaced in 1951), was now in a dreadful condition and it was clear reconstruction could not be delayed. From 1 March 1956 all east-going traffic (except trams) was diverted into George Street and a gyratory scheme introduced clockwise round the South Charlotte Street, George Street, Castle Street, Princes Street block and around St Andrew Square, this latter moving service 16 to Leith Street. To compensate for lack of bus transport eastwards in Princes Street extra trams were run on the outer circle of service 6. Resurfacing work was pushed ahead rapidly, the tram tracks left for the most part slightly below the adjoining finished road surfaces. Collapsible barriers were located where the discrepancy in level could be considered dangerous.

On 11 March 1956 service 7 was replaced by buses (same route) and tram service 17 withdrawn altogether. The latter gave rise to complaint by dockers, so a rush hour service was operated between Post Office and Granton via Bernard Street. (This ran without a service number, and white front window boards lettered 'Leith Docks' were carried.)

Leith tram depot was closed on 5 May 1956 and conversion as a bus garage commenced. Trams on services 13 and 14 found a temporary base at Shrubhill until 27 May when buses replaced services 6 and 19. Withdrawal of these from Tollcross depot then enabled services 13 and 14 to be operated from there. Old bus service 6 was renumbered 36 while the buses replacing tram service 19 carried number 49. Princes Street traffic was restored to normal on completion of the resurfacing programme, except for the West

No longer does the tram reign supreme in Princes Street. Six buses but only two trams. JWS 616 in the foreground right is ex-London, followed by Leyland LFS 481. Car 150 is on Marchmont Circle route 6. This car, because of its unique 'bucket' seats was always to be found on the Circle, so that they did not have to be reversed. (AWB Collection)

Car 180 was the only 'non-standard' car which lasted to the final days. There were hopes that because of its historical significance, it could be preserved, but this did not come about. By this time the Princes Street track to the west was lifted, the 28 service using the remaining lines to the east. 180 is on the shuttle from Hanover Street to the Infirmary, operated at visiting hours only. (AD Packer)

End, and Mound intersections, and east of St Andrew Street. To enable work to progress from St Andrew Street to the Post Office junction, remaining Princes Street services (11, 13, 14 and 28) were diverted via York Place plus service 16. This change was made on 1 June and track and overhead were immediately removed between St Andrew Street and Post Office. On 16 June Churchhill and Granton Circle trams 13 and 14 were withdrawn and track lifting, already effected in from Liberton to Salisbury Place continued on to the Post Office. A new bus service numbered 14 commenced on 17 June from Newington Station to Muirhouse via Post Office, Pilrig Street, Ferry Road, Goldenacre, and Granton. Tram service 16 was extended from Bernard Street to Granton, operating now all day, and thus replacing the northern section of the Granton Circle trams. The rush hour Post Office to Granton via Bernard Street trams were ended. Cowgate and Causewayside substations shut down their traction supply, and lines to the foot of the Mound were fed from McDonald Road (eastwards) and Dewar Place (westwards) respectively. On 17 June bus service 7 was extended from Liberton by Kaimes, Lasswade Road, and Kirkgate back to Liberton. Buses operating round this loop were numbered 37 in the opposite direction. Service 33 was diverted to East Preston Street and Old Dalkeith Road in lieu of Lady Road, and service 18 extended to Maybury Road at Barnton. The 18 had, on 1 April, been extended from Blackhall via March Road to Parkgrove Street.

The finale of the trams was now approaching. On Wednesday 12 September 1956 services 11 and 16 were replaced by buses, with old bus service 11 renumbered 41. These ran via Leith Street instead of York Place. In order to get rid of the 'sunken' track in Princes Street, tram service 28 was diverted to run by the Mound to Tollcross. Lifting of track from Tollcross to the West End and Mound then took place immediately. Operation of buses over Bernard Street swing bridge required resurfacing of the bridge, as its timber carriageway was not suitable for heavy traffic. (Since April 1955 it no longer opened for shipping). Leith substation and its Wardie satellite now ceased traction supply, McDonald Road taking over supply to Stanley Road and Granton Road Station. Only two tram services now remained, 23 Morningside Station to Granton Road Station and 28 Braids to Stanley Road, both now running via the Mound. Most of the overhead and track of abandoned routes had been swiftly removed, although north of Granton Road Station the overhead remained after track lifting was completed. Poles carrying lighting brackets were taken over by the Lighting Dept, all others were removed.

Last tram day was determined as Friday 16 November 1956, but the Suez crisis erupted just ahead of this. Tramway abandonment in some cities was deferred and it was hoped that Edinburgh might see sense and do likewise. All appeals were rejected; there was to be no reprieve.

During the last week the weather was fine and a vast amount of film must have been expended to record the trams. Children had to be photographed on the platform so that they could prove when they grew up that they had travelled on an Edinburgh tram. Special tickets on yellow paper overprinted 'Last Tram Week' were issued and a decorated tram toured the remains of the system, illuminated at night. All service cars flew trolley rope pennants, previously a joyous indication.

On the final day the restored horse bus appeared on the streets pulled by horses supplied by St Cuthberts Co-op Association, with crew in period uniform. A tour of the city and suburbs was made, attracting much attention; meantime tram services 23 and 28 continued, coping with the afternoon rush very much as usual. It was impossible to realise that there would be no trams running the following day.

The new bus service 23 commenced from Granton Road Station from 6.08pm, but trams continued to run until 7.29pm, this running only to the foot of the Mound, reversing there then proceeding to Shrubhill. At 7.05pm four cars ran from Morningside Station to Hanover Street, back to Tollcross then to Shrubhill, while the next four ran straight through to Shrubhill. Service 28 (being part day only) was not replaced by buses until the next day. The last through 28 from Stanley Road left at 6.57pm, preceded by the decorated tram and followed by two cars as far as Tollcross and three to St Andrew Street only, these then making their way back to Shrubhill. The last of these left Stanley Road at 7.44pm. The last three from Braids ran to Shrubhill direct. All spare trams at Tollcross depot plus old grinder 3 were run down to Shrubhill earlier. Ten trams (specially cleaned) were then sent up to the Braids to form the convoy of 'last trams' to Shrubhill. These quickly filled with those who had applied for special tickets for the memorable journey, although the normal fare was still charged. The very last of these, car 88, was preceded at 7.40pm by the decorated car, then followed from Morningside Station at 7.45pm by car 217, the final car of all, carrying town councillors and invited guests.

Vast crowds lined the entire route, long before the planned arrival at the foot of the Mound at 8.00pm. Pavements there and in Princes Street around Hanover Street were packed. Bus traffic was diverted by Market Street, Waverley Bridge and George Street. At the foot of the Mound the last three cars were stopped and joined by the horse bus. There, with BBC cameras in attendance, drivers James Pryde (car 88), William Moffat of the decorated car and James Kay (car 217) received inscribed controller keys from the

The 'last week tram' 172 was the last of a long succession of decorated trams and toured the remaining lines in the final days. Seen here in a dramatic pose at the foot of the Mound with Edinburgh Castle silhouetted against the skyline. (AWB Collection)

The last act on the final night, at the Mound when the final procession – hours delayed by crowds – eventually got to the spot where the official obsequies were held. Presentations from the Lord Provost to the 'last car' driver emphasised the end of an era of regulated railed electric transport – a civic asset thrown into oblivion; one which could not be replaced and one which – until the roads lobby prevailed – had provided cheap transport to ratepayers and which had contributed profits to the civic purse. (AWB Collection)

Lady Provost. She also handed over a suitably inscribed gold watch to James Kay and wallets to the other two. The ten preceding cars carried their loads only to Shrubhill's gates, then ran on by Pilrig Street to enter Shrubhill by Dryden Street.

The ceremony at the Mound over, the three cars and the horse bus made their way along Princes Street into St Andrew Square whence the horse bus made its separate way to Shrubhill. The three cars then processed through a blare of horns from the buses in St Andrew Square and midst more vast crowds along York Place and down Leith Walk. Pausing outside the Shrubhill gates, they eventually moved slowly through the throng and the gates were closed behind them. Generally the public behaved well, although the final car had been de-wired once or twice. Souvenir acquisition by the few who gained access to the depot was very limited. Many coins were flattened on the rails that evening, and much reminiscence appeared in the local press. The 'Scotsman' wistfully wondered if electric traction might not return again in time.

So an era ended. Traction current was shut down at 9.40pm and that very night the overhead was removed from Princes Street and the remaining islands uplifted. Car 217 was away on the scrap merchant's lorry first thing the following morning. Loading of the abandoned cars was now done inside Shrubhill, the other cars following daily. Fortunately car 35 was set aside for museum purposes. A tractor was used for moving cars for loading, following an unsuccessful attempt to use the 460 volt DC workshop supply.

Chapter 8

THE BUS OMNIPOTENT

The new 28 bus service reverted to its original route by West End and Leith Street, the original 28 now becoming 48. Fuel rationing following the Suez crisis brought bus service restrictions. From 17 December services 9, 14, 15, 17, 28 ,45, 46, and 48 became part day and not Sunday. Despite this service 26 had been extended to Clermiston Gdns from the 9th of the month. Part of Service 12 between Portobello and Niddrie was also thus subject to restricted operation. To compensate service 10 ran to Torphin, service 47 to Granton, while the 44 was diverted via Duddingston Road to Milton Road. Emergency legislation brought in to allow a temporary fares increase was implemented from 23 December, the minimum fare becoming 3d for four stages, and a maximum of 6d. The old fares were later restored but it was only a matter of time before these 'temporary' fares became permanent. The service cuts were restored also, although service 44 never returned to its original route.

Track lifting and road reconstruction proceeded at a pace dictated by funding availability, but the last overhead, at Churchhill was removed in December. It seemed odd to find track paving repairs still being carried out, this necessary where lifting was not imminent. Shrubhill depot also had to be made suitable for buses. The Department's head office in St James' Square, while conveniently situated, was in many ways unsuitable. New premises at 14 Queen Street were obtained and the headquarters relocated there on 13 January 1957. The radio control room and lost property office were also moved to Queen Street.

With a bus system now of over 118 miles, routes operating in 1957 were:

1	Leith Links to Corstorphine via Easter Road, High Street and Gorgie
2	Broomhouse to Newcraighall via Grassmarket & Prestonfield
2A	Broomhouse to Hay Drive
3	Saughton Mains to Moredun via Princes Street
4	Bingham Road to Fairmilehead or Hillend via Princes Street & Slateford
5	Morningside Station to Piershill via Grange & London Road
6	Marchmont Circle
7/37	Kaimes Circle to Newhaven via Foot of Leith Walk & Stanley Road
8	Gilmerton to Muirhouse via Broughton Street
9	Torphin Road to Granton via Broughton Street
10	Westgarth Avenue to Granton via Foot of Leith Walk & Ferry Road
11	Fairmilehead to Newhaven via Pilrig Street
12	Drum Brae South to Niddrie via Leith Walk, Fillyside and Portobello
13	Ravelston Dykes to Bernard Street via Drummond Place & Lochend
14	Newington Station to Muirhouse via Pilrig Street
15	Fairmilehead to Joppa via Princes Street
16	Braids to Granton via Foot of Leith Walk & Newhaven
17	Randolph Place to Granton via Muirhouse

18   Burdiehouse to Barnton via Melville Drive
19   Pilton to Broughton Street, George Street, Crewe Road Circle
20   Calder Road to Cramond (summer Sundays only)
22   Stenhouse to Blackhall via Dalry Road, Leith Walk & Newhaven
23   Morningside Station to Granton Road Station
25   Corstorphine to Eastfield via Princes Street & Seafield
26   Clermiston Gardens to Eastfield via Regent Road
27   Oxgangs Terrace to Crewe Toll via Mound & Hanover Street
28   Braids to Newhaven via Pilrig Street
29   St David Street to Comely Bank via Stockbridge
31   Corstorphine to Hyvots Bank via Princes Street
32   Waverley Bridge to Edinburgh Castle (summer only)
33   Saughton Mains to Fernieside (Little France) via Princes Street
34/35 Sighthill to Gorgie, Fountainbridge, Stockbridge, Leith, Lochend, Leith Street,
      High Street, Fountainbridge, Longstone, Sighthill (Circle)
36   Saughtonhall to Greendykes Road via Roseburn, Grassmarket & Prestonfield
39   Silverknowes to Greenbank Row via Mound
40   Portobello Town Hall to Newcraighall
41   Waverley Bridge to Barnton
42   Surgeon's Hall to Portobello Town Hall via Lady Road & Duddingston
43   St Andrew Square to Portobello Town Hall via Craigentinny
44   Eastfield to Juniper Green via Milton Road & Princes Street
45   Portobello Town Hall to Juniper Green via Willowbrae Road, High Street &
      Colinton
46   Portobello Town Hall to Juniper Green via Willowbrae Road, High Street &
      Fountainbridge
47   Randolph Place to Muirhouse via Drylaw
48   Goldenacre to Davidson's Mains or Silverknowes Promenade
49   Craigentinny Avenue North to Tollcross via Seafield & Melville Drive

The unnumbered service from Comiston Road to the City Hospital still ran at visiting
hours and specials were run from St Andrew Square to Easter Road, Tynecastle or
Murrayfield for matches. Night services were:

1   Foot of Leith Walk to Oxgangs Terrace
2   Portobello Town Hall to Morningside Station
3   Bonnington Terrace to Manse Road, Corstorphine via Broughton Street
4   Hay Drive to Crewe Road North via Stockbridge
5   Waverley to Sighthill Avenue
6   Gilmerton to Blackhall

Changes to services now became frequent. Service 26 was slightly extended to
Clermiston Road North on 31 March 1957, while on 28 July several alterations took
place, *viz* service 1 was extended to Meadowplace Road in Corstorphine; 16 was extend-
ed through Comiston to Oxgangs Bank and 22 extended to Sighthill via Stevenson
Drive; 15 was diverted to run by Whitehouse Loan, Strathearn Place and Churchhill.
Services 6 and 29 were combined, those covering the circle clockwise became service

The four Crossleys were used on the lengthy Eastfield to Juniper Green service, where 601 (GSF337) is seen near the terminus. (DLGH)

29 and diverted at Frederick Street via the existing route to Comely Bank, from there returning to resume the circle again in Princes Street. Those covering the circle anti-clockwise became service 24, the service no.6 was no longer used. From 28 July alternate journeys on service 39 were diverted via West Saville Terrace, Mayfield Road and Ratcliffe Terrace as service 38. This was not popular and ceased on 16 February 1958. A 3d minimum fare for three stages and 6d for over six stages came into effect on 21 July 1957. On 4 August service 48 was extended to Foot of Leith Walk (peak hours to Bernard Street) then later, on 10 November, at the other end to Parkgrove Street, Clermiston. On 9 March 1958 service 1 was extended from Meadowplace Road through Clermiston to link up with the 48 back to Foot of Leith Walk and Leith Links forming a new circular route (21). Service 48 ceased. Additional buses operated over the original service 1 route displayed that number. Another circular route was formed by extending service 42 via George IV Bridge and the Mound to St Andrew Square where it followed the route of service 43 back to Portobello. This retained the number 42, and service 43 was no longer used. This took effect on 16 February 1958. On 23 February followed an extension of service 8 to Silverknowes (to the Promenade in summer), while on 20 August service 14 was diverted from Newington Station via Dalkeith Road and Prestonfield to Hay Drive. Night services were improved, service 3 being extended to Meadowplace Road and service 4 to Muirhouse on 12 May, while service 6 was extended to Clermiston on 24 February. The night service fare then became 1/-.

Service 22 was extended through the Sighthill Industrial Estate at peak periods from 16 June 1958, 1d excess fare being charged on the extension of route. From 1 December the buses proceeded round this extension in the one direction only. Services 7 and 37 were altered from 13 July on weekdays, service 7 then proceeding to Newhaven via Ferry Road, returning by Lindsay Road. Service 37 ran in the opposite direction. From the same date service 12 was extended to Maybury and service 25 curtailed at Drum Brae South. Service 3 was extended to a new turning point at Gilmerton Station Road and service 23 extended to a new turning point about halfway along Balcarres Street from 13 August.

In 1958 off-peak travel declined markedly and frequencies were reduced at those times. There was public protest, and proposals that smaller buses should be used. One-man operation returned after 27 years, on 15 June, on service 40. The Ultimate type of ticket machine was tried experimentally on service 16; these issued a small printed ticket of a different colour for each value, *viz* 2d white, 3d yellow, 4d blue, 5d orange, 6d green.

Further economies in 1959 saw curtailment on weekday evenings and Sundays during the winter of service 13 at Sleigh Drive, service 15 at Morningside Station and service 31 at Saughtonhall Drive, from 8 February until 20 April. Also on 8 February service 41 was extended to cover the 39 route to Greenbank Drive. Service 39 was altered to follow Queensferry Road as the route to Silverknowes. Services 24 and 29 were now also extended to Craigleith Station. Services 4, 11 and 15 were extended from Fairmilehead to a new turning circle half a mile on the Biggar Road from 12 April. Service 11 was diverted to Princess Margaret Rose Hospital during visiting hours, with 1d additional fare, from 1 December 1958. From 17 May 1959 service 10 ran only at peak hours (except Saturdays) and not at all on Sundays. The summer extensions of service 4 to Hillend and service 8 to Silverknowes operated from the spring to the autumn holidays, and service 32 (Waverley to the Castle) ran as one-man operated from 28 June to 21 September. Summer weekend service 20 (Calder Road to Cramond) was cancelled. Further economy was achieved switching garages, so reducing dead mileage. Services 1, 21, 45 and 46 went to Longstone and 18, 23, 24, 27 and 29 went to Tollcross, while Central gained service 9.

Fares were again increased from 27 September 1959, five and six stages now 5½d and the 6d fare over six stages became 7d. The child's fare was increased from 2d to 3d. A service for dog-racing fans was provided as required from St Andrew Square to Beaverhall Road at a fare of 4d.

Services 17 and 47 were altered from 4 October 1959 when service 17 was re-routed via Crewe Road North, West Granton Road, Telford Road and Crewe Toll back to Randolph Place. Service 47 followed the same route in reverse. From 18 October services 11, 12 and 16 were diverted from Leith Street to York Place. A diversion of service 49 via Constitution Street, Charlotte Street, Links Place and James Place on weekdays except Saturday afternoon operated from 14 December 1959 to 18 April 1960 only. From 3 April 1960, 23 was rerouted at Goldenacre via Clark Road and Trinity Road to a terminus in Lennox Row returning by Stirling Road and Zetland Place to Trinity Road. From 25 September, the return was made by South Trinity Road instead of Zetland Place. (Screens read 'TRINITY'.) On this date service 9 was extended to Torphin Golf Club and from 5 December it was diverted via Redford Road, and Westgarth Avenue (except peak hours and Saturdays when service 10 covered these roads). From February there was further reduction in service frequencies on many routes in early morning, evening and Sundays. Service 16 was extended from 12 April at peak hours from Granton to Muirhouse and from 13 June service 49 was extended to King's Road Portobello.

Fares were again increased from 12 June 1960 to become, one or two stages 3d, three stages 4d, four stages 5d, five or six stages 6d, seven or eight stages 7d, nine to eleven stages 8d, twelve to fourteen stages 9d, over this 10d. A twelve journey Monday to Saturday ticket was offered at 8/- and the four-weekly season ticket at 50/-. The Sunday runabout ticket became 3/- with dogs and luggage charged 3d. Night bus fares became 1/3 but a permit allowed the use of two buses for a single fare.

Night buses were re-organised mainly as circular routes from 24 October 1960, operated by one-man single-deckers equipped with a radio to call assistance if needed. These were now:

1   Lochend, Leith Walk, Princes Street, Gorgie Road, Calder Road, Broomhouse Road, Corstorphine High Street, then to Princes Street, London Road and Marionville Road.

2   Portobello Town Hall to London Road, Leith Street, West End, Tollcross, Gilmore Place, Oxgangs, Craiglockhart, Tollcross, West End, Leith Street, London Road, Willowbrae Road and Milton Road West.

3   Foot of Leith Walk, Junction Street, Ferry Road, Newhaven Road, Pilrig, Leith Street, Princes Street to Drum Brae South, Queensferry Road, Princes Street and Leith Walk.

4   Hay Drive, Prestonfield Avenue, Dalkeith Road, Bridges, Princes Street, Frederick Street, Comely Bank, Crewe Road, Pennywell Road, Crewe Toll and back to Hay Drive by the outward route.

5   Hyvots Bank via Waverley, York Place, Broughton Street, Goldenacre to Granton Road, returning the same way to Newington then via Gilmerton Road to Hyvots Bank.

From 23 October service 13 became one-man operated and was re-extended to its former terminus at Bernard Street. Before passing on to 1961 it should be noted that most tram tracks had now gone, lifting in George IV Bridge being completed in March 1960. A short piece with the cable slot was retained as a relic in Waterloo Place (even if not quite in its correct position).

On 8 January 1961 the extension of service 11 to Princess Margaret Rose Hospital (visiting hours only) ceased and the Hospital became the regular terminus of service 15. From 16 January service 36 was withdrawn on Saturdays but a better service was provided on the other weekdays. Service 39 was extended to Silverknowes Promenade for the summer season.

A new Parcels Depot was built on a site in East London Street adjoining Central Garage. The building incorporated a transport museum to which preserved tram number 35 was moved along with other relics. These premises had to be vacated in 1962 and the Parcel Office returned to Shrubhill, with a larger museum, opened during the following year. Construction of a new garage to accommodate 130 buses at Marine Gardens in Portobello was also undertaken, opened on 9 December 1962. Service 39 and 41 were extended further along Greenbank Drive to the City Hospital gates from 22 October 1961. On 2 July 1961 the 4d fare became 4½d, and the 5d, 6d, and 7d fares were increased by 1d.

New buses were now equipped with fluorescent lighting, some including a lit advertisement panel on the off-side upper deck side. Heaters were also fitted and as these were popular, they were then gradually fitted to the older buses. The trams had, of course, had heaters years previously. A 36ft long single-deck 'standee' type bus was purchased. This had a rear entrance, where the conductor sat at a ticket desk, and two exits, front and cen-

Tram replacement Leyland PD2, 420 (LFS420) in new condition at the east end of Princes Street, at Waverley Steps. The smart new bus stop shows that conversion of the Stenhouse and Corstorphine tram routes has taken place, but trams can still be seen in Waterloo Place, dating this to the summer of 1954. (Gavin Booth)

tre. There were seats for 33 passengers and standing for 30. It went into use on service 16 on 29 April 1962, but did not find universal favour and soon disappeared from regular use. It re-appeared on 1 September 1963 on service 21 with the centre exit removed and now allowing only eight standing passengers. Eventually, in May 1969, it was converted to a coach for the Airport service.

Several service changes followed on 29 April 1962. Service 1 buses continued over the 21 route which now became service 1. Service 5 was extended via Northfield Broadway to a terminus in Milton Road (Brunstane) and altered to run via Regent Road instead of London Road. Service 44 reverted to the direct route to town along Milton Road West and service 46 became part-day only (not Sundays). The part-day extension of service 16 to Muirhouse had operated all day from 7 January and was now extended to Silverknowes. On 27 May, half of the 24 and 29 service was extended to Blackhall, the other half being curtailed at Comely Bank, until 4 November when all went to Blackhall. A one-way traffic scheme was introduced at Tollcross on 9 September, outgoing traffic using Earl Grey Street while incoming traffic used Ponton Street and Semple Street. From 12 November service 49 ran via London Road and Easter Road instead of Leith Walk. The visitors' service from Comiston Road to the City Hospital was withdrawn from 29 December. Some fares were again increased on 5 August 1962, the 7d fare becoming 7½d and the 8d and 9d fares increased by 1d. The opening up of Broomhouse Road made possible an extension of service 2 to Corstorphine where it was linked with service 12 back to Niddrie where the low bridge prevented formation of another circu-

One off (fortunately) Leyland PD3/2, PWS998, had a front entrance 72 seat body. Aesthetically disastrous it did pave the way for others of much improved appearance. Seen on tram replacement service 3 to Stenhouse, loading in Princes Street at Hanover Street in 1958. (Gavin Booth)

lar route. Service 25 was again extended to Maybury. On 24 March 1963 service 16 was extended from Oxgangs via Redford Road, now reconstructed, to Westgarth Avenue, Colinton.

In 1963, the first time for many years, the number of passengers carried showed an increase, but this was not maintained and with traffic congestion in the City becoming steadily worse, sustaining regularity became increasingly difficult. In the City centre long delays were endured daily. 1963 saw a change of manager when Mr Little left in September to succeed James Amos as Chairman of the Scottish Bus Group. Mr T Gray depute manager was appointed interim manager until his retirement on 20 July 1964, succeeded then by Mr Ronald Cox from Bournemouth. On 11 August 1963 the 4½d and 7½d fares were increased to 5d and 8d. Long 3d stages were introduced at the outer ends of some routes to help people to reach their nearest shops. On 15 December the 3d charge for luggage was abolished, also service 5 was restored to its original route by London Road and service 49 reverted to Leith Walk. The 49 was also diverted from its route by Melville Drive to run via East Preston Street and Dalkeith Road to Little France. More extensive alterations followed from 1 March 1964; service 39 was withdrawn and 24 and 29 extended to Silverknowes in lieu. Services 18 and 41 were linked at Barnton providing a service through Cramond, Barnton and Davidson's Mains. A new part-day service, 20, was started from Barnton to Hyvots Bank via Queensferry Road, George Street, Bridges, Liberton and Kaimes. The terminus of services 17 and 47 was removed from Randolph Place, the 17 becoming a circle via George Street, Bridges,

Melville Drive and Lothian Road, while the 47 followed the circle in the opposite direction. Service 27 was extended by Telford Road to Muirhouse.

Fares had to be increased again from 17 May 1964, and a more condensed scale was adopted, *viz* one or two stages 3d, three or four stages 6d, over four stages 9d. A useful Information Office at the top of Waverley Bridge came into use during 1964.

On the Fife and Glasgow holidays on 5 and 19 April 1965 an experimental 'Park-and Ride' scheme was tried but with only limited success. From car-parks at Carrington Road and Murrayfield buses ran to St Andrew Square, numbered 30 and 50 respectively. This lasted two years only. An Elderly Persons' Travel Concession scheme was introduced from 2 May for pensioners resident in the City permitting off-peak travel for a 3d fare. Fares generally were further increased from 30 May 1965 when two stages became 4d, 9d for five or six stages and over six stages 1/-. On 19 September, the long stage shoppers' concession cased. Following the spiral of fare increases traffic declined and service frequencies were reduced. Services 26 and 44 were linked at Eastfield from 13 June but the part-day 26 buses did not run through to service 44 but became service 28, terminating at Seaview Terrace. The stance for services 40, 45 and 46 was moved from Portobello Town Hall to nearby Lee Crescent on 19 September.

From 13 March 1966 services 26 and 28 were extended southwards to Clerwood Park at the top of the hill up from Corstorphine. Reconstruction of low bridges at Crewe Toll and Abbeymount removed restrictions on double-deck buses and from 17 July service 27 was able to proceed direct to Pennywell Road and Muirhouse, and was also extended to Silverknowes. Double-deck buses were provided for service 1 from 7 August. On 2 October service 24 was altered to return to town from Silverknowes via Ferry Road, Groathill Road North and Telford Road to rejoin its former route (29 in the opposite direction). A new peak hour circular service started on 3 October from Longstone via Stenhouse, Princes Street, North Bridge, Lawnmarket, Fountainbridge and Slateford to Longstone. This was numbered 38 clockwise, 39 anti-clockwise. Peak hour services such as this were indicated at stopping place 'flags' by a blue circle round the number. Use of the Parcels Service was declining and it closed on 28 May 1966.

On 9 January 1967 service 5 was extended via Greenbank Crescent to Oxgangs. Reconstruction of the low bridge at Niddrie enabled services 2 and 12 to be operated as a circular route from 16 July, service 14 being then extended to the west end of Newcraighall in place of service 2 with service 40 reduced to 30 minutes frequency. The latter had been run as two parts on some Sundays during the bridge reconstruction. There had been no increase in fares during 1966 but this respite ended on 6 August 1967 when one penny was added to all but the 4d fare and twelve or more stages became 1s2d. On 10 October service 20 was re-routed via Esslemont Road to Liberton Dams and on 9 April following the route was further changed from Esslemont Road to West Mayfield.

Labour unrest in the industry nationally came to Edinburgh with 'work-to-rule' sanctions from 23 October 1967, leading to a strike from 15-19 November. As a consequence the Corstorphine branch trains did brisk business (though they were being withdrawn at the end of the year). To assist erstwhile rail passengers from Balgreen Halt, bus service 36 was increased in frequency from 8 January 1968. To facilitate repair, the Dean Bridge was closed to outward traffic from April to June 1968, with bus services (including the Scottish Bus Group) diverted via Belford Road and Queensferry Terrace as they had run in 1922. Services 17, 19, 34 and 47 ran by Belford Road and Ravelston Terrace.

Passenger totals continued the inexorable decline; fewer people went home for lunch

– a tradition in Edinburgh that was encouraged by cheap tram fares. In common with other cities, increased car ownership reduced usage and the consequent increase in traffic volume created congestion, further delaying public transport. A seemingly endless spiral. The labour situation took time to settle, hence further reductions in frequencies could not be effected until 26 January 1969. Changes in services were also involved, services 25 and 46 being withdrawn and service 3 ceasing in the evenings and Sundays, while service 9 on Sundays ran only Colinton to Waverley. Service 15 stopped at 8pm and did not run on Sunday mornings. Other changes were – service 28 curtailed at Clermiston Crescent; service 31 extended via Femiehill Drive to join with the 33 at Little France; service 49 extended to Eastfield, and 45 diverted by Abbeymount and London Road to Meadowbank allowing use of double-deck vehicles. The route was soon altered to East Norton Place to avoid the turn at the top of Abbeymount. On the same date a new fare scale came into effect. One or two stages became 5d, three or four 8d, five or six 11d, seven to eleven 1s2d and over eleven 1s3d. The financial situation became such that during 1968 the idea of the Scottish Bus Group taking over the undertaking had been mooted, but not pursued. From 6 April 1969 services 26 and 44 ceased to run through from one to the other at Eastfield.

All services except 13, 32 and 40 now used double-deck vehicles. Nevertheless in the continuing search for economies and because of a shortage of staff, it was decided that one-man operation would have to be adopted for double deckers also. Fifty double deckers delivered in 1969 were therefore provided with exit doors near the centre and equipped with Setright ticket and change-giving machines. Illuminated 'Pay on Entry' signs were fitted beside the entrance doors and below the route screen. At both corners of the top deck front panel there were white vertical strips with three black circles similarly worded. A trial of double deck one-man operation was made on service 13 from

New generation of touring coach, in black and white livery. Leyland Tiger Cub coach NFS748 (fleet number 819) at the Waverley Bridge stance, 1957. (DLGH)

10 September, and then on 12 October services 3, 8, 31, 33, 45 and 49 followed. One of the new buses stood on Waverley Bridge during the preceding week to demonstrate the system. With the new double-deckers needed for these busier routes service 13 reverted to single-deckers on 5 October. Many earlier front entrance double-deckers were also equipped for one-man operation. Tollcross garage closed on 13 September 1969, its operation transferred to Central.

1970 saw services 38 and 39 replaced from 19 January by a new part-day Monday to Saturday service (30) from Wester Hailes (Hailesland Road, Inglis Green Road, Slateford Road, Fountainbridge, Johnston Terrace and Market Street to Waverley Bridge, the return journey going via the Mound.

An innovation was the introduction, on 16 March, of three one-man operated limited stop services running at, and in the direction of, peak hour traffic only. On the outward journey these only picked up in the City centre and set down only at suburban stops, with of course the reverse on the inward journey. A fare of 1s2d was charged. Service 73 ran from Princes Street (west) to Sighthill with town stops at Shandwick Place and Haymarket and the innermost suburban stop at Parkhead Gdns. Service 76 ran from Princes Street (west) to Clermiston Crescent with the first suburban stop at Drum Brae. Service 78 ran from Princes Street (east) to Gilmerton with town stops at North Bridge and Surgeon's Hall and the first suburban one at Moredunvale Road. The service numbers on the buses and stopping places were in black figures on yellow. On 16 March service 36 was extended to a new turning point at the south end of Greendykes Road. It now ran all day (not evenings or Sundays). The next conversion to one man operation came on 29 March with services 7 and 37. Another sign of the times was seen with employment of the first woman driver in April 1970. Some conductresses converted to driving but the number of women drivers remained low. Fares were further increased on 17 May 1970 and a more compact scale adopted which was suited to one-man operation; three stages became 6d, six stages 1s0d and any longer distance 1s6d. At the end of the school summer term the Scholars Permits of long standing which allowed a transfer on a child's fare were withdrawn in favour of Scholars' Season tickets available in different forms. Summer service 32 from Waverley to the Castle did not run this year and was not reinstated. The British Commonwealth Games were held in the City at the new Meadowbank Stadium from 17 to 25 July and gave the undertaking a busy summer. A special one-man operated service (50) ran Waverley Bridge to Meadowbank for that period. Service 41 was extended to the west end of the City Hospital Drive on 2 August and on the following day service 30 was extended along Hailesland Road, from 25 October becoming all day (including Sundays). Services 5 and 14 changed to one-man operations on 29 November and from the next day Limited Stop service 73 carried passengers either way morning and afternoon. Another useful service also started on 30 November for Christmas shoppers. This covered a circular route via Princes Street, Tollcross, Lauriston Place, Surgeon's Hall and the Bridges, fare 6d. It did not at first show a service number being known as the 'Shoppabus' shown on the destination screens of the one man single deckers used. It ran until 24 December. A new service from Wester Hailes to Corstorphine was proposed via Broomhouse Road, Ladywell Road and Manse Road to Meadowplace Road, but the routes through Corstorphine was considered unsuitable and the licence refused.

15 February 1971 was the date when the change to decimal currency took place. The latest fare scale was arranged to suit the new coinage and with ticket machines convert-

ed in advance the changeover was effected smoothly. Nevertheless there were some increases in fares from 28 March when the 2½p and 7½p fares became 3p and 8p respectively.

Since service 15 did not operate in the evenings, alternate journeys of service 11 were to the Princess Margaret Rose Hospital from 17 January 1971. On 21 March services 18 and 41 were altered to one-man operation. Service 40 was extended on 16 May from Portobello Town Hall via Joppa and Milton Road to the service 5 terminus (Brunstane). A new service round the suburbs started on 20 June. This (32) ran from Foot of Leith Walk via North Junction Street, Newhaven, Granton, Drylaw, Blackhall, Drum Brae North and Broomhouse to Wester Hailes Road at Clovenstone Road, diverting through Sighthill Industrial Estate at necessary times. It was one-man operated and ran every 15 minutes. The 'Shoppabus' service was reintroduced as service 6 on 9 August running 11.30am to 4.30pm and until 6.00pm during December. Further switches to one-man operation were effected whenever new buses were available – service 30 on 8 August, services 24 and 29 on 12 December 1971, service 20 on 24 January 1972 and service 42 on 23 April. As Wester Hailes expanded, service 30 was extended to Clovenstone Road from 19 March 1972, then on 29 October to the new Baberton Mains roundabout. From 19 March also, service 33 was extended via Murrayburn Drive to the new Wester Hailes shopping centre, while in evenings and Sundays, service 22 was cut back from Blackhall to Newhaven. Another service to Wester Hailes started on 20 March 1972 (43) from Waverley Bridge via Mound, Johnston Terrace, Fountainbridge, Slateford Road, Wester Hailes Road and Clovenstone Road to terminate at Wester Hailes Pk. Market Street was used on the inward journey to Waverley Bridge. It was one man operated, every 20 minutes and did not run in the evenings or on Sundays. The 43 was extended to Wester Hailes shopping centre on 29 October. The 33 was further extended to Westburn Avenue on 14 May 1972.

The number of passengers carried continued to decline with revenue trailing behind. The Airport coach service terminal was transferred from BEA's former office in George Street to Eastern Scottish bus station in St Andrew Square from 1 January 1969. Later the Information Office at Waverley Bridge was extended to provide waiting facilities for passengers on the Airport service and the terminus was transferred there from 4 July 1971. Traffic congestion in the City steadily increased, becoming a major problem despite the provision of many extra traffic lights. The system of traffic lights throughout Princes Street and the altered arrangements at the Hanover Street crossing, required service alterations from 19 March 1972 with service 42 diverted via Hanover Street and George Street in both directions. Service 41 was diverted to run via Mound, Hanover Street and George Street in both directions.

Inevitably fares went up again when the 5p, 8p and Night service fares were all increased by 1p on 9 April 1972. A new service (21) started on 30 July from Greendykes to Broomhouse via Prestonfield Avenue, Bridges, Princes Street, Ardmillan and Stevenson Road (Bankhead at peak periods). At the same time the 2A part route buses on service 2 ceased and service 36 was diverted to Hay Drive. On 29 July service 28 was withdrawn and service 15 extended to Eastfield. The Department's first Works Open Day was held on 7 October 1972 at Shrubhill. It was very successful, a free bus running from Waverley Bridge.

The Traffic Plan commissioned by the Corporation from Colin Buchanan Partners and Freeman, Fox, Wilbur Smith & Associates was published in October 1971 (the

'Standee' Leyland Leopard 101 (YSG101) was exhibited at the Scottish Motor Show. It was photographed (November 1961) in Glasgow's Cathedral Square at the Royal Infirmary. It was rebuilt several times, and is now preserved. (K Catford)

Buchanan Report). Although much attention was given to new roads, some emphasis was placed on improving public transport, and restricting parking in the City centre. Public meetings were held throughout the City to debate the Plan. One proposal was for an 'intermediate' ring road on the line of the South Side Suburban railway (which British Rail refused to relinquish) and certain other proposed roads. This aroused vehement opposition. The bias towards public transport seemed to find favour though this in turn led to pleas for better services. The Transport Department's problem was increasing congestion and the re-siting of bus stops even further away from main street intersections where most passengers wanted to be, especially those changing routes. The logic of this (while at the same time exhorting the use of public transport) did not commend itself to the Transport Manager, nor to many others. An Edinburgh Amenity and Transport Association was formed to support an improved public transport system. Regrets that there was no longer a tramway system began to resurface and Professor Hendry of Edinburgh University advocated (on behalf of the Association) a rapid transit rail system solution. For this he gathered much support, though not, apparently, among the City officials. The situation was now beginning to have a familiar ring. However, the Buchanan Report did include recommendations for 'Busways' which represented a small step in that direction. Three routes were proposed; those from Murrayfield and Gorgie converged to reach the old Lothian Road goods yard opposite the Usher Hall, following the abandoned rail trackbed. Another between Piershill and Abbeyhill was on the route of the rail loop which again British Rail were unwilling to relinquish. It was also proposed that buses and taxis only should be allowed on the Bridges and Princes Street. Other traf-

Leyland Atlantean prototype 801 (ESF801C) of 1966 heading east in Princes Street on service 16 to Silverknowes. (AJ Douglas)

Seddon 'Midibus' 103 (BWS103L) on service 60, the short-lived Dumbiedykes Circle, in St Andrew Square. (AJ Douglas)

fic was to be diverted to Queen Street with a tunnel at the West End leading to Coates Crescent. From the Bridges a parallel new road would replace the 'eastern flank' of the City Engineer's proposed Inner Ring Road to which such enormous public objection had been raised. The Queen Street proposal was also widely criticised as completely impracticable.

Actual achievements were creation of 'Clearways' on all main roads, followed later by much greater control of parking in the city centre. The latter was exceedingly unpopular but did secure an improvement in traffic flow and hence in bus service regularity. Construction of the suggested 'Busway' routes from Westfield Avenue and Angle Park Terrace to Lothian Road was put in hand, but these were not now to be for bus use exclusively.

In July 1973 Professor Hendry produced, for the Edinburgh Amenity and Transport Association, a plan for transport in the City with the main flows catered for by a light rail system. Routes proposed were a north circular using the old LMS Leith branch to Newhaven and the South Leith branch to Leith Walk, linking there to the LNER Leith Central branch, and a south circular line on the South Side rail track. There was a branch from this to Oxgangs plus one from the north line to Davidson's Mains. Another line was proposed from Granton using the LNER Granton branch and Scotland Street tunnel to Waverley station whence it was to continue south in a tunnel to near Newington, then on the surface to Burdiehouse. The plan also suggested a suburban service on BR tracks to Curriehill and to Turnhouse, and relaying the Corstorphine branch. There would be 50 stations. In some areas buses were to be used as feeders, but elsewhere buses were to be the main travel mode.

In September 1973 a document, 'Public Transport: The Options for Edinburgh' was published by the Scottish Association for Public Transport. Of two major proposals, one suggested designating 'Bus Priority Routes' on city centre streets and on main arterial routes. Suburban rail services were to be fundamentally restored. A ten-year programme was envisaged, including railway electrification and a new route (in tunnel) between Haymarket and Newcraighall. The alternative plan also included the Bus Priority Routes, but the BR involvement was reduced to Curriehill to Dalkeith and Wallyford and with fewer stations. The main feature of this proposal was construction over a 16-year period of an extensive Light Rapid Transit system serving most of the city and suburbs – mainly by circular routes. Surface running was envisaged with the Bus Priority Routes becoming Tram Priority Routes. Vehicles proposed were two-car articulated trams following the latest Continental practice.

The Corporation appeared to accept that the 'Buchanan' proposals would not satisfy public opinion, but as the rail-based schemes required massive public financial funding, this was sidestepped by the commissioning of yet another report. This, by Consulting Engineers De Leuw Chadwick O'Eocha, was presented in 1975 and also advocated a light rail system for principal routes. Included were lengths of 'elevated' track. Unsurprisingly this was considered unacceptable, and indeed totally unnecessary.

The reorganisation of Local Government was approaching and as transport was to become a Regional function no action was taken. Professor Hendry was now working on a new plan 'Road and Rail, 1975' which included a (partly underground) light rail route from Granton to Burdiehouse, and an electrified BR route from Curriehill to Joppa.

Changes within the Corporation Transport organisation fall to be recorded, from 1973. The Limited Stop services were successful and two more started on 15 January 1973 at

By 1973 Leyland Atlanteans were standardised to this design with panoramic windows. The signs on either side of the destination screen show this to be a one man operated, pay on entry service Number 42 (BFS42L). (AJ Douglas)

a flat fare of 9p. On these two services (70 & 75) single deck vehicles were used, and passengers were required to have the correct fare as no change was given. Service 70 ran from Waverley Bridge via Mound, Johnston Terrace, Fountainbridge and Slateford to Wester Hailes. The 75 from Princes Street (east) ran to Eastfield. Another new service (60) started on 28 January from St Andrew Square to Dumbiedykes via North Bridge, St Mary's Street and Holyrood Road to Viewcraig Street, returning by High Street, Mound and George Street. Small 25-seat Seddon Midibuses were used. From 22 July the route was extended to the foot of Holyrood Road in lieu of Viewcraig Street. The service ran at 20-minute frequency until 7.00pm only.

These three services, plus service 6, were the subject of trials of four fare-collection systems, observed by the Corporation's Work-study Dept. All four systems, Videmat, Autofare, Setright and Almex incorporated a farebox into which the fare was deposited. Passengers quickly became accustomed to providing the correct coinage, sometimes when necessary pairing up with others before boarding – very un-Edinburgh behaviour! In addition to legal tender the new fareboxes also collected 36 foreign coins, 11 washers and two other (undefined) items.

The experimental battery-electric bus owned by the Department of the Environment was briefly used on service 6. Service 4 became one-man operated from 14 January 1973, services 17 and 47 on 29 April, and 44 on 20 May. Service 10 was extended to Torphin (all day) and from Granton to Muirhouse at peak hours, from 8 August. As a consequence of development of Turnhouse Airport the main road (A9) beyond the Airport was closed permanently. The Kirkliston services of Eastern Scottish ran via Glasgow Road from 2 August, leaving Turnhouse without a service. This was remedied by a new Corporation service (25), from Charlotte Square, also from 2 August, operated initially by one-man single deckers, then later by Seddon Midibuses.

Ronald Cox, the Transport Manager, departed in April to join the new Greater Glasgow Passenger Transport Executive. His successor in Edinburgh was R E Bottrill, who had been at Portsmouth. Mr Cox was, no doubt, pleased to be aware that passenger numbers had started to increase; the decline had at last been halted. In the summer of 1973 the new Manager proposed that fares be increased to 4p, 7p and 10p, but the Transport Committee favoured a scale of 4p up to six stages, 8p above. This was rejected by the Traffic Commissioners as it appeared to rely upon a rating subsidy. A fare increase did come into effect from 3 February 1974; 4p for three stages, 7p for six, and 10p over. The Council agreed to the OAP concession fare being replaced by free travel at all times, effective from 1 October. The Social Work Dept made an appropriate contribution to the Transport Dept finances.

The 'Exact Fare' system using Bell-Punch Autofare equipment was introduced on service 30 on 30 September and the next day on service 43. In place of the 'Pay on Entry' indication, these services displayed a blue arrow on a white background. Fares were placed in a hopper, the driver then providing a small ticket from a dispenser. Tickets were coded 1 to 4 for fare values of 3p, 4p, 7p,and 10p respectively. Another Limited Stop service (77) commenced on 3 December 1973 from Princes Street (east) to Oxgangs Bank.

The Autofare system was extended to Limited Stop services 70, 73 and 77 in February 1974 and applied to other services on conversion to one-man operation (if not so already) thus

4 March	service 3	18 August	26
17	31, 33	25	8
24	17, 32, 47	15 September	24, 29
31	14	22	18, 41
7 April	7, 37	30	20
26 May	23, 27	6 October	22
23 June	42	28	75
22 July	49	3 November	13, 25, 40, 60
28	45	4	Night services
4 August	5	9 March 1975	19
12	78	13 April	11

Setright fareboxes were used for Night services and on service 77 from 2 March 1975. Service 60 was altered on 6 January 1974 to run from Waverley Bridge to Holyrood via Mound, High Street, Market Street, returning by Holyrood Road, St Mary's Street, High Street, and Market Street. The Seddon Midibus initially used proved unpopular and was replaced by a normal single decker. From 6 October the route was extended via Abbeyhill to Meadowbank, returning via Spring Gardens. From this date service 13 was shortened to operate Lochend to Charlotte Square only, though for a time some journeys continued to Craigleith Rise. A new 'Hail-a-Bus' service (61) was operated Frederick Street to Ravelston Dykes where it took a route including Succoth Place, Cumlodden Avenue, Campbell Road and Craigleith Avenue North then back along Ravelston Dykes, stopping anywhere on request. Seddon Midibuses were used from this time on service

40. On 6 October service 32 was extended from Foot of Leith Walk via Portobello to Hay Drive, and at the other end from Wester Hailes to Hyvots Bank via Colinton, Oxgangs, Fairmilehead and Kaimes. At the end of May 1974, a fuel delivery strike affected Corporation services only minimally. Only the Shoppabus was withdrawn. It did reappear, but only irregularly (as a result of staff shortages) until December, when it disappeared for good. Vandalism on buses had reached alarming proportions with bus crews being subjected to unacceptable levels of violence. To emphasise their concerns staff withdrew all services after 9.30pm on 25-28 July.

Traffic arrangements at Tollcross were altered from 7 July following widening of Earl Grey Street, with a bus lane for north bound services. This was the first dedicated bus lane in the City. Service 4 was now extended to Hillend at all times, and service 40 was cut back to Newcraighall from 8 September. With rampant inflation a further increase of fares became unavoidable, taking effect on 18 April 1974 – less than seven months since the last. All fares were increased by 1p. The next increase came just six months later, on 23 February 1975, the scale becoming 6p, 10p, and 13p.

The new Western Approach Road built along the former railway from Lothian Road to Angle Park Terrace was opened on Sunday 15 December 1974, with limited stop services 70 and 73 transferred to it from the following day. Service 70 then ran by Gorgie Road and Longstone Road instead of Slateford Road. A special service (51) ran by the Western Approach to Murrayfield on International match days. New Limited Stop services started on 14 April 1975; 71, Princes Street (east) to Oxgangs, 72, Hanover Street to Oxgangs replacing the 77 which was withdrawn, 79, Princes Street (east) to Fairmilehead. On the previous day several services were altered; the 7 and 37 reverted to their old separate routes to Newhaven, but the 7 was diverted from its Kaimes circle to link with the 11 at Fairmilehead, and service 37 was extended to Burdiehouse; service 15 was diverted to Swanston Drive; service 20 diverted by Hope Park Terrace, Mayfield Road, Liberton Brae and Lasswade Road to Gilmerton; service 31 was diverted via Kaimes and Captains Road in place of service 20; and service 32 was extended between Hay Drive and Hyvots Bank forming an outer circular route.

CHAPTER 9

THE REGIONAL REGIME

Reorganisation of Scottish local government from 16 May 1975 brought major changes, with transport becoming a Regional function. Edinburgh Corporation Transport Department was no more – the undertaking becoming Lothian Region Transport. Assets passed to the Region while the financial deficit of c£2m remained with Edinburgh District Council as successors of the Corporation. This, not surprisingly gave rise to some hard feelings. The City coat of arms on the buses was replaced by Lothian Region's new 'crest'. The legal lettering was changed within days. There was again a proposal at this time that the whole undertaking be sold to Eastern Scottish Omnibuses Ltd, but nothing transpired.

Services operated at the time of transfer were:

1   Leith, High Street, Corstorphine, Ferry Road, Leith Circular
2   Broomhouse, via Grassmarket, to Niddrie (linked with service 12)
3   Saughton Mains to Gilmerton
4   Bingham Road, via Slateford to Fairmilehead or Hillend
5   Oxgangs to Brunstane
7   Fairmilehead, Kaimes Circle to Newhaven via Foot of Leith Walk, Junction Street and Stanley Road

Lothian Region Transport Leyland Cub 169 (MSC169X) turning into Princes Street from Waverley Bridge on the short-lived 85 service to Turnhouse. (AJ Douglas)

LRT Leyland National 106 (YFS106Y) at the foot of the Mound on service 49 bound for Eastfield. (AJ Douglas)

8   Gilmerton via Broughton Street to Silverknowes

9   Colinton via Broughton Street to Granton

10   Colinton via Foot of Leith Walk to Muirhouse

11   Kaimes, Fairmilehead Circle via Pilrig Street to Newhaven

12   Niddrie via Foot of Leith Walk to Broomhouse (linked with service 2)

13   Lochend to Charlotte Square or Craigleith Rise

14   Muirhouse to Newcraighall

15   Eastfield to Fairmilehead

16   Silverknowes via Newhaven & Morningside to Colinton

17/47 Muirhouse Circle – Melville Drive Circle

18   Burdiehouse to Barnton (linked with service 41)

19   Pilton, Broughton Street, Crewe Road, Pilton Circle

20   Barnton to Hyvots Bank

21   Greendykes to Broomhouse

22   Sighthill via Foot of Leith Walk to Newhaven

23   Morningside via Mound to Trinity

24/29 Marchmont Circle, Stockbridge, Silverknowes Circle

25   Charlotte Square to Turnhouse

26   Clerwood to Eastfield

27   Oxgangs via Mound to Silverknowes

30   Waverley Bridge via Fountainbridge to Wester Hailes

31   Ferniehill Drive to Corstorphine

32   Hyvots Bank, Colinton, Corstorphine, Granton, Leith, Niddrie, Hyvots Bank

33   Ferniehill Drive to Wester Hailes

1984 Leyland Olympian 762 (B762GSC) has the LRT logo on the bonnet in its all-over advertising livery. Passing the end of the Western Approach Road at Lothian Road by the Usher Hall. (AJ Douglas)

34/35 Sighthill, Fount'bge, Stockbridge, Leith, Lochend, Fount'bge, Sighthill
36   Saughtonhall to Hay Drive
37   Burdiehouse via N Junction Street to Newhaven
40   Newcraighall via Portobello and Eastfield to Brunstane
41   Barnton via Mound to Greenbank (linked with service 18)
42   Portobello, Lady Road, Mound, Craigentinny, Portobello Circular
43   Waverley Bdge via Fountainbridge and Kingsknowe to Wester Hailes
44   Eastfield to Juniper Green
45   Portobello via Colinton to Juniper Green
49   Little France via Seafield to Eastfield
60   Waverley via Holyrood to Meadowbank
61   Frederick Street to Ravelston Dykes 'Hail-a-bus'
70   Limited Stop Waverley Bridge Wester Hailes
71   Limited Stop Princes Street to Oxgangs
72   Limited Stop Hanover Street via Lauriston to Oxgangs
73   Limited Stop Princes Street to Sighthill
75   Limited Stop Princes Street to Eastfield
76   Limited Stop Princes Street to Clermiston
78   Limited Stop Princes Street to Gilmerton
79   Limited Stop Princes Street to Fairmilehead
Service numbers 6, 28, 38, 39, 46, 48, 50-9, 62-9, 74 & 77 were not in use.
Single deck buses were in normal use on services 25, 40, 60 and 61, while only services 1, 2, 9, 10, 12, 15, 16, 21, 34, 35, and 36 had conductors with Setright ticket machines.

SOME CONCLUDING NOTES

What changes have transpired since the start of this story! From the dark evening when Willie Elliot's Musselburgh horse coach started off from Waterloo Place without him, coming to a halt at Portobello twelve minutes later, his inside passengers quite unperturbed thinking only 'Willie is driving unusually fast tonight'. Some older readers may recall the laborious business of getting the hood up on a charabanc when it came on to rain (though sometimes the crew would rather keep on running, in the hope that the rain would go off!); and starting the engine before leaving the terminus by swinging the starting-handle.

Until the thirties it was the rule rather than the exception for the conductor to call out the stopping-places. This useful practice has gone – as have conductors! A few old hands kept it up, and some may recall the embellishments regularly added by a worthy on car service 12 – 'Next stop the Zoo, for the monkeys...' The Zoo gave him plenty scope, but he had some pithy comment for most stops. Even on bus service 9 in the fifties the practice persisted!

This work is an attempt only to record the past – those interested in daily passenger movements into and out of the City will find a useful survey in the magazine of the Scottish Geographical Society vol 69 no 3.

There is at present a proposal for a 'guided bus' route for a small part of Edinburgh's transport system. Why not turn the wheel the full circle, as some English cities have been able to, and restore to Scotland's capital modern, rail-borne, pollution-free public transport, fit for the twenty-first century and a re-invigorated Capital City?

To this end there has been set up the 'New Edinburgh Tramways Company' which is actively campaigning to restore a modern tramway to the streets of the Capital. This proposes a modern urban transport nucleus for the city in the new century. The proposed first route is very similar to the line of Edinburgh's first, 1871, horse tramway line from Newhaven to Haymarket. Perhaps the wheel has indeed turned the full circle.

Appendix 1

ROLLING STOCK – TRAMCARS

Top deck covers ordered by the Corporation for the cable cars from Hurst Nelson & Co were slightly longer than the lower saloons, with four side windows and a more curved roof. Balcony canopies were symmetrical, of full width. As the bulkhead doors were central, new semicircular turn stairs were provided. These new top covers were fitted to cars 3, 4, 16, 20, 31, 33, 58, 101, 116, 117, 118, 147, 154, 155, 156, 158, 159, 160, 163, 168, 174, 182, 183, 185, 192, 193, 194, 198, 201, 207 and 208. After reconstruction the weight was increased to 8ton 16cwt.

Mr Pilcher planned to convert as many as possible of the cable cars to electric operation. In April 1921 the first, car 36, appeared with a new Hurst Nelson top cover, extended balconies and lengthened platforms with drivers' vestibules. Cushioned seats were provided in the lower saloon. Two cable car bogies were fitted with 27hp electric motors and new disc wheels. It was then put to work on the Leith section lines, part of the Edinburgh undertaking since November 1920. In July car 33, which had already received a Hurst Nelson top cover, was similarly reconstructed, but it retained its cable bogies and continued in use on the Murrayfield to Nether Liberton route. Cars 115, 178 and 185 were thus reconstructed, but on four-wheeled electric trucks; 115 had a new type

Standard open top cable car 208 of Brown Marshall build photographed at the entrance to Shrubhill car shed. The newly applied Corporation coat-of-arms dates this to immediately after the change of ownership, ie 1919-20. Unusually this car has a grip wheel at both ends. Normally this was transferred by the driver to the front platform. (EOC)

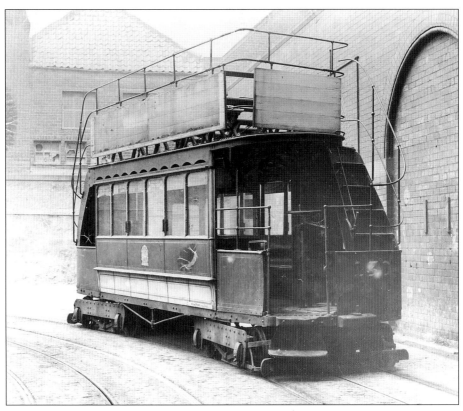

Cable car 130 at Shrubhill in early Corporation days. This was one of the former Northern Section cars, not normally to be found on the City lines. (EOC)

of Brill truck, the other two with 8ft 6in wheelbase Peckham trucks and 32hp motors. These four cars, 36, 115, 178 and 185 were initially painted in Leith style, with small number transfers. Cars 33, 36 and 192 had a single window on the platform vestibule corners, the others two narrower ones.

Thus the initial electric stock consisted of the 38 Leith cars, four Slateford cars and the four new conversions. To avoid duplication all Leith cars had their numbers increased by 230. The Slateford cars were renumbered 229, 230, 268 and 269. They were removed from their old bogies and mounted on new trucks; a Peckham for 229, a Brill (as the Leith cars) for 230 and new 7ft 6in Brush trucks for the other two. In 1922 the body of 229 was reconstructed like a Leith open-topper but without platform vestibules. It may not have operated thus as it was soon provided with vestibules like the other converted cable cars. Cushion seats were fitted in its saloon. The other three Slateford cars were reconstructed in 1926 as normal open-top cars with vestibuled platforms, but without the cushioned seats.

Having tried these Peckham, Brill and Brush trucks, and the converted cable bogies – which though lighter and faster were found to be heavier on current – Pilcher proposed that 37 cars be fitted with bogies for use on the hilly routes, the others to have four-wheel trucks. It was however felt that standardisation presented greater benefits and the bogie proposal was ruled out. The Peckham truck was chosen as standard, and the converted

Top covered car 154 at Murrayfield terminus. This has had a Corporation repaint with more elaborate livery than that favoured by the company. (EOC)

The ultimate in cable cars. Number 33 as rebuilt in 1921 in preparation for electrification, but running on cable bogies in the short term. An electric car in all but means of propulsion it now has lengthened top deck, and enclosed platforms with front exits. At Murrayfield with driver J. Berwick. (Late J Berwick)

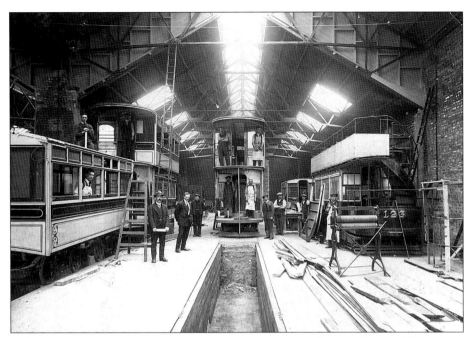

Reconstruction of cable cars in hand at Shrubhill, a photograph full of interest. From the left, a new top deck sitting on a pair of ex-cable bogies, top covered cars 168 then 4, another top deck and on the right Northern section car 123 with the Corporation crest just visible beside the top deck canopy propped awaiting fitting. (EOC)

cable bogies were soon discarded although the Brill and Brush trucks remained. Peckham type trucks were supplied by Hurst Nelson and Brush, with 26-inch diameter wheels. In some cases 27in wheels were used, this eventually becoming standard. Wheelbase was 8ft 6in with two Metropolitan-Vickers type MV101 40hp motors. Axle-boxes rode on patent Peckham pendulum links that gave very steady motion. Magnetic track brake shoes were fitted, energised from the rotating motors through the controller connections, though the first truck on car 178 did not have these, its electric brake being plain rheostatic (*ie* the rotating motors dissipated their generated current in resistances). In many later trucks motors were 50hp MV101B. A number of these were fitted with roller bearings, becoming MV101BR. The motors on 115's Brill truck, and those on the converted cable bogies were by GEC.

Cable cars that had previously been fitted with new Hurst Nelson top covers were being reconstructed similar to car 33, for use for the last few months of cable operation. In June 1922 as the first stage of electrification approached they were quickly put on Peckham trucks, fitted with controllers and run on the new Liberton and Churchhill electric routes. These twenty cars were numbers 3, 4, 20, 31, 33, 116, 117, 118, 147, 155, 168, 174, 182, 183, 192, 194, 198, 201, 207 and 208. The balance of the standard cable cars (except 43 which had been out of use since 1916) were all similarly reconstructed, on Peckham electric trucks. Provision of cushion seats was soon stopped. The reconstructed cars were 27ft 8in long overall and seated 20 in the saloon and 36 upstairs. New top deck covers were provided by various builders, but some Brown-Marshall cars remained open top with 40 seats and central trolley mast. The Dick-Kerr and Shrubhill built cars were the last to be converted, most used latterly on the Portobello route. Cars

Car 36 was, in April 1921, reconstructed like 33 on page 113 but was mounted on experimental electrified cable car bogies. Photographed on trial at Stanley Road on the former Leith lines it was said to be prone to derailment and heavy on power consumption. The car number is in the small blue-shaded Leith style transfers. (EOC)

Another of the earliest conversions was car 178, mounted for comparison purposes on a Peckham truck (without track brakes). Seen here on Granton Road overlooking the harbour with the Fife coast beyond. (EOC)

Car 84, seen in Shrubhill, was placed in service in January 1923. It was a former Northern section car (probably 126) which had received a virtually new body in 1916. It soon became a works car, and was scrapped as early as 1928. (EOC)

54, 59, 66 and 72 retained a shallow step into the lower saloon that later proved troublesome in the wartime blackout. Car 222 of the former type was dealt with in a unique manner. Its original 1907 top cover was retained, the bulkheads removed and new vestibuled ends built enclosing the stairs. It thus became all enclosed but was not to be confused with 'Crystal Palace' cable car 37 which was converted in the normal fashion with a new top cover. Car 222 seated 42 on the top deck and was erroneously licensed for 22 in the lower saloon (which had cushion seats).

By June 1922 six new cars (from an order for sixteen) had been delivered and were placed to work in Leith. These were slightly longer than the converted cable cars, with four windows aside in the lower saloon and top saloons. They seated 22 in the lower saloon, on wooden seats, and 36 upstairs. Overall length was 29ft 9in and weight 9ton 9cwt. The stairs turned 90 degrees to a small landing at the top. Otherwise they were similar to the converted cable cars. Numbered 121-136, the lower decks were built by Messrs McHardy & Elliott Ltd, with top covers from the Hurst Nelson order. They ran on standard Peckham trucks. Substantial orders for standard cars were then placed (with other firms) and these began to appear in the summer of 1923, Following completion of cable car conversions early in 1924, Shrubhill works then commenced construction of similar new cars.

All standard cars and ex-cable cars were fitted with narrow doors beneath the stairs, which could be opened by the driver. This was intended for use as a front exit at busy stopping places, but as the benefit was limited, they soon fell out of use. One of the new Shrubhill cars (53) was fitted with similar doors to the platforms, worked by air. These also proved inconvenient and were soon removed. On all cars a chain was hung on the dash, which was put across the entrance by the conductor when the car was fully loaded, and always hung across the driver's platform.

New cars and ex-cable cars were fitted with roller blind destination screens above the driver's window, and also carried a side window route board. A lantern was fixed below the balcony roof, above the top of the stairs, showing to the front and side two coloured glasses for route identification. These conformed to the service number, which initially had been displayed on a board, as on the cable cars. From August 1923 an extension was fitted below these lanterns with a sloping mirror behind, and the service number displayed by a stencil. Open-top cars had this mounted on a post at the top of the stairs. The route number stencil, when added, was put above the coloured glasses. Former Leith cars were also so provided.

Cars were painted in much the same livery. Waist panels and dash panels, and the panel above the side windows on the converted cable cars, were madder (otherwise known as maroon) with gold lining bordered by a thin white line with corner ornamentation. Other panels were white with brown lining bordered by a thin red line, forming scrolls at the ends of the top deck panels. Window pillars were white with a thin red or black line, though in some cases parts of the lower saloon corner pillars were madder. The roof was black, with initially the edge painted white. Rocker panels were lettered 'Corporation Tramways' in gilt lettering with red shading, the number in the centre of the dash being similar. Railings *etc* on balconies were red, trucks were red picked out with black lined white. The white paint-work aged to a cream or yellow tone, following subsequent re-varnishings. Grinder car number 1 remained green with white lining and gilt lettering shaded blue as it had been in Leith days.

Controllers were either by BTH or Dick-Kerr with the former predominating. There

Manufacture of standardised tram bodies at Shrubhill c.1925. As can be seen parts were prefabricated, not built as individual cars. (EOC)

were two exceptions, 9 and 172, which had Metropolitan-Vickers controllers. All cars were equipped with the usual hand brake, sand pedal, gong pedal, and lifeguard equipment. The resistance boxes were tight under the stairs and the circuit-breakers mounted on the lower saloon bulkheads. Contrary to normal practice, headlamps were not fitted, just a small lamp alongside the destination box. When this was to the rear a red glass was swung over it. On cars built after 1924, this lamp was put above the outer of the two corner windows, and earlier cars were subsequently altered. Electric bell pushes were fitted. The driver was provided with an inner mirror plus an outer one giving him a view of the steps. A small outside mirror was also fitted to the centre of the top deck for use by the conductor, but these were soon removed.

Some non-standard cable cars now require to be examined. These were the three reconstructed Northern section cable cars, 123, 125, and 126(?), plus a fourth one (number unknown) which retained its six windows; prototype cable car 112, and three of the converted horse car types, 15, 17, and 19. All other Northern car numbers had been used for the new standard cars so these were renumbered, respectively, 75, 76, 84, and 86. Of these, 75 was stripped of its seats and stairs though the decency board remained. Fitted with chutes and hoppers for track-salting duties, it ran on the Peckham truck without track-brake shoes ex 178. The remaining three had their reversed stairs altered to normal pattern and with only minor changes resembled the old Slateford cars in their original form. Running on Peckham trucks they saw use in passenger service for just a year or so, then in 1924 they also were reconstructed as salt cars. Stripped of top-deck fittings and stairs, platform vestibules were now provided. Number 75, already a salt car, was then dealt with similarly. Number 112 was also used in passenger service, on a Peckham truck, until becoming a salt car in 1924. In this case the removal of top-deck fittings, stair *etc* and provision of platform vestibules was not undertaken until 1927. The three former horse cars did not see use as electric passenger cars. Car 19 was fitted up first as a rail grinder car with water tanks, but this equipment was later removed, it then becoming another salt car. Number 17 was equipped as a grinder car, while 15 became a salt car. All three were provided with Peckham trucks, but retained their upper deck panels and stairs until 1924 when they were stripped of these, and then provided with platform vestibules. Brackets for snow plough side extension arms were later fixed to the truck of 19 but then were later removed. Provision was made for attaching snowploughs to the fronts of all salt cars when required. When the salt and grinder cars were vestibuled they were repainted madder overall, unlined. They retained their trolley masts (except 19), though most lost them later.

Ex Leith grinder car 1 was also fitted with platform vestibules but these did not extend beyond the platform. It exchanged its original Brill truck with 19's Peckham and was repainted in 'works car' over-all madder. It later received canvas side sheets, finally replaced by metal sides.

In the summer of 1923 number 177 was the subject of an interesting experiment, suggested by Councillor Mancor, with a rubber ring insertion in the wheels. Unfortunately this attempt at resilience and quietness was not successful. 49 was for a time fitted with a roller-blind destination screen in the middle side window, while an advertising route indicator was tried in 117. 225 ran without track-brake shoes for a while, and 47 got the new Brill truck from 115. Two types of roller bearing axle boxes were tried, an SKF set on 105 and for a time 208, and a Hoffman set on 27 briefly, and then on 45 until 1930, and finally, from 1933, on 89.

All Leith cars lost their advertisement panels in 1923 and in 1924-5 all their top-covered cars were rebuilt and fitted with platform vestibules. Those that already had platform vestibules got new ones and new metal dash plates. The opening roofs on numbers 261-3 disappeared. Trucks were lengthened to 7ft 6in and some cars got new electrical equipment. Earlier they were fitted with magnetic track-brakes for the Edinburgh lines. 247 was provided with a new shorter wheelbase Peckham type truck. The first car reconstructed, 262, lost its headlights, but these were retained on all others. All were painted in standard style with red-shaded dash numerals. Only a few of the Leith open-toppers were thus painted, and none was reconstructed. About this time the Milne reversible cushion seat was marketed and fitted in the top saloons of all new cars after 1925, then to all earlier standard cars and most of the ex-cable cars.

Air operated track brakes were required on the Comely Bank, Mound, and Hanover Street routes; the first sets by G D Peters & Co Ltd, were fitted to the Dick-Kerr ex-cable cars (except 222) and to cars 37, 46, 48, 53, and 192. Later sets went to 143-4 and 332-41. The compressor and air reservoir were placed under the lower saloon seats, the driver's control mounted between the controller and brake handle. As the hand brake on these cars would not be used for service stops, they were provided with a driver's seat carried on folding brackets attached near the controller. In 1925 similar air brakes to operate on the wheels were introduced and the cars so fitted are listed. Peters provided 60 sets, Westinghouse 37 sets.

In 1926 further new cars were being built at Shrubhill with numbers reaching 353, with all formerly blank numbers filled. The oldest of the ex-cable cars were now being broken up, but where new deck saloons had been fitted they were reused. For the next

Bow collector experiments were carried out using car 67 on the Portobello route. Seen here outside Portobello Depot. (EOC)

Pantograph collection was tried for a short time, also on the Portobello run. Car 73 is seen at Joppa. The bowler-hatted figure in the saloon is Robert Shaw, Overhead Superintendent. (EOC)

two years no increase in stock was made, new cars built at Shrubhill replacing ex-cable cars, taking the same numbers, using old top saloons where suitable. Car 36 (completed in October) was the first replacement with a slightly modified design. The front exit under the stairs had a step down to a well inside in lieu of the outside step, and the folding doors extended down to cover this. Another innovation was the introduction of transverse cushion seats, Milne type, in the lower saloon. These were arranged in four rows of double seats on one side with single seats on the other plus longitudinal fixed cushioned seats for two over the sandboxes in the corners, total seating becoming 20. The conductor's bell-pushes were moved from the window rail to the ceiling. The next three cars, 33, 185, and 208, were similar to 36 but did not initially have the new seating, though they were soon altered. Subsequent cars had the transverse seats but the well inside the front exit was shallower and the outside folding step reappeared. Cars built after 1927 were slightly wider and had a small radius turning under the rocker panel. Most new cars were fitted with wheel air brakes, though some ran without this for a short time. The transverse seating was very popular and older standard cars were altered. In some cases an end window on one or both sides of the lower saloon was made to open. On car 36, and some others, the gear ratios were altered to give higher speed; HS was then stencilled inside the dash.

By 1929-30 the few remaining open top cars were used only at peak times, but since traffic was still increasing, the fleet was expanded by seventeen cars, plus replacement cars also built. Numbers 354-366 were standard type, except on 357, 358, and 360-6 where the front exit was omitted. This also applied to replacement cars 79, 101, and 198.

A few earlier cars were also treated thus. Some of these new cars had white panelled ceilings in the saloons, but these were eventually replaced by the usual brown. New build 367-370 had totally enclosed top deck saloons without bulkheads, the top of the stairs enclosed by a partition and sliding door. Tubular electric heaters were provided, with seating for 38. The service number was displayed on a roller blind above two concentric discs with coloured glasses in a box over the stairs. On 367 the route number was initially alongside the colour lights and the lining out was simplified, with all fancy scroll-work omitted. On the other three all window pillars were dark brown, this then becoming standard for all new cars. As the top deck panels were now continuous round the car, the lining was likewise, with scrolls and red lining omitted. All had a single, wide window to the platform corners (like old 36), and this also became standard practice.

Further cars replacing ex cable cars, and utilising their old top decks, were built in the old form but now the balcony ends were enclosed. As the saloon bulkheads remained, the stairs were not partitioned off, and the box containing number screen and colour discs was fitted in the corner window above them. A full drop window was provided in each top deck end, useful for dealing with refractory trolley-heads. Opening it in other circumstances incurred the displeasure of the driver from the draught created. Tubular electric heaters were fitted in the top saloon and the seating capacity remained unchanged. The top deck window pillars were brown. The front exit under the stairs was omitted. Number 70 was the first to be turned out in this form, followed by another seven, after which the new lower saloons became the same as 368-370. New cars replacing open-top ex cable cars were similar to 368-370 throughout. Two of these replaced ex

Car 367 was the first new car built with fully enclosed top deck, put out in August 1929. Top deck window woodwork was soon painted brown. Photographed at the top of Craighall Road. H L Mittell, later chief draughtsman, who was a major influence on design development, is the centre figure on the top deck. (EOC)

The special truck used under 371 (soon renumbered 266) was by EMB Ltd, without axle box hornways. Unusual was the position of the motors, at right angles to the usual layout and with worm drives. (EOC)

Car 264 was the 'sister' to 371 and also incorporated unique features. The upper deck side panels were initially painted in 'aluminium' or silver colour (originally unlined, but soon divided as shown here, at Granton Square). 'Edinburgh Corporation' in small block letters on the rocker panel was another short-lived variation. In this case the car was put out on a Maley & Taunton swing-link truck. (EOC)

Leith cars (264 and 266), the latter originally numbered 371. It had moquette seating with a floral design, and Metropolitan-Vickers controllers. The earlier standard cars now began to have their ends enclosed and the front exit removed. Where they did not already have transverse seating in the lower saloon this was now fitted.

The body of old car 177 was reconstructed to carry a welding set for track repairs, the middle of each side being removed and the platforms shortened. It was mounted on an old Leith truck and given number 2. To assist with the nightly rail grinding programme, in 1931 open top car 230 had its track brake shoes replaced by grinding blocks. Not being provided with water tanks it operated following one of the regular grinders. Soon 269 replaced it on this duty until 1934, then only the regular grinders were used, with outlying lines done during daylight. 269 was later stripped of its top deck fittings and stairs, but it was never repainted in works car livery.

This was a period of many innovations and experiments. First, livery; car 131 appeared in November 1930 with its top deck colours transposed; 222 was similarly treated in June 1931, but meantime 270 (and new cars 119 and 161) had appeared similarly, but with the upper top deck panel painted unlined brown. On 270 the lining to the top deck madder panel was in red, while on 161 the rocker panel was also painted madder. In July 1931 followed 264, newly built, with both top deck panels painted 'aluminium'. This bare effect was relieved by red lining added within a few weeks. None of these liveries was perpetuated. In June 1931 'Corporation Transport' which had superseded 'Corporation Tramways' on the rocker panels gave way to 'Edinburgh Corporation', in small black letters on the bottom left hand corner. Eight cars, 106, 161, 200, 264, 291, 308, 310, and 316 were so treated before the wording was altered, in August to 'City and Royal Burgh of Edinburgh'.

In August 1931, 75hp motors were fitted to car 162. These were later on 317, then on new car 261. These produced a fine turn of speed capable of well over 30mph. 162 also had two pairs of track-brake shoes for a time. Other short-term experiments were a motor field-shunt to give increased speed; divided motor armatures; hollow axles and special wheel centres; lighter trolley-booms with different tensions. The 'anti-galloping bars' were removed from the trucks of many cars, with, on the first dozen, additional small coil springs.

New car 177 appeared in June 1931 with a number of novel features, and on a new truck. Instead of side window route boards, a roller blind was provided in the top-light beside the platform entrance. 'Numa' air bells replaced the electric bells, and 'Ashanco' ventilators were fitted to the lower saloon. The lighting circuits were arranged with fifteen 40-volt lamps in series, the holders fitted with a 'bridging' device which came into action in the event of a lamp failure. This arrangement allowed additional lamps at the top of the stair. In the saloons the lamps were enclosed in rectangular fittings. This 'long-series' arrangement was later applied to a number of other cars, the two additional lamps on the lower deck circuit being located on the saloon ceiling panels. On 177 bright metal work, such as handrails, controller-top, *etc*, hitherto brass, was chromium-plated, this later becoming standard.

Number 177's truck was the first of three supplied by the EMB Co Ltd. The second was used on 371, while the third, a Peckham P35 type, went also to 177 which lost its original truck to another new car. The first two were of the 'Flexible Axle' type, but that under 371, was the most unconventional. The truck side members were swept up over the axleboxes, which were located only by the heavy underslung springs, not guided by hornways. 75hp MV107 fully-sprung motors drove the axles by a worm drive; internal expanding shoes worked on brake drums inside the wheels. This arrangement gave a quieter and smoother ride, but there were resultant maintenance problems, and after a few months the motors, drive, and brakes were replaced by orthodox equipment. This truck finished its life in 1934 under car 110. All three EMB trucks had SKF roller bearings and two pairs of track-brake shoes, though a single pair was later provided to the first and third examples. The outside ground clearance of the first two trucks was inadequate for the central guard strip on Bernard Street opening bridge, and they were kept off that route.

The air-brake system on these three trucks was also of EMB design. The controller shaft extended through a valve box on the controller top, the first notch on the 'brake' side of the controller applying air to the track brakes. Further movement in that direction energised the track-brake shoe magnets in the normal way. Air was applied to the wheel-brakes by a lever from the right side of the valve box, but this was automatically released if the controller handle was moved either way from the 'off' position. Further, the wheel-brake lever could only be applied against a heavy spring if the controller was not in the 'off' position. Any risk of skidding the wheels by applying wheel and track-brake at the same time was thus avoided. There was also a separate air cock (painted red) giving direct track-brake application for emergency use from either platform. Three pressure gauges were provided, in a frame behind the hand brake handle.

Earlier, 367 when new, had been provided with a similar EMB brake, but without air operation of the track-brakes, and only two pressure gauges. This was followed by Maley & Taunton air brake for wheels and track shoes, on 168, with principles the same as EMB. In the M & T layout the wheel brake was operated by a lever on a separate small valve at the driver's right hand. The M & T brake was chosen as standard, and by 1933 all service cars were fitted, older types of air brake and the EMB brakes being abandoned. When these new air brakes were installed, an adjustable one-legged seat was provided, fitted into a floor socket. A few open balcony ex cable cars received the M & T brake (as listed), but most of the bodies proved too fragile and the air brakes were removed.

The last two EMB trucks were painted red without lining out, this style then becoming standard. They were followed by a Maley & Taunton 'Swing-link' truck under 264, with Hoffman roller-bearings and GEC motors. Three pairs of GEC controllers were obtained, one pair being used on this car, the others on 16 and 109. A Peckham truck (by the Brush Company) was fitted to car 151 which differed by having under-slung springs.

The most remarkable development was for a completely new, modern, design of car. Accordingly the council authorised expenditure of £4,000 for one car. The body was built by Shrubhill and included many unusual features. Mounted on a steel frame, with timber infill, each side of both lower and upper saloons was built as one piece, with pillars extending from frame to roof. These pillars were of duralumin channels, again with wood infill, those beside the driver' screen similar. Longitudinal rails were of duralumin or aluminium angles incorporating an aluminium alloy sheet between frame and seat rail of the lower saloon. Plywood was used for the other interior side panels, while lower saloon bulkheads were of teak, as were the principal roof-sticks of both saloons. The upper saloon floor was of laminated wood panels, the lower saloon being normal tongued and grooved timber. The roof was 'Masonite' covered with an aluminium sheet. The sides were flat, the lower saloon having five windows each side. The upper deck was

Edinburgh's special car 180 was unveiled to an appreciative public in March 1932 – a radical departure from all cars which had preceded it. Here in Shrubhill it is put through a tilt-test – the 'swing meter' reading 22½ degrees. (EOC)

one long saloon, access being by a staircase partitioned off from the platform, with a sliding door at platform level. The entrance was inset from the corner pillars, hence the folding step, when lowered, did not project. Platform corner windows were of curved glass. The lower saloon had transverse seats for two, staggered on both sides of the gangway, the sandbox seats at the ends seating two and three, a total of 26. The usual arrangement applied on the upper deck except that the centre pair were single with two grab rails from floor to ceiling. Single seats were provided opposite the top of the stairs, the upper deck seating being for 38. All seats were of a wider type, blue leather in the lower saloon and red in the upper, the side panelling and pillars in Rexene to match, and the ceilings panelled in white. Lighting was in enclosed fittings. Ashanco ventilators and Numa air bells were provided, plus tubular electric heaters in both saloons. There was a headlamp with dimming device, a brake-stop-light, and an air operated screen wiper for the driver. The car was put on the EMB truck taken from 177, with EMB air-brake, and Metropolitan-Vickers controllers. Its weight, complete, was 13 tons. Perhaps the most striking feature was the livery, bright red with grey window pillars, lined in silver edged with blue, below the windows of each deck. Such a departure attracted much attention, and soon earned it the nickname 'Red Biddy'. Numbered 180, the car appeared on service 12, on Sunday 3 April 1932. After a few days however, the M & T truck and air-brake from number 264 replaced the EMB equipment, which then found its way to 197. The red livery was retained until 1935.

Arc windscreen wipers were henceforth gradually fitted on all the standard cars. (180's original wiper had a parallel action.) The top of the driver's window was already rather low and this alteration made it more so. New cars built in 1933 and onwards, (except 6, 34, 81 and 206) therefore had the destination box set higher, projecting slightly above the upper deck floor.

In 1932 three Brill trucks (all differing slightly) were obtained second-hand from Ayr Corporation, after that system closed down, and put on cars 25, 27 and 50. Air brakes were not fitted. These were used only till 1934. Also in 1932 the salt cars were relieved of their Peckham trucks being then placed on ex Leith trucks. Nine ex Leith cars, 232-238, 243 and 247 now received Peckham trucks, while 248 received that formerly on 247. Many of the ex Leith cars, and most open-top cars, had now been scrapped, and Shrubhill was busy building new cars to the current 'standard' design as replacements. To keep pace with requirements, external orders were placed.

Firstly, at the end of 1932, came cars 250-259, from R Y Pickering & Co Ltd, Wishaw, of wooden construction and similar to the standard design but fitted with air bells, screen wipers, brake stop lights, and headlamps (though the first few ran for a week or two without). Maley & Taunton trucks were provided, except 256 that had yet another new type, English Electric FL32 with English Electric motors and Hoffman roller bearings. These ten were followed by 260 and 265, generally similar to 180, but of all-metal construction, built by Metropolitan-Cammell. These had flat corners to the platforms, and M & T trucks, and were painted in the usual style except for window pillars that were white. Lining out was similar to 180. Later, 260 had the lower half of the top deck painted white, while on 265 the upper half of the top deck and all above became white, and the lower deck window pillars brown. The roofs of these all-metal cars were provided with duckboards for the use of depot staff, but to deal with any trolley difficulty in service, they were equipped with a bamboo pole carried on hooks under the edge of the body.

The next development was delivery of two cars from Metropolitan-Cammel in February (260) and March (265) 1933. Differing liveries gave the cars differing appearances. At Joppa looking east. (EOC)

Also at Joppa, on route 12, is car 265. The 12 was the route often chosen to run in new cars. (EOC)

Next in 1933 came another unique Shrubhill product – 261– a hybrid – like the 250-9 design but with flat sides and slightly 'streamlined' body. (EOC)

All standard cars having now been equipped with transverse seats and enclosed balconies, the same procedure was applied to the ex cable cars of Dick-Kerr and Shrubhill build. None of the older ex cable cars were so dealt with. The lining out on the remaining old cars was much simplified. Car 222, with its fully enclosed top deck, had the seating improved, with transverse seating in the lower saloon. From October 1933, brown was adopted for the lower deck window pillars of all cars.

Early in 1933 reconstruction of the Peckham trucks, with cross-tying of the motors to the Maley & Taunton system (to assist in steadying the running) was commenced. 'Anti-galloping bars' and tie-bars were removed, a guard bar being fitted in place of the latter, although a few cars ran without this for a time. As this now involved trucks not remaining with the same body, they received a 'Rebuilt Truck Number' with the date, on a metal plate which was fixed to the inside of one side frame. Number 1, dated 11/2/33, appeared on the truck of car 328.

Regenerative control was tried in 1933, with Metropolitan-Vickers controllers on car 203. The arrangement was for the motors to act as generators while running downhill or stopping, the energy being returned to the overhead thus easing the load on the power station, as well as saving wear on brake gear. There were difficulties with a line fed by rectifiers, and the only route supplied throughout by rotary machines was that to Levenhall. So, although lacking in hills from which most advantage could have been gained, 203 was put to work on service 21. After a year economies were such that a fur-

Six further cars came from Metro-Cammel in May – June 1934 (241, 2, 4-6, 9). Delivered by rail in two sections, 241 came to grief while being unloaded at the LMS Leith Walk goods depot, just yards from Leith Depot. (EOC)

ther eleven cars were altered for that route. Occasionally lack of other cars close to absorb the current would produce a rise in voltage too great for the lamps at night. The transition to and from regeneration often produced jerk in running which gave rise to severe complaint from some regular passengers who campaigned for 'better cars'. Early in 1939 the regenerative cars were withdrawn and reverted to normal with the Pickering cars transferred to Portobello depot in their place.

Newly delivered 242 is followed up Granton Road by 'standard' car 43. (EOC)

While still continuing to turn out the 'standard' car, another new design was built at Shrubhill during 1933. This was 261, generally similar to the Pickering type except that the lower saloon was straight-sided thus accommodating double seats on both sides. The City crest on the side panels had a red diamond-shaped background. It was now decided that the 'standard' design incorporating top deck saloons from ex cable cars be ended and designs were prepared for a new standard Edinburgh tram, incorporating many features of the recently supplied cars.

Twelve more all-metal cars were ordered, six from Metropolitan-Cammell, and three each from Hurst Nelson, and English Electric. The 'Met-Cams' were similar to the earlier two but improved by having a 'domed' roof. They were fitted with turntable type seats of a comfortable design in both saloons. One 249, had folding doors to the platform, but these were later removed. The Hurst Nelson cars also had domed roofs, but the ends were rounded like 180, and seating was also similar. The three English Electric cars resembled those from Hurst Nelson, but the ends were distinctly sloped back in 'streamline' fashion, resulting in a foreshortened upper saloon, losing two seats in the process. As the roof curved down, the end windows were smaller, hence the service number box was installed behind the main panel, on the front, with the colour discs to the off side. One of these English Electric cars, 267, acquired the English Electric truck from 256, while M & T trucks were got for the others. The City crest was again enclosed in a diamond lined in the ordinary colour, while window pillars were in white. On all these new cars destination screens were set up a little into the panel above, and in the case of these Hurst Nelson and English Electric cars (also 261), the upper deck paint work was curved up over. The last old standard car to be built, 191, was painted similarly.

On some older cars the top saloon full-drop side windows were replaced by metal framed half-drop windows. There were many variations including quarter-drops and

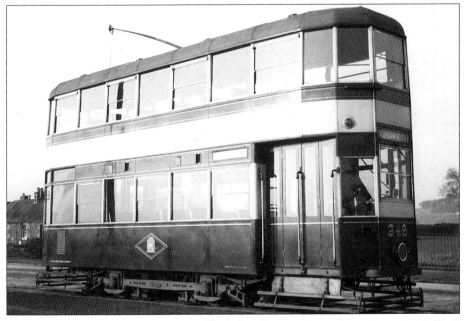

Car 249 of this batch was fitted when new with platform doors, an innovation not perpetuated. North Gyle terminus, Corstorphine on 10 November 1935. (DLGH)

Three of the 1934 English Electric cars were of this streamlined design, arriving in August and September. At Braids Terminus on 29 October, looking to Greenbank. (EOC)

The first of the Shrubhill 'final standard' design – car 69 – with its proud driver, David Corsie. Details of the original livery can be clearly seen. (EOC)

winding types. Sometimes only certain windows were altered, others becoming fixed, while many cars were never altered at all.

On 24/3/34 (the form in which shown), the practice was started of stencilling on the back of the stair the date of the overhaul of the truck, normally a week's work for which the body was lifted off. This ceased at the end of October 1937.

The last open-top car was scrapped in 1934, and at the end of that year the first of the new standard Shrubhill cars appeared. These were similar in appearance to the Hurst Nelson cars, though rather neater. They were *not* all-metal cars, as has been sometimes claimed, their design being more akin to the composite construction of 180. There were differences from 180 as the lower and upper saloons were built separately with the side panels of both consisting of 'Armourply' (plywood faced with aluminium sheet). The lower saloon seated the usual 24, the upper saloon 38. Some had the old narrow style seats in the upper saloon, while 88 had these throughout. Cars 56 and 150 had 'turntable' seats in the lower saloon, the former of Nesta type, the latter by Peters. The 'popularity' of car 150 was such that it was kept on the Marchmont Circle (where seats were not reversed). Ordinary electric bells were fitted, and except on the first few, headlamps had a plain yellow glass only. Rebuilt 'Peckham' trucks were provided. With these cars there was yet another painting change. The madder upper deck panel was brought to the point above the destination screen, and the lower deck gold lining brought to a point below the headlamps, also curving down at the platform end. All window pillars were brown. Soon however the pointed madder panel gave way to a wider sweep, the width of the destination screen, while the gold line was instead broken at each side of the car number. The white and madder sections of the upper deck were then reversed, this becoming the standard style for all cars. None of the few remaining open balcony or ex Leith cars (which finally disappeared in 1936) received this style.

A problem with these new cars with enclosed staircases was the draught created down the driver's back. An answer was found by a hinged door which he could draw across the middle of the platform, the draught dissipating behind.

Further twenty new all-metal cars were provided in 1935, eight by Hurst Nelson and six each by English Electric and Metropolitan-Cammell. These were of the so-called 'streamline' design as per the earlier three from English Electric. These had moquette turntable seats in the lower saloon, the 'Met-Cams' having their own make, the others of the Nesta type. Five years later however, these were replaced by the Milne seats, though with moquette upholstery in most cases. The 'Met-Cams' (which at first ran from

Standard car 164 of 1935 construction was initially painted in this style which prevailed for a short period only. On the right can be seen salt car 5. (EOC)

Appearing after the first of the standards were 20 cars of streamlined appearance, from three differing builders, each design being slightly different. Car 19, here on route 11 en route to Braids (but without the destination screen having been changed) was of the English Electric batch of six. (AWB Collection)

228 was the highest numbered former 'Dick Kerr' cable car, seen in Shrubhill depot in the 1930s. It was not replaced until May 1947. (DLGH)

Former cable car 66 was originally built by the District Tramway Co. Edinburgh's concessions to war-time conditions are illustrated – a small headlight and a white line from the fender round the body. The car was soon to be scrapped, in May 1942. (DLGH)

Portobello depot) had the number screens on the near side corner instead of the front. They had M & T trucks in which rubber blocks replaced the small coil springs, while the others ran on rebuilt Peckham trucks. Numbers 21-4 later received modified M & T trucks.

These new cars were (unusually for Edinburgh) numbered 11 to 30 in one series, so to achieve this twenty-three cars were renumbered. Ex Leith grinder 1 and welding car 2 retained these numbers but the other 'works' cars were renumbered 3-10. Details were:

Old No	3	5	6	7	13	15	16	17	18	19	20	23
New No	75	76	84	86	169	4	61	3	182	5	184	41

Old No	24	25	26	27	28	29	75	76	84	86	112
New No	78	172	112	73	151	138	6	7	8	9	10

By 1939 the tram fleet had become quite standardised. All odd trucks had been discarded, except that on 197 which lasted a little longer, leaving only Peckhams and M & Ts, plus the ex Leith trucks on works cars. All service cars were now totally enclosed, equipped with transverse seating, screen wipers, electric heaters to the upper deck (and lower saloon on flush-sided cars), and M & T air-brake. Numa air bells were being discarded (while 158 had continuous bell strips instead of bell pushes). Trafficator arms were tried temporarily on 82, and a lap valve for the air-wheel brakes on 88. During 1935-7 car 81 was the subject of experimental work on regeneration under the auspices of Maley & Taunton. The equipment was used in service on car 162 for a time in 1938, and then abandoned.

Wartime livery for McHardy & Elliot/Hurst Nelson built car 125, at Fairmilehead terminus. These were the first all new cars built for the electrification and were also the first to be scrapped after the war, 125 going in January 1950. (E Fielding)

On some older cars, the waist and rocker panels were replaced by a flush panel with a flat beading formed into a diamond around the City crest. On most of these cars plain unshaded dash numerals were used. This was applied to various cars from 1938. The diamond beading was omitted in some cases, then beading was omitted altogether after the war. The unshaded numerals were used on some cars until after the war.

By the end of 1937 Shrubhill had built 46 of the new standard cars. Material was then ordered for a further 38, to replace all remaining ex-cable cars. These differed in minor details only, including the use of brown seating and panelling in the upper saloon, and moquette seating in the lower saloon. Construction continued slowly during the war, with at least one car turned out each year (except 1944). The final six appeared in 1950.

One of the eleven cars purchased from Manchester Corporation. These were in poor condition and even after refurbishment served only a few more years. (G Fairley)

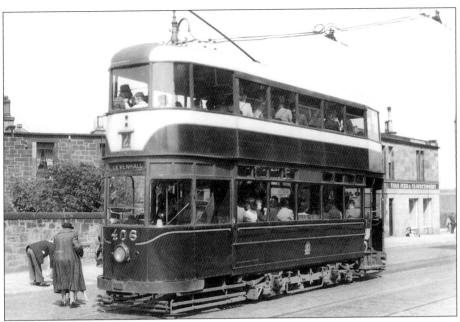

These ex-Manchester cars worked in service only on route 21 to Levenhall. Car 406 came to Edinburgh in August 1948 and looks much the better of its repaint. Photographed at Joppa, 25 June 1950. (DLGH)

Some of the old salt cars were scrapped during the war, and the former welding car was adapted for this work, while another (10) was built from the remains of the old 51. Some had their trolley masts removed. After the war their use was discontinued, and all except this new one were scrapped. It replaced old grinder 3, taking its number. Both it and number 1 were then fitted with 'destinations' TRACKWORK. The salt cars had found limited use. Though overhauled each summer they often failed in winter duty. Number 5, having no track brake, had been confined to Leith.

Following fitting of headlights during the war, the obsolete bullseye lights on the vestibules were removed, as were the brake-stop lights. From 1946 the rocker panels of older cars were painted madder.

At this time there was a need for additional cars, and eleven were purchased from Manchester Corporation. These arrived, complete with trucks, in 1947-9, mostly in a sorry state. Manchester and Edinburgh numbers were:

Manchester	173	676	196	125	558	217	389	231	242	349	381
Edinburgh	401	402	403	404	405	406	407	408	409	410	411

All were thoroughly rehabilitated and turned out on Peckham trucks with M & T air-brakes and the usual Edinburgh fittings. They resembled the standard car design but were slightly longer and were in service restricted to the relatively straight Levenhall route. They did not have an enclosed staircase, instead there was a trap door in the floor which was let down over the top of the stairs at the driver's end.

Electric heaters fell out of use during the 1947 power shortage, and were then gradually removed from the cars. The oldest of the standard cars went for scrapping in 1949,

Works car number 1 was the former Leith Corporation water and grinder car. Seen in Claremont Park with Leith Links behind, in its original green livery but now in Edinburgh Corporation ownership. (EOC)

Number 1 was reconstructed several times and is seen here on 24 September 1934 working on the new tracks out to Maybury terminus, Corstorphine. (DLGH)

122 being the first. No replacements were constructed. The first batch was broken up behind Shrubhill, but after 1953 cars were sold complete to J. N. Connell Ltd who removed them to their works in Coatbridge for scrapping.

During 1949 six sets of Timken roller bearings were obtained, then twenty-five sets of Hoffman make; six SKF sets arrived in 1950, a further twenty-five Timkens in 1951-2. These were fitted to Peckham trucks which then had their coil springs replaced by rubber blocks. Soon after all M & T trucks were withdrawn (Nos 11, 12 and 16 had received M & T trucks in 1948). Peckham trucks, rebuilt and un-rebuilt, with ordinary or roller bearings, were used for all types of car and were interchanged between cars frequently.

Salt car 19 – seen in Dryden Street – had a long history. Converted from a cable car it had started life as a horse car many years before. It later became 5 in the works car list. (EOC)

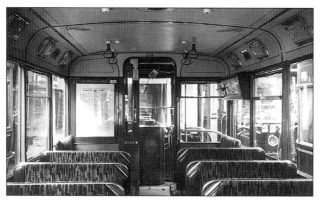

Lower saloon of '1934 standard' car, in this case number 218. Note the moquette covered seats. 16 April 1939. (DLGH)

Top deck of (probably) tram 178 – note the metal framed half-drop windows. Most of these cars originally had wooden framed one-piece windows which could be fully let down. (EOC)

Top deck of Shrubhill built 'Red Biddy' – car 180 – showing its open construction without bulkheads. (EOC)

The odd Met-Vick and GEC controllers and most other non-standard items also disappeared. By 1951 no major repairs were being carried out and cars were withdrawn accordingly. Repainting also ceased. Before we come to the end the various decorated cars have to be mentioned.

At Christmas 1933 for three weeks, car 74 was fitted up with 2,500 lamps forming slogans which varied from seasonal greetings to travel and parcels slogans. Early October 1934 saw 'Telephone Week', with car 58 equipped for Post Office advertising. For a Royal visit in July 1934, car 50 was prepared with 7,500 sprays of artificial flowers on a 'grass' background. There followed a more ambitious project for the Coronation in May 1937. Car 40, prior to scrapping, was stripped to lower saloon waist level and a large crown built. New dash plates were fitted, the whole finished in gold with blue lettering. Car 221, when withdrawn from service in February 1939, was painted 'aluminium', advertising an RAF Exhibition and lit by concealed lamps. For the next two months the slogan became 'National Service' then in June

In the first Departmental museum, tram 35 was the main exhibit – albeit a static one. With good fortune car 35 is again in running order and has operated in Blackpool and Glasgow. (AWB Collection)

'Safety Week'. After a period of inactivity, 221 re-appeared in June 1940 for 'Savings Week', painted gold, and with the floodlighting removed.

Finally for the 'Last Tram Week' in November 1956, car 172 was painted white with the City crest on one end and the old Edinburgh and District Tramways Company crest on the other, with appropriate wording and lighting.

An Edinburgh electric car can still be seen, as number 35 has been preserved. It operated at the Glasgow Garden Festival of 1988, and on the tramway of Blackpool Corporation. The car is presently at the National Tramway Museum at Crich, Derbyshire.

Lower saloon of tram 178, built at Shrubhill in 1927. Note the fluted lampshades and the bulkhead adverts. (EOC)

Table of Tram Types, Building Dates and Other Details

Tramcar fleet list – Key to type references:

A   Former Cable Car built by Brown-Marshall, top cover by
      1   McHardy & Elliot
      2   Hurst-Nelson
      3   Craven

B   Former Cable Car built by Brown-Marshall, open top

C   Former Cable Car, Northern section, open top

D   Former Cable Car built by Milnes, top cover as type 'A'

E   Former Cable Car built by Milnes, open top, ex-Slateford electrified cars

F   Former Cable Car built by EDTCo, top cover by McHardy & Elliot

G   Former Cable Car built by ERTCW, top cover by McHardy & Elliot (not 222)

H   Standard Electric Car built by
      1   McHardy & Elliot (top cover by Hurst Nelson)
      2   Leeds Forge (of Bristol)
      3   English Electric
      4   ECT
      5   ECT (built with enclosed balconies)

J   Standard Electric Car built by Pickering (without upper saloon bulkheads)

K   Standard Electric Car built by ECT (without upper saloon bulkheads)

L   Former Leith Car built by BTH, top cover by
      1   Brush
      2   BTH

M   Former Leith Car built by Brush, top cover by Brush

N   Former Leith Car built by Brush, open top

P   Cars built by ECT, 1932-3

Q   Steel Cars built by
      1   Metropolitan-Cammell
      2   Metropolitan-Cammell, domed roof
      3   Hurst Nelson

R   Cars built by ECT, 1934-50

S   Steel Cars, streamlined ends, built by
      1   Hurst Nelson
      2   English Electric
      3   Metropolitan-Cammell

T   Former Manchester Car

W   Works cars
      1   Former Leith water car
      2   Welding car
      3   Grinder car, former cable car, former horse car
      4   Grinder car, former cable car
      5   Salt car

a   Earlier type of air-brakes for track shoes

b   Earlier type of air-brakes for wheels

c   These, with all cars of types F,G,H,J,K,P,Q,R,S,&T received M&T air-brakes

d   Illustrated in this volume

e   These cars still in stock, 16 November 1956

f   Specific mention in text (sometimes more than once)

Depot Code: G – Gorgie; L – Leith; P – Portobello; S – Shrubhill; X – Tollcross

Table of Tram Types, Building Dates and Other Details

Nos		Year New	Type		Notes	Year Scrapped	Depot 1930	Depot 1945
1	(i)	1923	D1	c	Salt car, later 10	1935	X	
1	(ii)		W1		Grinder ex Leith 60	1954	S	S
2	(i)	1923	A1			1935	L	
2	(ii)	1931	W2		Welding car ex 177			S
3	(i)	1922	A2			1926		
3	(ii)	1927	H4	b	Renumbered 75(ii)		L	X
3	(iii)		W3		Grinder ex 17(i)		S	
3	(iv)		W4	f	Grinder ex 10(iii)	1956		S
4	(i)	1922	A2	c		1935	L	
4	(ii)		W5		Salt car ex 15(i)	1941		
5	(i)	1923	F		Renumbered 76(ii)		L	
5	(ii)		W5		Salt car ex 19(i)			
6	(i)	1923	A1			1931	L	
6	(ii)	1933	H5	f	Renumbered 84(iii)			
6	(iii)		W5	f	Salt car ex 75(i)			
7	(i)	1924	H4	b	Renumbered 86(ii)		X	
7	(ii)		W5		Salt car ex 76(i)	1943		G
8	(i)	1923	A1			1935	L	
8	(ii)		W5		Salt car ex 84(ii)	1946		G
9	(i)	1922	A3	f		1935	X	
9	(ii)		W5		Salt car ex 86(i)			G
10	(i)	1923	A1			1935	L	
10	(ii)		W5	f	Salt car ex 112(i)	1942		
10	(iii)		W5		Salt car ex 51(i). Renumbered 3(iv)			
11	(i)	1923	A1			1934	G	
11	(ii)	1935	S1	f		1956		L
12	(i)	1923	A1			1935	P	
12	(ii)	1935	S1	f		1956		L
13	(i)	1923	F		Renumbered 169(ii)		P	
13	(ii)	1935	S1			1956		L
14	(i)	1922	A1			1935	L	
14	(ii)	1935	S1			1956		L
15	(i)	1923	W5	f	Salt car. Renumbered 4(ii)			
15	(ii)	1935	S1			1956		L
16	(i)	1922	A2			1930		
16	(ii)	1932	H5	f	Renumbered 61(ii)			
16	(iii)	1935	S1	f		1956		L
17	(i)	1923	W3	f	Grinder. Renumbered 3(iii)			
17	(ii)	1935	S1			1956		L
18	(i)	1922	B			1928		
18	(ii)	1928	H4	b	Renumbered 182(ii)		L	
18	(iii)	1935	S1			1956		L
19	(i)	1922	W5	f	Salt car. Renumbered 5(ii)			
19	(ii)	1935	S2			1956		L
20	(i)	1922	A2			1927		
20	(ii)	1928	H4	b	Renumbered 184(ii)		S	
20	(iii)	1935	S2			1956		L
21	(i)	1923	A1			1935	X	
21	(ii)	1935	S2	f		1956		L
22	(i)	1922	A3			1935	L	
22	(ii)	1935	S2	f		1956		L
23	(i)	1923	A1			1929		
23	(ii)		D1	c	Former 268(i). Renumbered 41(ii)			

Table of Tram Types, Building Dates and Other Details

Nos		Year New	Type		Notes	Year Scrapped	Depot 1930	Depot 1945
23	(iii)	1935	S2	f		1956		L
24	(i)	1923	B			1928		
24	(ii)	1929	H4	b	Renumbered 78(ii)			
24	(iii)	1935	S2	f		1956		L
25	(i)	1923	F	f	Renumbered 172(ii)		L	
25	(ii)	1935	S3			1956		L
26	(i)	1923	D1	c	Renumbered 112(ii)		S	
26	(ii)	1935	S3			1956		L
27	(i)	1924	F	f	Renumbered 73(ii)		X	
27	(ii)	1935	S3			1956		L
28	(i)	1924	H4	b	Renumbered 151(ii)		L	
28	(ii)	1935	S3			1956		L
29	(i)	1923	A1			1933	S	
29	(ii)	1933	H5		Renumbered 138(ii)			
29	(iii)	1935	S3			1956		L
30	(i)	1923	A1	c		1935	L	
30	(ii)	1935	S3			1956		L
31	(i)	1922	A2			1929	X	
31	(ii)	1930	H5			1955		X
32	(i)	1923	A1			1934	S	
32	(ii)	1935	R			1956		X
33	(i)	1922	A2	f		1926		
33	(ii)	1927	H4	bf		1954		L
34	(i)	1922	A3			1931	S	
34	(ii)	1933	H5	f		1955		X
35	(i)	1923	F			1947	S	
35	(ii)	1948	R		Preserved	e		L
36	(i)	1922	A2	f		1926		
36	(ii)	1926	H4	bf		1950	G	L
37	(i)	1924	F	a		1947	X	
37	(ii)	1949	R			e		L
38		1924	H4			1955	L	L
39	(i)	1923	D1	c		1937	S	
39	(ii)	1938	R			1956		P
40	(i)	1923	D1	cf		1936	L	
40	(ii)	1937	R			1956		G
41	(i)	1923	A3			1935	L	
41	(ii)		D1		Former 23(ii)	1936		
41	(iii)	1936	R			1956		P
42	(i)	1922	B			1928		
42	(ii)	1928	H4	b		1954	L	P
43		1924	H4	b		1953	L	L
44	(i)	1922	A1			1931	P	
44	(ii)	1932	H5			1955		X
45	(i)	1923	D1	cf		1936	S	
45	(ii)	1936	R			e		P
46	(i)	1923	D1	a			X	
46	(ii)	1932	H5			1955		L
47	(i)	1923	F	f		1942	S	
47	(ii)	1946	R			e		
48	(i)	1924	F	a		1947	X	
48	(ii)	1950	R			e		L
49	(i)	1923	F	f		1947	P	

Table of Tram Types, Building Dates and Other Details

Nos		Year New	Type		Notes	Year Scrapped	Depot 1930	Depot 1945
49	(ii)	1950	R			e		L
50	(i)	1923	F	f		1947	P	
50	(ii)	1950	R	f		e		L
51	(i)	1923	F		Became Salt car 10(iii) in 1942			
51	(ii)	1945	R			e		L
52	(i)	1923	F			1939	P	
52	(ii)	1939	R			e		P
53		1924	H4	af		1954	X	P
54	(i)	1923	F	f		1940	P	
54	(ii)	1940	R			1956		P
55	(i)	1923	D1			1935	L	
55	(ii)	1935	R			1956		G
56	(i)	1922	A1			1935	P	
56	(ii)	1935	R	f		1956		G
57	(i)	1922	B			1927		
57	(ii)	1928	H4	b		1955	S	L
58	(i)	1922	A2			1927		
58	(ii)	1928	H4	b		1955	L	G
59	(i)	1923	F	f		1943	P	
59	(ii)	1947	R			e		L
60	(i)	1922	B			1928		
60	(ii)	1929	H4	b		1955	L	L
61	(i)	1923	A1			1935	L	
61	(ii)		H5		Former 16(ii)	1955		L
62	(i)	1923	D1			1935	L	
62	(ii)	1935	R			1956		X
63	(i)	1923	D1	c		1937	S	
63	(ii)	1938	R			1956		P
64		1924	H4	b		1953	L	G
65	(i)	1923	D1			1930	P	
65	(ii)	1932	H5			1955		P
66	(i)	1923	F	f		1942	P	
66	(ii)	1946	R			e		L
67	(i)	1923	D1			1935	P	
67	(ii)	1935	R			1955		G
68	(i)	1923	D1			1931	S	
68	(ii)	1932	H5			1955		L
69	(i)	1923	B			1934		
69	(ii)	1934	R	f		1956		G
70	(i)	1922	A3			1929		
70	(ii)	1929	H5	bf		1955	X	L
71	(i)	1923	A1			1935	L	
71	(ii)	1935	R			1956		G
72	(i)	1923	F	f		1940	P	
72	(ii)	1941	R			e		L
73	(i)	1923	D1			1935	L	
73	(ii)		F		Former 27(i)	1945		
73	(iii)	1947	R			e		L
74		1924	H4			1953	L	L
75	(i)	1922	C	f	Salt car, Renumbered 6(iii)			
75	(ii)		H4		Former 3(ii)	1955		X
76	(i)	1922	C	f	Salt car. Renumbered 7(ii)			
76	(ii)		F		Former 5(i)	1938		

Table of Tram Types, Building Dates and Other Details

Nos		Year New	Type		Notes	Year Scrapped	Depot 1930	Depot 1945
76	(iii)	1938	R			1956		P
77	(i)	1923	B			1928		
77	(ii)	1928	H4	b		1954	S	L
78	(i)	1923	A1			1935	P	
78	(ii)		H4		Former 24(ii)	1954		X
79	(i)	1923	D1			1929		
79	(ii)	1930	H4	f		1955		X
80	(i)	1922	A3			1933	L	
80	(ii)	1933	H5			1955		L
81	(i)	1923	D1			1932	L	
81	(ii)	1933	H5	f		1955		P
82	(i)	1923	D1	c		1936	L	
82	(ii)	1937	R	f		1956		L
83	(i)	1923	D1			1934	L	
83	(ii)	1935	R			e		G
84	(i)	1923	C	f	Salt car	1928		
84	(ii)			f	Salt car. Former 146(i). Renumbered 8(ii)			
84	(iii)		H5		Former 6(ii)	1954		L
85	(i)	1923	A1			1931	L	
85	(ii)	1932	H5			1955		X
86	(i)	1923	C	f	Salt car. Renumbered 9(ii)			
86	(ii)		H4		Former 7(i)	1953		L
87		1923	H2			1953	X	X
88	(i)	1923	B			1934	P	
88	(ii)	1935	R	f		e		L
89	(i)	1923	A1			1932	L	
89	(ii)	1933	H5			1955		X
90		1923	H2			1954	X	P
91	(i)	1923	A1	c		1936	X	
91	(ii)	1937	R			1956		P
92		1923	H2			1953	X	X
93		1923	H2	b		1954	X	X
94	(i)	1923	D1			1933	X	
94	(ii)	1934	H5			1955		L
95		1923	H2			1954	X	X
96		1923	H2			1954	X	P
97		1923	H2			1954	X	P
98		1923	H2			1954	X	X
99		1923	H2			1953	X	X
100	(i)	1922	A3			1933	X	
100	(ii)	1933	H5			1953		L
101	(i)	1922	A2			1929		
101	(ii)	1930	H4	bf		1955		L
102		1923	H2			1953	X	X
103	(i)	1923	D1			1935	S	
103	(ii)	1935	R			1956		G
104	(i)	1923	D1			1929		
104	(ii)	1930	H5	b		1955	S	G
105	(i)	1923	D1	f		1935	G	
105	(ii)	1935	R			1956		P
106	(i)	1922	B			1927		
106	(ii)	1928	H4	bf		1955		G
107	(i)	1922	B			1930	P	

Table of Tram Types, Building Dates and Other Details

Nos	Year New	Type		Notes	Year Scrapped	Depot 1930	Depot 1945
107 (ii)	1930	K	b		1956		G
108	1923	H2			1954	P	L
109 (i)	1923	A1				S	
109 (ii)	1932	H5	f		1955		L
110	1923	H2	f		1953	P	L
111 (i)	1922	A1			1935	S	
111 (ii)	1935	R			1956		P
112 (i)	1922	C	f	Salt car. Renumbered 10(ii)			
112 (ii)		D1	c	Former 26(i)	1935		
112 (iii)	1935	R			1956		P
113	1924	H4	b		1953	X	P
114 (i)	1922	A1					
114 (ii)	1927	H4	b		1954	L	P
115 (i)	1922	A2			1927		
115 (ii)	1927	H4	b		1954	L	L
116 (i)	1922	A2			1929		
116 (ii)	1930	H5			1955		X
117 (i)	1922	A2			1927		
117 (ii)	1927	H4	b		1955	G	X
118 (i)	1922	A2			1926		
118 (ii)	1931	H5			1953	S	X
119 (i)	1922	B			1930		
119 (ii)	1931	E	f		1955		P
120 (i)	1923	A1			1935	L	
120 (ii)	1936	R			1956		R
121	1922	H1			1950	G	L
122	1922	H1			1949	L	L
123	1922	H1			1950	L	L
124	1922	H1			1951	L	L
125	1922	H1			1950	L	L
126	1922	H1			1951	L	L
127	1922	H1			1951	S	L
128	1922	H1			1950	L	L
129	1922	H1			1949	L	L
130	1922	H1			1950	L	L
131	1922	H1	f		1949	L	X
132	1922	H1			1951	L	L
133	1922	H1			1951	L	X
134	1922	H1			1952	L	X
135	1922	H1			1951	L	X
136	1922	H1			1949	L	X
137 (i)	1923	A1			1935	P	
137 (ii)	1935	R			1956		G
138 (i)	1923	A1			1935	P	
138 (ii)		H5		Former 29(ii)	1956		G
139	1924	H4	b		1953	L	G
140	1924	H4	b		1953	L	L
141	1924	H4	b		1955	L	X
142	1924	H4	b		1953	L	G
143	1925	H4	a		1950	X	G
144	1925	H4	a		1953	X	P
145 (i)	1922	B			1934	P	
145 (ii)	1935	R			1956		L

Table of Tram Types, Building Dates and Other Details

Nos	Year New	Type		Notes	Year Scrapped	Depot 1930	Depot 1945
146 (i)	1923	B		Became Salt car 84(ii) in 1929			
146 (ii)	1929	H4	b		1954		G
147 (i)	1922	A2			1927		
147 (ii)	1927	H4	b		1954	S	G
148 (i)	1922	A1			1933	P	
148 (ii)	1934	H5			1955		L
149 (i)	1922	A3			1931		
149 (ii)	1931	H5			1955		P
150 (i)	1922	A1			1935	L	
150 (ii)	1935	R	f		1956		X
151 (i)	1922	A1	f		1935	P	
151 (ii)		H4		Former 28(i)	1953		G
152 (i)	1922	A1			1933	P	
152 (ii)	1934	H5			1956		L
153 (i)	1922	B			1928		
153 (ii)	1928	H4	b		1953	P	X
154 (i)	1922	A2			1927		
154 (ii)	1928	H4	b		1953	L	X
155 (i)	1922	A2			1929		
155 (ii)	1930	H5	b		1955		G
156 (i)	1922	A2			1929		
156 (ii)	1931	H5			1956		G
157 (i)	1922	A3			1935	L	
157 (ii)	1935	R	f		1956		G
158 (i)	1922	A2			1930	L	
158 (ii)	1931	H5	f		1956		L
159 (i)	1922	A2			1933	L	
159 (ii)	1934	H5			1955		L
160 (i)	1922	A2			1935	L	
160 (ii)	1935	R			1956		G
161 (i)	1923	B			1930		
161 (ii)	1931	K	f		1955		P
162 (i)	1922	B			1930		
162 (ii)	1930	K	f		1955		P
163 (i)	1922	A2			1929		
163 (ii)	1930	H5	b		1955		L
164 (i)	1922	A3			1935	L	
164 (ii)	1935	R			1956		G
165 (i)	1923	A1			1935	P	
165 (ii)	1935	R			1956		G
166 (i)	1923	B			1930		
166 (ii)	1931	K			1955		P
167 (i)	1922	B			?		
167 (ii)	1931	K			1955	L	P
168 (i)	1922	A2			1929		
168 (ii)	1930	H5	f		1955		P
169 (i)	1922	A3			1935	L	
169 (ii)		F		Former 13(i)	1947		
169 (iii)	1950	R			e		L
170	1923	H2			1954	S	X
171	1923	H2			1955	L	X
172 (i)	1922	A3	f		1935	L	
172 (ii)		F		Former 25(i)	1947		

Table of Tram Types, Building Dates and Other Details

Nos	Year New	Type	Notes	Year Scrapped	Depot 1930	Depot 1945
172 (iii)	1950	R	f		e	L
173 (i)	1922	A3		1935	X	
173 (ii)	1936	R		1956		P
174 (i)	1922	A2		1927		
174 (ii)	1928	H4	b	1955	S	P
175 (i)	1922	A3		1933	S	
175 (ii)	1934	H5		1955		L
176 (i)	1923	B		1928		
176 (ii)	1928	H4	b	1954	P	L
177 (i)	1922	B	f	Became Welding Car 2(ii) in 1931		
177 (ii)	1931	K	f	1956		L
178 (i)	1922	A2	f	1926		
178 (ii)	1927	H4	b	1954	S	G
179 (i)	1922	B		1928		
179 (ii)	1928	H4	b	1953	L	P
180 (i)	1922	B		1931		
180 (ii)	1932	P	f		e	L
181 (i)	1923	B		1928		
181 (ii)	1929	H4	b	1955	L	L
182 (i)	1922	A2		1935	L	
182 (ii)		H4		Former 18(ii)	1954	L
183 (i)	1922	A2		1927		
183 (ii)	1927	H4	b	1955	G	L
184 (i)	1922	A3		1935	S	
184 (ii)		H4		Former 20(ii)	1955	L
185 (i)	1922	A2	f	1926		
185 (ii)	1927	H4	bf	1954	S	L
186 (i)	1923	A1		1933	L	
186 (ii)	1933	H5		1954		L
187 (i)	1922	A3		1926		
187 (ii)	1927	H4	b	1954	S	L
188 (i)	1923	B		1928		
188 (ii)	1928	H4	b	1955	P	P
189 (i)	1922	A3		1935	L	
189 (ii)	1935	R		1956		G
190 (i)	1923	B		1934	L	
190 (ii)	1935	R		1956		X
191 (i)	1922	A3		1933	S	
191 (ii)	1934	H5		1955		L
192 (i)	1922	A2	af	1926		
192 (ii)	1927	H4	b	1954	S	L
193 (i)	1922	A2		1933	L	
193 (ii)	1933	H5		1955		G
194 (i)	1922	A2		1927		
194 (ii)	1928	H4	b	1955	S	P
195 (i)	1922	A1		1935	S	
195 (ii)	1936	R		1956		P
196 (i)	1922	B		1928		
196 (ii)	1928	H4	b	1956	G	L
197 (i)	1922	A1		1933	P	
197 (ii)	1933	H5	f	1955		P
198 (i)	1922	A2		1929		
198 (ii)	1930	H4	bf	1956		P

Table of Tram Types, Building Dates and Other Details

Nos	Year New	Type	Notes	Year Scrapped	Depot 1930	Depot 1945
199 (i)	1922	A3		1935	L	
199 (ii)	1936	R		1956		P
200 (i)	1922	B		1927		
200 (ii)	1928	H4	bf	1955	P	P
201 (i)	1922	A2		1929		
201 (ii)	1930	H5	b	1956		L
202 (i)	1923	A1		1934	G	
202 (ii)	1935	R		e		G
203 (i)	1922	A3		1931	X	
203 (ii)	1933	H5	f	1954		P
204 (i)	1922	B		1934	L	
204 (ii)	1935	R		1956		X
205 (i)	1922	B		1928		
205 (ii)	1928	H4	b	1955	G	L
206 (i)	1923	A1		1932	S	
206 (ii)	1933	H5	f	1955		P
207 (i)	1922	A2		1931	L	
207 (ii)	1931	H5		1955		P
208 (i)	1922	A2		1926		
208 (ii)	1927	H4	bf	1954	L	G
209 (i)	1923	G	a	1941	X	
209 (ii)	1943	R		e		L
210 (i)	1923	G	a	1944	X	
210 (ii)	1947	R		e		L
211 (i)	1924	G	a	1940	X	
211 (ii)	1941	R		e		L
212 (i)	1923	G	a	1939	X	
212 (ii)	1940	R		e		L
213 (i)	1923	G	a	1941	X	
213 (ii)	1942	R		e		L
214 (i)	1923	G	a	1939	X	
214 (ii)	1940	R		1956		L
215 (i)	1923	G	a	1939	X	
215 (ii)	1939	R		e		L
216 (i)	1924	G	a	1939	X	
216 (ii)	1939	R		e		L
217 (i)	1924	Q	a	1944	X	
217 (ii)	1947	R		e		L
218 (i)	1923	G	a	1937	X	
218 (ii)	1938	R		1956		L
219 (i)	1924	G	a	1947	X	
219 (ii)	1948	R		e		L
220 (i)	1923	G	a	1939	X	
220 (ii)	1939	R		e		L
221 (i)	1924	G	af	1943	X	
221 (ii)	1939	R		e		L
222 (i)	1922	G	bf	1938	L	
222 (ii)	1939	R		e		L
223 (i)	1923	G	a	1939	X	
223 (ii)	1939	R		e		L
224 (i)	1923	G	a	1947	X	
224 (ii)	1947	R		e		L
225 (i)	1923	G	af	1947	X	

Table of Tram Types, Building Dates and Other Details

Nos	Year New	Type	Notes	Year Scrapped	Depot 1930	Depot 1945
225 (ii)	1950	R		1956		L
226 (i)	1923	G	a	1938	X	
226 (ii)	1938	R		1956		L
227 (i)	1924	G	a	1939	X	
227 (ii)	1939	R		e		L
228 (i)	1923	G	a	1947	X	
228 (ii)	1948	R		e		L
229 (i)		E	f	1934	S	
229 (ii)	1935	R		e		L
230 (i)		E	f	1934	S	
230 (ii)	1935	R		1956		L
231 (i)		L1		1933	L	
231 (ii)	1934	Q3		1956		L
232 (i)		L1	f	1936	L	
232 (ii)	1936	R		1956		X
233 (i)		L1	f	1936	L	
233 (ii)	1936	R		1956		X
234 (i)		L1	f	1936	L	
234 (ii)	1936	R		1956		X
235 (i)		L1	f	1936	L	
235 (ii)	1936	R		1956		X
236 (i)		L1	f	1936	L	
236 (ii)	1936	R		1956		X
237 (i)		L1	f	1936	L	
237 (ii)	1936	R		1956		X
238 (i)		L1	f	1936	L	
238 (ii)	1937	R		1956		X
239 (i)		L1		1933	P	
239 (ii)	1934	Q3	f	1956		L
240 (i)		L1		1933	P	
240 (ii)	1934	Q3		1956		L
241 (i)		L1		1933	P	
241 (ii)	1934	Q2		1952		L
242 (i)		L1		1933	P	
242 (ii)	1934	Q2		1955		L
243 (i)		L1	f	1936	L	
243 (ii)	1937	R		1956		L
244 (i)		L1		1933	L	
244 (ii)	1934	Q2		1952		L
245 (i)		L1		1932	L	
245 (ii)	1934	Q2		1951		L
246 (i)		M		1933	L	
246 (ii)	1934	Q2		1952		L
247 (i)		M	f	1936	P	
247 (ii)	1937	R		1956		L
248 (i)		M	f	1936	L	
248 (ii)	1937	R		1956		L
249 (i)		M		1933	L	
249 (ii)	1934	Q2	f	1952		L
250 (i)		N		1931		
250 (ii)	1932	J		1956		L
251 (i)		N		1931		
251 (ii)	1932	J		1956		L

Table of Tram Types, Building Dates and Other Details

Nos	Year New	Type	Notes	Year Scrapped	Depot 1930	Depot 1945
252 (i)		N		1931		
252 (ii)	1932	J		1956		L
253 (i)		N		1931		
253 (ii)	1932	J		1955		L
254 (i)		N		1931		
254 (ii)	1932	J		1956		L
255 (i)		N		1931		
255 (ii)	1932	J	f	1952		L
256 (i)		N		1931		
256 (ii)	1932	J		1956		L
257 (i)		N		1931		
257 (ii)	1932	J		1955		L
258 (i)		N		1931		
258 (ii)	1932	J		1953		L
259 (i)		N	f	1931		
259 (ii)	1932	J		1955		L
260 (i)		N		1931		
260 (ii)	1933	Q1	f	1956		L
261 (i)		L2		1932	L	
261 (ii)	1933	P	f	1955		L
262 (i)		L2	f	1933	L	
262 (ii)	1934	S2		1956		L
263 (i)		L2		1933	L	
263 (ii)	1934	S2		1956	L	
264 (i)		M		1931	L	
264 (ii)	1931	K	f	1955		L
265 (i)		M		1932	L	
265 (ii)	1933	Q1	f	1956		L
266 (i)		M		1931	L	
266 (ii)		K	f	Former 371	1954		L
267 (i)		M		1933	L	
267 (ii)	1934	S2	f	1955		L
268 (i)		E	f	1929	L	
268 (ii)	1929	H4		1955		X
269 (i)		E	f	1935	S	
269 (ii)	1935	R		1956		G
270	1923	H2		1953	X	X
271	1923	H2		1953	X	L
272	1923	H2		1954	S	X
273	1923	H2		1953	L	X
274	1923	H2		1954	P	X
275	1923	H2		1954	S	X
276	1923	H2		1953	S	X
277	1923	H2		1955	G	L
278	1923	H2		1953	S	L
279	1923	H2		1953	S	X
280	1923	H2		1954	L	X
281	1923	H2		1955	L	G
282	1923	H2		1954	S	G
283	1923	H2		1954	S	G
284	1923	H2		1954	P	G
285	1923	H2		1954	X	G
286	1923	H2		1954	P	G

Table of Tram Types, Building Dates and Other Details

Nos	Year New	Type	Notes	Year Scrapped	Depot 1930	Depot 1945
287	1923	H2		1954	G	G
288	1923	H2		1953	G	G
289	1923	H2		1954	G	G
290	1923	H2		1954	G	G
291	1923	H2		1955	S	G
292	1923	H2		1955	P	G
293	1923	H2		1955	S	X
294	1923	H2		1953	G	X
295	1923	H2		1953	L	X
296	1923	H2		1953	S	X
297	1923	H2		1954	S	X
298	1923	H2		1953	S	X
299	1923	H2		1955	S	X
300	1923	H2		1953	X	X
301	1923	H2		1954	X	G
302	1923	H2		1954	X	G
303	1923	H2		1953	X	G
304	1923	H2		1954	X	G
305	1923	H2		1953	G	G
306	1923	H2		1953	P	X
307	1923	H2		1954	L	X
308	1923	H2	f	1955	G	X
309	1923	H2		1955	X	X
310	1923	H2	f	1954	P	X
311	1923	H2		1953	X	X
312	1924	H3	b	1954	L	X
313	1924	H3	b	1955	G	G
314	1924	H3	b	1953	S	L
315	1924	H3	b	1954	S	G
316	1924	H3	bf	1955	S	G
317	1924	H3	bf	1953	L	L
318	1924	H3	b	1953	L	L
319	1924	H3	b	1953	S	L
320	1924	H3	b	1953	L	G
321	1924	H3		1955	G	X
322	1924	H3		1954	G	X
323	1924	H3		1955	G	X
324	1924	H3	b	1951	S	L
325	1924	H3	b	1953	S	L
326	1924	H3	b	1955	G	L
327	1924	H3	b	1953	S	G
328	1924	H3	bf	1953	G	L
329	1924	H3	b	1953	S	L
330	1924	H3	b	1954	S	L
331	1924	H3	b	1953	S	G
332	1925	H4	a	1954	X	G
333	1925	H4	a	1955	X	G
334	1925	H4	a	1955	X	L
335	1925	H4	a	1953	X	G
336	1925	H4	a	1953	X	G
337	1925	H4	a	1953	X	G
338	1925	H4	a	1954	X	G
339	1925	H4	a	1953	X	G

Table of Tram Types, Building Dates and Other Details

Nos	Year New	Type	Notes		Year Scrapped	Depot 1930	Depot 1945
340	1925	H4	a		1953	X	G
341	1925	H4	a		1955	X	G
342	1926	H4	b		1953	L	G
343	1926	H4	b		1953	L	G
344	1926	H4	b		1953	L	G
345	1926	H4	b		1953	L	G
346	1926	H4	b		1955	L	G
347	1926	H4	b		1955	L	G
348	1926	H4	b		1953		G
349	1927	H4	b		1950	S	G
350	1927	H4	b		1954	S	G
351	1926	H4	b		1953	S	G
352	1926	H4	b		1953	L	G
353	1926	H4	b		1955	S	L
354	1929	H4	b		1954		L
355	1929	H4	b		1955		L
356	1929	H4			1956		L
357	1929	H4	bf		1955		L
358	1929	H4	bf		1955		L
359	1929	H4	b		1956		L
360	1929	H4	bf		1955		P
361	1929	H4	bf		1955		P
362	1929	H4	bf		1955		P
363	1929	H4	bf		1955		P
364	1929	H4	bf		1956		P
365	1929	H4	bf		1955		P
366	1929	H4	bf		1955		P
367	1929	K	f		1955	L	P
368	1930	K			1955		P
369	1930	K			1956	X	P
370	1930	K	b		1955	L	P
371	1930	K	f	Renumbered 266(ii)			
401		T		Purchased 1947	1954		
402		T		Purchased 1947	1954		
403		T		Purchased 1947	1954		
404		T		Purchased 1947	1954		
405		T		Purchased 1948	1954		
406		T		Purchased 1948	1954		
407		T		Purchased 1948	1954		
408		T		Purchased 1949	1954		
409		T		Purchased 1949	1954		
410		T		Purchased 1949	1954		
411		T		Purchased 1949	1954		

Appendix 2

ROLLING STOCK – BUSES

Three charabancs and twelve 35/40hp buses were ordered from Leyland in the Spring of 1919. The 27-seat charabancs, which were painted grey, arrived in August and used Edinburgh licence numbers 1-3 as fleet numbers; registrations were B8725 and S9257-8. The buses were numbered 4-15 (S9309-20), with rather box like Leyland bodies, flat roofed and with a narrow rear entrance. The saloon (seating 31) was divided, the rear forming a smoking area. Behind the driver was a partition and on his nearside was a hinged seat for two passengers, also reached by a door on the nearside. All windows had top-lights with the nearside over the windscreen and the rear containing destination screens. Livery was madder, with white window pillars. The Magistrates inspected No5 on 24 November, but at 25ft long it exceeded the maximum allowed in the by-laws. However as a precedent had already been established, the necessary licences were issued. Further six 27-seat Leyland charabancs came early in 1920, numbers 16-21 (SG53, 1196, 1299, 1300 and 1524-5).

Additional thirty Leyland chassis were delivered in 1920 and early 1921, with bodies from three builders:

Leyland numbers 22-33 (SG1649-53, 2133-6, 2801-3)

Lincoln Lorries, Louth numbers 34-9 (SG2139-41, 2277-8, 2804)

Cowieson, Glasgow numbers 40-50 & 150 (SG1654, 2142, 2138, 2137, 2273-6, 2805-8)

The Corporation's first charabanc Leyland B8725 of August 1919. The lettering on the rear panel is 'Corporation Tramways No 1'. (EOC)

Number 5 Leyland from the initial batch of buses, photographed in the first garage at Shrubhill. The building was originally the horse tram body building department of the Street Tramways Company and horse tram track can be seen below the rear wheel of the bus. (EOC)

SG1300 originally had a charabanc body but was fitted in 1921 with this Cowieson central entrance body. Although the destination screen says 'Cramond' the bill in the front window reads 'Football Match Tynecastle' which seems more accurate as the photograph was taken outside the 'Diggers' in Angle Park Terrace. (EOC)

Leyland 28, (SG2134) was one of those rebuilt with the entrance at the front for operation by driver only on lightly trafficked routes, although this location has not been identified. Robert McLeod, the Traffic Superintendent who ten years later was to become Manager, is seen on the right with bowler hat. (EOC)

In September 1920 thirty buses were ordered to replace cable cars on the hilly Northern routes where greater power was required These were AEC Y type with Tyler 40/45 hp engines (some later had 45 hp AEC engines). 'Standard' bodies were built by E&H Hora of London, numbered 157-186 (SG2008-15, 2221-6, 2267-72, 2325-30 and 2809-12). Sprags were fitted to prevent run-back but were removed after a short time. SG2812 is thought to have burned out when descending Hanover Street in April or May 1921, its chassis then used for a lorry. It is also possible that AEC lorry No10 (SG54) ran with a bus body for a short time about 1923, though this has not been confirmed. Likewise there is no physical evidence of SG2812 actually being bus 186, but this is the only satisfactory interpretation of the few known facts.

The Council wanted to see a double deck bus, and on 27 September 1920 inspected an AEC K type. Mr Pilcher however advocated a large capacity single decker, and submitted a design for a 42-seat bus. The double-decker was left in abeyance, and an order placed with Cowieson for six bodies to Pilcher's design (but shortened to fit normal control chassis on which they would take the place of charabancs during the winter). Pilcher's design had a wide entrance near the centre of the body divided by a central handrail. They now seated 32, hence were little improvement on the original design. Six Leyland charabancs were ordered, but of the accepted longer length, giving an additional row of seats (for 33). These were numbered 186-191 (SG2813-5, 7, 6, 8) and arrived in May 1921.

The first Cowieson centre-entrance body was numbered 151 and was mounted on one of the short Leyland charabanc chassis given registration number SG2819. This number has not been explained, but may have been former charabanc 16 or 17 re-registered erro-

AEC number 165 (SG2221) was one of thirty purchased for use on the former Northern and Mound tram routes. It has side boards for the Easter Road to Ardmillan route, and was photographed in Henderson Row in front of the former cable car depot which was converted to a bus garage. (EOC)

neously. When inspected by the Hackney Carriage Inspector on 24 June 1921 he refused to accept it. However, in July after fitting additional guards to the rear wheels, a temporary three-month licence was granted. At the end of October an annual licence was issued, and two more centre-entrance bodies (152-3) replaced the charabanc bodies on SG1299 and SG1300. Number 155 was also noted later. After the winter these centre-entrance bodies (151-6) were removed and laid aside, only to reappear as will be relat-

Forward control AEC 192 (SG4869) had a Cowieson body but was not accepted by the Corporation. It thereafter received an open-top double deck body. Seen near St Anne's Church, Corstorphine. (EOC)

The Corporation's first double deck bus was number 193 (NO 5027). Not only had the AEC a London style body, it was also painted London red. Purchased in 1922 it is seen in Princes Street. (EOC)

ed. SG2819 reverted to a charabanc with its original registration number. There was much press comment regarding the Corporation buses which were compared unfavourably with those of the SMT. The centre-entrance type was particularly unpopular.

A larger capacity single-decker, generally to Pilcher's design, was built by Fry on an AEC S type chassis and following inspection by the council in February 1922, was offered to the Corporation for three months free trial on the Corstorphine route. The driver was in the forward-control position beside the engine protected only by a metal dash plate and light windscreen. The entrance, of normal width, was near the front, there being one window ahead of it and four behind. The internal layout was probably similar to the Cowieson centre-entrance bodies but with a rear-facing seat against the front bulkhead. This bus, 192 (SG4869), was painted red and carried only the 'legal' lettering. Also on free trial and also run for three months on the Corstorphine route (adorned with AEC and Peric Motor Co advertisements) was a red London type AEC S type, 54-seat open-top double-decker 193 (NO5027). Despite the restrictions of the open top in the Scottish climate, the council still wanted its double-decker, so it was purchased at a reduced price at the end of June then fitted with a small windscreen. Its licence was issued on 4 July. Single-decker 192 was rejected and an alternative sought. This materialised in October also numbered 192, and still carrying registration SG4869, but now with a similar red double-deck body built by Fry.

As it was to be four years before any additions were made to the bus fleet, mention should be made to alterations to the existing vehicles. Drivers' doors were blocked off at an early date, the two high steps and the narrow entrances gave rise to complaint, so in 1921 a third step was incorporated in entrances to all buses, also entrances were widened on numbers 7, 8, 9, 11, 14, 15, 25 and 29, and possibly others. In late 1922 number 28 was altered for one-man operation by moving the entrance to the front, alongside the driver. The original rear entrance was removed but an emergency door and folding step was provided in its place, with a lift-up seat inside. The seating capacity was reduced to 30. Numbers 4, 22, 37, 40 and 46 were altered likewise. Later, in 1929, six AECs were similarly altered, *viz* 158, 161-2, 168-70 and all but the last two were fitted with folding doors. Before this 32 and 38 exchanged bodies. Many original bodies were now being broken up and to keep some of the old buses going a little longer, the six centre entrance Cowieson bodies were resurrected, and fitted to numbers 13, 33, 42, 48, 49 and 50. The partition was moved further back to make a smaller smoking compartment , while later the seats in this compartment (except on 42) were rearranged to mostly face forwards. A Cowieson front entrance body was subsequently fitted to 49.

In 1922 Michelin beaded-edge pneumatic tyres were tried for a few months on 47. During the second half of 1922 three others were fitted with straight-sided pneumatic tyres, and a further three in 1923 (6, 7, 8, 23, 24 and 40). These were successful and soon all the Leylands were so fitted. Some had the front and rear wheels altered at different times. Most AECs were changed also but 157, 159, 163-5, 172, 174-5, 178, 182 and 184 were withdrawn in 1927, still on solid tyres.

About 1928 the service number on the roof was replaced by a roller-blind number in the top-light above the driver. Earlier some buses had the destination screen arranged centrally between the two front top-lights (4, 13, 46, 168, 169, 170 and 181). Later, surviving buses had the waist band, and the inside of the roof, painted white, including 5, 8, 9, 11-13, 29, 31-4, 37-8, 42, 45-6, 48-50, 150, 158, 161-2, 167-8, 170-1, 177 and 179-81. At the end of 1930 charabancs 1-3 and 16-8 were converted to lorries as were sev-

In 1926 the Corporation purchased the Annandale Street Industrial Hall premises for use as their Central Garage. It is seen here, still with its original stage and before the doors were heightened to allow double deck vehicles in. An interesting selection of twenty-five Leyland and AEC vehicles, all now on pneumatic tyres. (EOC)

Dennis 14-seat charabanc purchased in 1926, on the Arthur's Seat circular tour at Dunsapie Loch. Livery was grey, lined red. (EOC)

eral earlier withdrawn. Remaining charabancs were then painted bright red with a darker red band above. Two vehicles were re-numbered in 1930, 11 to 31 and 38 to 8.

By the time the next new vehicles were supplied, in 1926, design had improved. First came three neat Dennis 14-seat charabancs with grey painted bodies by Vickers, 501-3, (SF6028-30). More striking were eight Leyland Lion PLSC1s with 29-seat Leyland bodies. The new Lions had a cut-away rear entrance, forward of which was a partition. Between the partition and the entrance was a longitudinal seat for two on each side, then a forward-facing seat for two on the off-side and a seat for four across the back, this forming a smoking section. There was also a front entrance with a hinged door at the top of the steps. All windows had top-lights except the rear where there were two windows, with the destination screen centrally. The roof was domed, and the white ceiling gave a bright appearance inside. The driver's cab was completely enclosed. These were robust and lively acquisitions, numbered 504-11 (SF6258-61, 6330-1, 6470-1). Also obtained were four AEC 507 double-deckers with Brush bodies similar to the existing two, but with enclosed driver's cab. They were painted in standard livery. They took numbers 153-6 (SF6521-4) and ran on solid tyres initially, though pneumatic tyres were later fitted to the front wheels, and subsequently to the rear wheels. Destination screens were added early in 1931, by which time the original two double-deckers had been scrapped (they also received pneumatic tyres, about 1929).

The 1927 additions consisted of fourteen more Leyland Lions, this time PLSC3 with 32-seat bodies by Croall and by Hall Lewis. The numbers were 512-7 (SF8495-8500) with Croall bodies, and 518-25 (SF8989-96) with Hall Lewis bodies, except 521 which was by Croall. Another new type was six Karrier six-wheelers WL6/1 with similar Hall

Leyland Lion PLSC3 (SF8495), number 512 of 1927. Seen at the foot of the Mound, outside the Royal Scottish Academy, then terminus of the route 11 to Blackhall and Davidson's Mains. (EOC)

Lewis bodies seating 39. Seating reflected that of the PLSC1s, but with longer seats over the wheel-arches. The dash was also higher and provided with louvered ventilators. These were 526-31 (SF8997-9 and SF9002-4).

In 1928 came four more Leyland Lion PLSC3, eight more Karriers, and another type (the precursor of a long sequence) – eight Daimlers. The latter were type ADC 423. All

Also in 1927 were purchased six Karriers with Hall Lewis bodies. The first, SF8997, number 526, photographed in Green Street at the side entrance to the Central Garage. (EOC)

bodies were by Croall, similar to the preceding ones but there were variations in the seating of the Daimlers, and the dash panels of the Karriers were lower. A service number screen was incorporated in the destination screen-box, and the box set into the roof instead of being above it. All earlier buses were subsequently likewise altered. There were also three further Dennis, with 14-seat open coach bodies. These were grey, with a yellow waist panel added early in 1930. Licence numbers from old buses were now re-used:

Leyland:	Nos 10, 26 (soon renumbered 24), 151-2, (SC1126-9 respectively)
Daimler:	Nos 157, 9-60, 47, 163-6, (SC1130-7 respectively)
Karrier:	Nos 172, 4-5, 532, 178/82, 533, 184, (SC1138-45 respectively)
Dennis:	Nos 14 (soon renumbered 26), 35, 9, (SC1146-8 respectively)

Number 172 was destroyed by fire when quite new and replaced by another, registered SC2216.

The last Leylands for many years, PLSC3s, were added in 1929. These were 30, 6, 194-7, 183, 200, 198-9 (SC3401-10) with Cowieson bodies, and 535, 772-3, 771, 770 (SC3411-5) with Croall bodies. A solitary Daimler CF6 with Croall body, 534, (SC3416) followed, then fourteen AEC Reliance, also with Croall bodies, 774-87 (SC3417-30). The only body difference in these was a large oval rear window. (The AECs had Holt heaters.)

Yet another new make appeared in 1930, four Morris Viceroy 20-seat coaches (painted red) followed by three Morris Dictators with similar 24-seat bodies by Mitchell. These also were red, and carried a destination board above the windscreen illuminated by cowled lamps. The former were 581-4 (SC7281-4), the latter 48-50 (SC8747-9). Standard livery was subsequently adopted. Buses supplied in 1930 were all Daimlers, CF6, with

AEC Reliance 739 of 1929 (SC3422) had Croall bodywork. Seen in South St David Street with two Edinburgh institutions behind, the Scott Monument and, to the right, Jenner's Store. (EOC)

Cowieson bodies. These took numbers 4, 5, 7, 9, 11, 12, 13, 170, 15, 22, 23, 25, 27, 28, 33, 36, 37, 38, 40, 41, 42, 43, 44, 46, 167, 171, 14, 173, 176, 177, 179, 180, 181, 185, 192, 193 (SC7285-7320). In some cases the old buses with these numbers, *eg* 5, 13, 33, 37, continued in traffic so there was duplication of some numbers for a month or two. Near the end of the year a further Daimler appeared, a CH6 with fluid flywheel, and similar body by Hume. This was 169 (SC8791) with only 29 seats.

In 1931 the City licensing system ended and the new Traffic Commissioners' small oval white enamelled number plates were fixed to the rear of all buses. For the next few years these, with their M prefix, were used as fleet numbers. As on the trams, the old form of lettering was discarded in favour of the small 'City and Royal Burgh of Edinburgh' low on the front near-side. Both series of Dennis and the remaining old charabancs were now painted red like the later coaches. Of the pre-1926 fleet only six buses and nine charabancs survived into the new scheme. The Karriers were not found successful and some had already been scrapped. The remainder, together with the double-deckers and pre-1926 vehicles disappeared by the end of 1931, the Dennises the next year. The 1931 buses comprised a Crossley Alpha (SC9901), an Albion Viking PMB28 (SC9902), a Daimler CP6 (SC9903), fourteen Daimler CF6 (SC9904-17), and three Morris Dictators (SC9918-20). All of their 31-seat bodies were built locally by Alexander Motors. New features were enclosed light fittings and air bells for the conductor.

By 1932 the new Ministry of Transport requirements regarding exits *etc* required a change in body work design. Hence the nine CH6 Daimlers (FS2159-67) had 32-seat Cowieson bodies generally similar to the Alexander Motors' ones of 1931 but with no entrance at the front. There was, however, a front offside emergency door. There were two similar Morris Dictators (FS2157-8) but the body of the latter was of all-metal construction by Metropolitan-Cammell with a flatter roof. Another six Morris Dictator 24-seat coaches were added (FS2151-6). Their Alexander Motors' bodies had an emergency door between two windows in the back, moquette seating, a higher roof with an opening portion and a double destination screen at the front. Air bells were fitted and they

SC7299 was a Daimler type CF/6, new in 1930 and is seen ascending Market Street. Behind on the skyline, Nelson's Monument and the turrets of Calton Jail. (EOC)

Ravelston Dykes terminus c.1931 at the north end of Murrayfield Road, with new Morris Dictator 48 (SC8747) with coach body. (EOC)

were pained in the red coach livery. Later the coach door was replaced by a bus entrance at the front and standard livery adopted.

Over the next two years only a few buses were purchased, but much experimental work was carried out. Leyland SC3407, AEC SC3423, and Daimler SC9903 were for a short period only adapted to use tar oil as fuel. AEC SC3430 received a Beardmore oil engine in August 1933, for which the bonnet was slightly extended. Two Morris Dictators with metal 34-seat front entrance Metropolitan-Cammell bodies arrived in the early part of 1933 (FS4422 and FS5936). The emergency exit was at the rear. They had rather flat roofs without service number provision initially. The former eventually had one under the canopy.

The Corporation's first closed top double-decker appeared in July 1933, a Morris Imperial with Park Royal 'low-bridge' body, seating 50. The platform was enclosed and a service number screen provided back and front with destination screen below at the front, and above the platform (FS6340, plus another, FS9611, the next year). The second had a body by Metropolitan-Cammell with minor differences, seating one less on each deck. Meanwhile four more single-deckers were added, all different. FS7032 was a Morris Dictator, FS7033 a Daimler CP6 both with English Electric 34-seat bodies similar to those of 1933. FS7036 was a Daimler COG5 with a Weymann body of massive appearance. This bus had a Gardner oil engine, while WS637, another Daimler CH6 with a similar 32-seat Roberts body had a Tangye oil engine. Finally in October 1934 came an AEC 'Q' (WS1506) with a 39-seat Weymann body with front entrance. An AEC Ricardo oil engine was fitted. The window pillars of SC7287 were painted brown in 1933 but this was not repeated.

Seen in Central Garage, FS2156 was one of the Morris Dictator coaches which received a front entrance body rebuild to make it more suitable for service operations. (DLGH)

Further oil engines were obtained and all AEC Reliances (except that with the Beardmore engine) were fitted with four cylinder AEC oil engines in 1934. During 1934-5 Gardner five-cylinder oil engines were fitted to all the 1932 Daimler and Morris buses, to the Albion, and to SC8791 and FS7033. WS637 also received one in 1936, as did the Morris Imperials. The Crossley was fitted with an oil engine (of that make) in 1934. A Thornycroft engine was tried in one of the 1930 Daimlers (SC7301). This had its bonnet extended and, in 1935, received a larger Daimler radiator. During the following year this was changed for a Thornycroft radiator, but during 1937 reverted to its original form, with petrol engine.

The Daimler-Gardner combination with MCW all-metal body became standard, five cylinder engines for single-deckers and six cylinder for double-deckers. In 1935 sixteen 54-seat Metropolitan-Cammell highbridge type double deckers were got, generally similar to FS9611 (WS6371-85). 1936 added single deckers WS9502-21 with 36-seat Weymann bodies. These had the usual front screens and a destination screen over the entrance.

The necessity of an improved identification other than by the Traffic Commissioners' 'M' number was apparent, so a scheme was drawn up, with each type numbered separately with a prefix letter:

A   Daimler single-deckers with oil engines.
B   AEC.
D   Daimler single-deckers, petrol engines.
G   Daimler double-deckers (later including other makes).
L   Leyland.
M   Morris (all types).
X   Other makes.

Each sequence started at eleven, it being intended that renewals would take lower numbers: so that if the first (say) ten buses were replaced by (say) fifteen new ones, there

A solitary AEC "Q", WS1508 was operated by the Corporation for a short period. Seen here at the foot of the Mound, with the Doric columns of the Royal Scottish Academy behind. (EOC)

Waverley Bridge terminus, 1936, with Daimler COG5 registration WS9508. Fleet number A30 can be discerned in small characters above the headlight. The elegant Edinburgh skyline behind leads the eye to the Castle, on the extreme right. (EOC)

Daimler COG6 double deck bus of 1936, seen at Hay Drive terminus among some basic inter-war local authority housing architecture. (EOC)

would be numbers available. Double-deckers WS6371-86 were thus numbered G11-26. Single-deckers WS9502-21 took numbers A24-43, the numbers A11-23 being allocated to the older vehicles. These numbers were in fairly small figures on the dash and on the rear near-side waist panel. These numbers were gradually applied to older vehicles: the list on pages 179-180 giving details. The issue of 'M' number plates ended in 1939.

Not content with decorated trams, Edinburgh Transport also decorated buses. This out-of-service Leyland Lion, running on trade registration plates, was photographed for the 1938 Hospital charity parade. The photo is in Holyrood Park, on Queens Drive near St. Leonard's School. (EOC)

A44-53 and G27-41 followed in 1937, the same as their predecessors but with moquette seating. More arrived in 1938, A54-68 and 69-88; G42-51 and 52-61. The 1937 and 1938 double-deckers seated one or two less and the last batch had a ventilator in the top of the top deck front window.

No new buses were ordered in 1939 and with war-time controls there were no additions until 1941 when the first of a mixed bag of vehicles 'unfrozen' by the Ministry of Supply were delivered. These were G9-10, AEC Regents with Park Royal utility double-deck bodies, single-deck X13-4, Tilling Stevens H5LA4s with Willowbrook bodies, and X15, a Bristol L5G with Bristol body. Another two 'unfrozen' double-deckers followed in 1942, G7 a Bristol K5G with Northern Counties body, and G8, a Leyland Titan TD7 with Pickering utility body. The double-deck Bristol and AECs had the top deck waist panel of white curved down at the front, like the tramcars. The single-deck Bristol and Tilling-Stevens had a front entrance, though the former was altered to the usual cut-away rear entrance in 1948.

Next, in 1942, some war-time utility buses were delivered, Bedford OWBs with SMT bodies to the standard front entrance 32-seat design. These were X7-10 (in a dark grey-brown livery), followed by X1-6 and X16-25 in 1943. Double-deckers obtained in 1943 were G62-3, Daimler CWG5 with Massey bodies, and G64-5 similar but CWA6 types with AEC 7.7 litre engines; also G1-6 Guy Arabs with Gardner 6LW engines and Pickering bodies (except G2-3 with bodies by Massey). G62-3 ran in grey livery for their first few months. The original idea of reserving numbers 1-10 had been abandoned and these were now used, before adding higher numbers. More Daimler CWA6s followed in 1944-5, G66 with a Massey body, G67-70 with Northern Counties bodies and G71-8 with Brush bodies.

A number of standard 'A' buses, and all the Morris coaches, were taken over by the War Department at the beginning of the war, while G44 and G46 were borrowed by London at the critical period of 1940-1. All except the Morris coaches returned. Two former Dundee Daimler COG5 single-deckers, badly damaged in WD service, were on offer. These were accepted and rebuilt at Shrubhill to virtually Edinburgh standard pattern. They were prepared in grey, fully lined and varnished, numbered A23 (the first A23 had been withdrawn in April 1940) and A10. The grey livery was applied to all Bedfords, to G4, 5, 6 and 63, and also to a pre-war bus (A51). As the war continued there was increasing difficulty in keeping older vehicles operating. The AECs were the oldest vehicles, surviving until 1943. The 1930 Daimlers had sleeve-valve engines that were difficult for spares so finally petered out at the end of that year. Much 'make do and mend' was required, and D55 acquired a second-hand Albion engine. Producer-gas operation has already been referred to.

After the war new bodies by Northern Counties were fitted to G1-6 in 1948/9, while the bodies of G1, 3, 4 and 5 replaced those on G64-5, 63 and 66 respectively. G71 was wrecked in 1945 and subsequently fitted with a reconstructed single-deck body with a front entrance, originally on M18. As a single-decker it was renumbered A11 (the original A11 having been scrapped). A12 was reconstructed as a 26-seater in 1947 and with additional external mouldings was used on the airport service. A14 was withdrawn in 1944 but the others, A13, A15-9 and A47 were fitted (in 1949) with new 36-seat bodies by Alexander of Stirling. They were generally similar to the immediate pre-war pattern but with larger front service number screen, while that on the rear was central. A20 was badly smashed in 1948 and then received a rebuilt body that may have come from the

Crossley scrapped some years before. During 1949-50 several of the Daimler single-deckers were rebuilt at Shrubhill similar to the Alexander ones, most with a new curved front panel.

The first post-war deliveries in 1945-6 were twenty-seven Guy Arab II double-deckers with Gardner 6LW engines (G79-105) of which G88-92 had Weymann bodies, the others Northern Counties bodies with a domed roof and, except for G81-7, ventilators to the top deck front windows. The service number screens were larger than hitherto. Larger screens were also fitted to several older double-deckers. On G93-105 however, a new arrangement of screens with two larger screens was adopted. The service number was shown in that on the offside, and two or three points on the route in the other. Earlier double-deckers were duly altered similarly. These were followed by seventeen Daimler CVD6 double-deckers and the first of sixty-two similar CVG6s. The CVD6s, G106-12 of 1947-8 had Northern Counties bodies similar to those on the Guys, while G113-22 of 1949 had Metropolitan-Cammell bodies to a design used by Birmingham Corporation, with deeper top deck windows. The CVG6s, G123-84 of 1949-50 had these Birmingham-style Metropolitan-Cammell bodies.

With the vast post-war demand for new vehicles, buses of any make were acceptable so the first new single-deckers of 1948 were ten Guy Arab IIIs (A131-40). These had 35-seat Metropolitan-Cammell bodies generally similar to the reconstructed pre-war Daimlers. They were followed at the end of the year by ten Daimler CVG5s with similar bodies (A89-98). Four Crossley single-deckers were acquired (A1-4). They were built for another operator, and had Roe 34-seat front entrance bodies, with the emergency door in the rear. They were turned out in chocolate colour without white relieving, but were repainted in standard livery in 1950. Also in 1950 fifteen Bristol L6B single-deckers appeared with Brockhouse bodies similar to the Daimlers (A162-76). Old Bristol X15 was now renumbered A161. Seven Bedford OWBs with Duple Vista coach bodies came in 1949-50. These took numbers X2, 9, 18 and 22-5, older vehicles carrying these numbers being renumbered X32-8. New Duple coach bodies were provided for X4, 6, 7, 8,10, 19, 20 and 21 and new seating provided in the others. The standard livery was restored with, on some, a down-swept mid panel. All the Duple bodied Bedfords were, in 1952, fitted with Perkins P6 diesel engines. The few remaining grey buses were soon repainted in standard colours.

Fifteen Guy Arab III double-deckers with Northern Counties bodies, G200-14, and seventeen AEC Regent III double-deckers with Brockhouse bodies, G221-37, were delivered over 1949-51. The Brockhouse bodies, built at Clydebank, were to a Park Royal design.

Few old vehicles were withdrawn during the early post-war years as every vehicle was needed to cope with the traffic demands. In 1949, with delivery of new vehicles resumed, withdrawal of the first of the 1935-6 Daimler double-deckers started, then followed in 1950 by withdrawal of the 'unfrozen' vehicles (except A161). In 1951 the first of the un-rebuilt 1936-8 Daimler single-deckers went although it was 1957 before the last had gone. The final 1937-8 Daimler double-deckers survived until 1956.

In May 1951 a straightforward scheme of numbers without prefixes was adopted. These were now shown in larger figures just behind the cab or bonnet below the waist panel, and in the same position as before on the rear. The renumbering was straightforward. The 'G' series vehicles retained their numbers, those in the 'A' series having six hundred added. The Bedford coaches kept their old 'X' numbers. A list of numbers under

Hillend, terminus of the short route to Firrhill via Fairmilehead. AEC Regent G9, with Park Royal body work was photographed c 1942. The vehicle is wrongly registered DFS when it should have been DSF. (AWB Collection)

the new scheme is given on pages 182-184, with details of registration numbers *etc*.

From 1952 large orders were placed to cover tramway conversion requirements. Mr Little was interested in the Continental-style single-deck standee bus and in 1951-2 trials were made with 801, a Leyland Royal Tiger PSU1/13 with 31-seat rear entrance Alexander body and 802, a Leyland Olympic HR44 with MCW 32-seat rear entrance body. They were hired from August 1951 then purchased the following year (they were always in ECT livery). Another demonstration vehicle (also in ECT livery) arrived at the end of 1951, a Daimler Freeline G6H/S with Duple 36-seat two-door body, registration number LRW377. It received number 800, but was returned to the makers after a short time. Numbers 801-2 were rebuilt as front entrance coaches in 1955 becoming 37- and 36-seaters respectively. A new coach livery of white and black was applied to all coaches from 1955, including the remaining Bedfords. In 1952 numbers 803-18 appeared, Leyland Royal Tiger PSU1/17 40-seat Leyland built saloons with cut away rear entrance. They were initially used on the Comely Bank tram replacement but soon transferred to other routes. Between 1957 and 1960 they were rebuilt with front entrances, numbers 803-5 and 814-8 as 37-seat coaches; 806-13 as 43-seat buses. Before long these also became coaches, 806, 809-11 seating 37, the others 41.

The double-deckers of 1952 were 240-60, Leyland Titan PD2/12s with eight feet wide Leyland bodies seating 56 (58 in 251-5). In 1961-3 they were rebuilt with glass-fibre fronts and 59 seats. Also in 1952-3 came numbers 301-60, ex-London Transport utility Guy Arabs with Gardner 5LW engines. The chassis were completely rebuilt, and new full-fronted 55-seat eight feet wide bodies fitted. The lower decks of these were by Duple of Hendon and the upper decks by Nudd Bros & Lockyer of Kegworth. These lightweight buses were placed in service between November 1952 and July 1953, a useful low cost stopgap in the early stages of the tram-bus conversion. In 1958-9 they received Leyland style glass-fibre fronts, lasting until 1967-9. Number 314 was fitted with a 6LW engine in 1963 and is preserved in its original condition.

An interesting vehicle in the ECT fleet from April 1953 to December 1954 was 185, an ex-Birmingham 1939 Leyland Titan TD7c with Leyland 52-seat body. It had a Leyland 0.350 engine and Wilson preselective transmission relative to Leyland's developments of their first rear-engined double-deckers.

More Leyland double-deckers, all eight feet wide, followed in 1954 with one hundred Titan PD2/20s with Metropolitan-Cammell Orion bodies, numbers 401-500 obtained for tram replacement. (They weighed only 6ton 12cwt.) In 1955-6 followed 501-600, then 701-800 in 1956-7. To make way for these 731-40 and 761-76 were renumbered 831-40 and 861-76 in 1956.

In 1954 numbers 62-70 and 72-8 received new Alexander full-front 58-seat bodies and Gardner 5LW engines. In 1959 they received Leyland style glass-fibre fronts, remaining in use until 1967. Of all the full-fronted bodies only 301-60 had waist panels and a white panel over the lower saloon windows. 575 was turned out unpainted aluminium but soon received a madder band between the decks. Numbers 781, 792-800 were turned out similarly, but normal livery was applied in 1959. 642 and 645 had their waist band over painted madder about 1953.

Three new coaches were bought in 1955, 819-21, Leyland Tiger Cub PSUC1/2s with Alexander 41-seat front entrance bodies in the white and black livery.

To complete tramway replacement in November 1956, seventy Guy Arab IVs with

Sight-seeing tours recommenced soon after the war. This is Bedford ASF358 on a fine day with its fabric roof folded back. It is turning off Princes Street at the RSA. Note the Rolls Royce taxi on the right. (AWB Collection)

Alexander 63-seat bodies entered service that year, 901-70. 959 received a Gardner 6LX engine in place of the 6LW unit in 1958 and ran in a cherry-red livery during 1959-61.

Two buses arrived at the end of 1957, after being exhibited at the Scottish Motor Show. 822 was an Albion Aberdonian MR11L with Alexander 43-seat front entrance body. In 1958 it became a mobile exhibition unit, but reverted in

Edinburgh Castle was, and is, a magnet for tour buses and in summer months the Corporation ran a shuttle service to and from Waverley Bridge. Daimler A54 leads a trio of vehicles on what would today be a very quiet day at the Castle, but tourism was, when this photograph was taken, only an embryo industry. (EOC)

1959 to service as a 37-seat coach. The other, 998, was a Leyland Titan PD3/2 to the newly authorised 30ft length, with an Alexander 72-seat forward-entrance body and an unusual 'Homalloy' glass-fibre front.

The first post-war buses to be withdrawn were the Weymann-bodied Guy Arabs 88-92 in 1954, followed by some of the Northern Counties-bodied ones in 1957 (though some survived further 10 years). The four Crossleys (601-4) went in 1957, the re-bodied Bedford coaches in 1958, the newer ones in 1959. In 1959 thirty-six pre-war single deck Daimlers were still in regular service, some dating back to 1932 (though in rebuilt form). Following trials fifty new single-deckers were obtained allowing withdrawal of the last pre-war buses. The new buses, 1-50, were Leyland Tiger Cub PSUC1/3s with stressed skin Weymann bodies seating 44 (number 26 sat 47). Guy Arabs 1-6 were renumbered 81-6. Fifty more PSUC1/3s followed in 1960-1 (51-100). These were 47-seaters like 26, except for 56 which had 45 seats plus luggage space at the front. 51-5 and 57-62 were converted thus in 1961 for one-man operation. Vehicles between 62 and 97 had their numbers increased by 300 to accommodate these. With these new Tiger Cubs available, the remaining post-war single-deckers, Britsols, Daimlers and Guys, were withdrawn. Other double-deck withdrawals were AECs 221-37 in 1960, Daimler CVD6s 106-22 in 1960-2, and Guy Arabs 200-14 in 1962.

Five more 30ft long Leyland Titans were delivered early in 1959, all with Alexander 72-seat front entrance bodies. 261-4 were synchromesh gearbox PD3/3 models, while 999 had a fully-automatic gearbox PD3/2, delivered in an all scarlet livery, running thus until 1962. 264 ran from 1959 to 1962 in a variation of livery incorporating more madder. For a short period during 1959 Leyland 256 ran in an all madder livery, relieved only by a single white band. 261-4 were renumbered 994-7 in 1971 and, with 998-9 were sold to Highland Omnibuses in 1974.

An unusual single-decker was bought in 1961 (101) a Leyland Leopard PSU3/2R, to the newly authorised 36ft length. It had an Alexander 'continental' type body with 33 seats and space for 30 standing. There were three doors, a wide rear entrance that led to a platform behind the rear axle from where passengers passed a seated conductor, and narrower front and centre exit doors. It ran on service 16 for some time then in 1963 transferred to single-deck service 1, later to the 45 and 46. It was never popular, and in 1969 was converted to a 45-seat coach for the Airport service (in white and black livery). In 1975 it reverted to normal livery as a one-man bus.

Fifty Leyland Titan PD2A/30s appeared in 1961-2, 601-50. These were of 27ft length with Alexander rear entrance bodies (66 seats) and glass-fibre fronts. Twelve new Bedford coaches with Duple bodies came in 1963. These were 25-seat VAS1 models 201-3, and 41-seat SB5s 204-12. The Bedford-Duple combination then became standard for some time, with SB5s 219-21 and VAS1 222 in 1964. Also in 1964 came 52-seat VAL14 six-wheelers with twin-steering front axles, 213-8, and similar VAL70s 223-5, 228-30 and 235-7 in 1968-70. 45-seat VAM70s 231-4 arrived in 1969-70, 45-seat YRQs 238-42 in 1971, and 53-seat YRTs 204-8, 214-8 and 243-7 in 1972-3. There were also two Ford R226s with 52-seat Duple bodies (226-7) of 1968. All these coaches had Duple body styles, Bella 1963-4, Viceroy 1968-72, and Dominant 1973. Most of the early Bedfords and the Fords had short lives, although 201-3 and 222 were reseated as 25-seat buses in 1975 and painted in bus livery.

The next double-deckers were fifty Leyland Titan PD3/6s (30ft long) with Alexander 70-seat front entrance bodies (651-700) delivered in 1964. On these a larger 'route' box had screens listing six intermediate points. The arrival of these allowed the withdrawal of many of the remaining 1949-50 Daimlers.

Early in 1965 trials were conducted with three double-deck demonstrators, viz AEC Renown 7552MX, Daimler Fleetline 565CRW and Leyland Atlantean KTD551C. Existing Leyland PD3/6, 684, was also included in the trials. The outcome favoured the rear-engined models and in the interests of standardisation Leylands were ordered, 25 Atlanteans, plus 25 Titan PD3A/2s. The first Atlantean, 801, had an Alexander 74-seat body and 7ft 11in long panoramic windows. The remainder followed in 1966, 802 with panoramic windows and 803-25 with normal length windows. The PD3A/2 Titans arrived in 1966, with 70-seat Alexander front entrance bodies and glass-fibre fronts. They were placed on service 1, releasing 48 of the Tiger Cub single-deckers, 1-8, 10-21 and 23-50, which were sold to the Ulster Transport Authority (9 and 22 were withdrawn in 1963 after accident damage). Older single-deckers 801-22 were renumbered 102-23, though 104-19 carried these numbers only briefly prior to withdrawal. The former Leyland demonstrators (now 102-3) and Tiger Cubs (120-2) were withdrawn in 1968. The final five of the 1949 Birmingham-style CVG6 double-deckers were withdrawn in 1967, with number 135 retained for preservation.

The Leyland Atlantean with Alexander double-deck body now became the standard, from 1967 with panoramic windows. The 1967 deliveries were 851-99, PDR1/1s with 74-seat front entrance bodies, and 900, a 33ft, PDR2/1 with front entrance 82-seat body. From 1969 a two-door, front entrance and centre exit, layout was adopted seating 75. Deliveries were 301-50 in 1969, 351-400 in 1970, 251-300 in 1971-2, and with AN68/1R chassis and Alexander AL style body, 1-50 in 1972-3, 901-50 in 1973-4 and 401-50 in 1975.

1969 saw the first of the Guy Arab IVs 901-70 withdrawn, all having gone by 1973. The first of the Leyland PD2s went in 1970, withdrawal continuing but with almost 100 still in stock in 1975 when Lothian Region Transport came into being. Several withdrawn Leylands and Guys were adapted as driver training vehicles. Bristol 761 was driver training modified in 1953 until withdrawn in 1961. Guy Arab 83 was used 1958-67,

'Utility' Bedford DWS131 (X3) was painted in normal service livery for a short time. Seen here descending the Mound. (RL Grieves)

joined in 1961 by single-deck Guy Arabs 839-40 which lasted until 1970. Two of the Guy Arab IVs, 901 and 903, were training vehicles 1970-2, then were sold to Sunderland Corporation (for the same duties). In 1972 Leyland PD2/20s 705 and 707 became trainers, later joined by 480, 731, 733, 734, 771, 775-8 and 796-800. 707 was withdrawn in 1974, the others then numbered T1-15 in numerical order. These driver-training vehicles later received a distinctive livery with larger white areas. Two former driver trainers are

The fleet number (G80) of Daimler CVG6 can just be distinguished above the registration plate GSG12. The driver's white topped summer cap is leaning against the windscreen. Ascending the Mound with the National Gallery to the right c.1949. (RL Grieves)

Tour coach meets service bus on the Royal Mile outside the City Chambers. On the right is Bristol FWS161, fleet number (then) 868. (DLGH)

preserved: Guy Arab III single-decker 839 is privately preserved (as 739) and Leyland PD2/20 480 is retained by Lothian Region Transport.

A batch of ten Seddon Pennine IV midibuses with 25-seat Pennine Coachcraft bodies was bought in 1973 (102-11) to operate in narrow streets, for school transport, crew transfers, *etc*. Ten Bedford YRTs with 49-seat Alexander Y type coach bodies (112-21) were bought in 1975, but after a year in white and black coach livery, were repainted in white with a low madder strip then used on service routes. The last Bedfords, and the last three Atlanteans were delivered just days before Edinburgh Corporation was transformed into Lothian Region Transport. The three Atlanteans were, in fact, not used before the demise of the Edinburgh Corporation Department.

Edinburgh Corporation Motor Bus Fleet List
1931-1939

Reg	Old	'M'	New	Reg	Old	'M'	New
S9316	31	388	-	SC1135	164	309	D17
SG1300	19	396	-	SC1136	165	310	D18
SG1524	20	263	-	SC1137	166	311	D19
SG1525	21	264	-	SC1140	175	312	-
SG2135	29	389	-	SC1142	178	313	-
SG2139	34	391	-	SC1143	182	314	-
SG2274	45	393	-	SC1144	533	315	-
SG2278	8	392	-	SC1146	26	316	-
SG2802	32	390	-	SC1147	35	317	-
SG2813	186	265	-	SC1148	39	318	-
SG2814	187	266	-	SC3401	30	319	L27
SG2815	188	267	-	SC3402	6	320	L28
SG2816	190	268	-	SC3403	194	321	L29
SG2817	189	269	-	SC3404	195	322	L30
SG2818	191	270	-	SC3405	196	323	L31
SF6028	501	271	-	SC3406	197	324	L32
SF6029	502	272	-	SC3407	183	325	L33
SF6030	503	273	-	SC3408	200	326	L34
SF6258	504	274	-	SC3409	198	327	L35
SF6259	505	275	-	SC3410	199	328	L36
SF6260	506	276	-	SC3411	535	329	L37
SF6261	507	277	-	SC3412	772	330	L38
SF6330	508	278	-	SC3413	773	331	L39
SF6331	509	279	-	SC3414	771	394	L41
SF6470	510	280	-	SC3415	770	332	L40
SF6471	511	281	-	SC3416	534	333	D20
SF6251	153	282	-	SC3417	774	334	B11
SF6522	154	283	-	SC3418	775	335	B12
SF6523	155	284	-	SC3419	776	336	B13
SF6524	156	285	-	SC3420	777	337	B14
SF8495	512	286	-	SC3421	778	338	B15
SF8496	513	287	L11	SC3422	779	339	B16
SF8497	514	288	L12	SC3423	780	340	B17
SF8498	515	289	L13	SC3424	781	341	B18
SF8499	516	290	L14	SC3425	782	393	B19
SF8500	517	291	L15	SC3426	783	343	B20
SF8989	518	292	L16	SC3427	784	401	B24
SF8990	519	293	L17	SC3428	785	344	B21
SF8991	520	294	L18	SC3429	786	345	B22
SF8992	521	295	L19	SC3430	787	400	B23
SF8993	522	296	L20	SC7281	581	346	M28
SF8994	523	297	L42	SC7282	582	347	M29
SF8995	524	297	L21	SC7283	583	348	M30
SF8996	525	298	L22	SC7284	584	349	M31
SF8999	528	397	-	SC7285	4	350	D21
SF9002	529	299	-	SC7286	5	351	D22
SC1126	10	300	L23	SC7287	7	352	D23
SC1127	24	301	L24	SC7288	9	353	D24
SC1128	151	302	L25	SC7289	11	354	D25
SC1129	152	303	L26	SC7290	12	355	D26
SC1130	157	304	D12	SC7291	13	399	D55
SC1131	159	305	D13	SC7292	170	356	D27
SC1132	160	306	D14	SC7293	15	357	D28
SC1133	47	307	D15	SC7294	22	358	D29
SC1134	163	308	D16	SC7295	23	359	D30

Edinburgh Corporation Motor Bus Fleet List
1931-1939

Reg	Old	'M'	New	Reg	Old	'M'	New
SC7296	25	398	D54	FS2157	-	287	M11
SC7297	27	360	D31	FS2158	-	313	M12
SC7298	28	361	D32	FS2159	-	263	A11
SC7299	33	362	D33	FS2160	-	264	A12
SC7300	36	363	D34	FS2161	-	266	A13
SC7301	37	364	D11	FS2162	-	267	A14
SC7302	38	365	D35	FS2163	-	285	A15
SC7303	40	366	D36	FS2164	-	299	A16
SC7304	41	367	D37	FS2165	-	282	A17
SC7305	42	368	D38	FS2166	-	268	A18
SC7306	43	369	D39	FS2167	-	283	A19
SC7307	44	370	D40	FS4422	-	4321	M16
SC7308	46	371	D41	FS5936	-	2115	M17
SC7309	167	372	D42	FS6340	-	4706	M33
SC7310	171	373	D43	FS7032	-	4964	M18
SC7311	14	374	D44	FS7033	-	4970	A21
SC7312	173	375	D45	FS7036	-	396	A22
SC7313	176	376	D46	FS9611	-	943	M32
SC7314	177	377	D47	WS637	-	1675	A20
SC7315	179	378	D48	WS1508	-	2434	B25
SC7316	180	379	D49	WS6371	-	2723	G11
SC7317	181	380	D50	WS6372	-	2725	G12
SC7318	185	381	D51	WS6373	-	2727	G13
SC7319	192	382	D52	WS6374	-	2736	G14
SC7320	193	383	D53	WS6375	-	2753	G15
SC8747	48	384	M25	WS6376	-	2754	G16
SC8748	49	385	M26	WS6377	-	2754	G17
SC8749	50	386	M27	WS6378	-	2757	G18
SC8791	169	387	A23	WS6379	-	2760	G19
SC9901	-	2895	X11	WS6380	-	2763	G20
SC9902	-	2938	X12	WS6381	-	2765	G21
SC9903	-	2896	D70	WS6382	-	2766	G22
SC9904	-	1445	D56	WS6383	-	2770	G23
SC9905	-	1485	D57	WS6384	-	2773	G24
SC9906	-	1486	D58	WS6385	-	2778	G25
SC9907	-	1487	D59	WS6386	-	2779	G26
SC9908	-	1903	D61	WS9502 - 20	-	5302-20	A24-A42
SC9909	-	1902	D60	WS9521	-	5301	A43
SC9910	-	2044	D65	ASC301-310	-	5321-30	A44-A53
SC9911	-	2043	D64	ASC311-325	-	5331-45	G27-G41
SC9912	-	2042	D63	BSC15-29	-	5761-75	A54-A68
SC9913	-	2041	D62	BSC77-86	-	5776-85	G42-G51
SC9914	-	2176	D66	BWS203-223	-	6293-6312	A69-A88
SC9915	-	2177	D67	BWS224-233	-	6313-22	G52-G61
SC9916	-	2545	D68				
SC9917	-	2546	D69				
SC9918	-	2897	M13				
SC9919	-	2898	M14				
SC9920	-	2899	M15				
FS2151	-	265	M19				
FS2152	-	269	M20				
FS2153	-	270	M21				
FS2154	-	312	M22				
FS2155	-	314	M23				
FS2156	-	2317	M24				

Edinburgh Corporation Motor Bus Fleet List
Wartime Additions

No.	Reg	Make	Body	Builder	Note
G9	DSF983	AEC Regent	H56R	Park Royal	
G10	DSF984	AEC Regent	H56R	Park Royal	
X13	DSF985	Tilling Stevens	B30F	Willowbrook	
X14	DSF986	Tilling Stevens	B30F	Willowbrook	
X15	DSF987	Bristol L5G	B34F	Bristol	W
G8	DSF988	Leyland TD7	H56R	Pickering	
G7	DSG228	Bristol K5G	H56R	N Counties	
X7	DSG750	Bedford OWB	B32F	SMT	X
X8	DSG751	Bedford OWB	B32F	SMT	X
X9	DSG752	Bedford OWB	B32F	SMT	
X10	DSG753	Bedford OWB	B32F	SMT	X
A23	DSG837	Daimler COG5	B36R	ECT	
A10	DSG965	Daimler COG5	B36R	ECT	
G62	DWS82	Daimler CWG5	H56R	Massey	
G63	DWS83	Daimler CWG5	H56R	Massey	Y
G4	DWS126	Guy Arab 6LW	H56R	Pickering	Y
G5	DWS127	Guy Arab 6LW	H56R	Pickering	Y
G6	DWS128	Guy Arab 6LW	H56R	Pickering	Y
X6	DWS130	Bedford OWB	B32F	SMT	X
X5	DWS131	Bedford OWB	B32F	SMT	
X4	DWS132	Bedford OWB	B32F	SMT	X
X3	DWS133	Bedford OWB	B32F	SMT	
X2	DWS232	Bedford OWB	B32F	SMT	
X1	DWS233	Bedford OWB	B32F	SMT	
X16	DWS234	Bedford OWB	B32F	SMT	
X17	DWS235	Bedford OWB	B32F	SMT	
G3	DWS312	Guy Arab 6LW	H56R	Massey	Y
G2	DWS313	Guy Arab 6LW	H56R	Massey	Y
X18	DWS373	Bedford OWB	B32F	SMT	
X19	DWS374	Bedford OWB	B32F	SMT	X
X20	DWS375	Bedford OWB	B32F	SMT	X
X21	DWS376	Bedford OWB	B32F	SMT	X
X22	DWS377	Bedford OWB	B32F	SMT	
X23	DWS378	Bedford OWB	B32F	SMT	
X24	DWS379	Bedford OWB	B32F	SMT	
X25	DWS380	Bedford OWB	B32F	SMT	
G1	DWS415	Guy Arab 6LW	H56R	Pickering	Y
G64	DWS420	Daimler CWA6	H56R	Massey	Y
G65	DWS421	Daimler CWA6	H56R	Massey	Y
G66	DWS422	Daimler CWA6	H56R	Massey	Y
G67	DWS544	Daimler CWA6	H56R	N Counties	Y
G68	DWS545	Daimler CWA6	H56R	N Counties	Y
G69	DWS546	Daimler CWA6	H56R	N Counties	Y
G70	DWS547	Daimler CWA6	H56R	N Counties	Y
G71	DWS928	Daimler CWA6	H56R	Brush	Z
G72	DWS929	Daimler CWA6	H56R	Brush	Y
G73	EFS128	Daimler CWA6	H56R	Brush	Y
G74	EFS129	Daimler CWA6	H56R	Brush	Y
G75	EFS130	Daimler CWA6	H56R	Brush	Y
G76	EFS131	Daimler CWA6	H56R	Brush	Y
G77	EFS132	Daimler CWA6	H56R	Brush	Y
G78	EFS133	Daimler CWA6	H56R	Brush	Y

W: Renumbered A161 in 1949. X: New Duple C29F body in 1949. Y: Change of body later – see text.
Z: Became single deck A11 later – see text.
The conventional body code is used – number of seats prefixed by B – bus, C – coach, H – normal height double deck, and with suffix F – front entrance, R – rear entrance, D – dual doors.

Edinburgh Corporation Bus Fleet List
May 1951 to May 1975

Number	Registration	New	Make	Body	Bodybuilder	Withdrawn	Notes
1	DWS415	1943	Guy Arab 6LW	H56R	N Counties	1962	1
2	DWS313	1943	Guy Arab 6LW	H56R	N Counties	1962	1
3	DWS312	1943	Guy Arab 6LW	H56R	N Counties	1962	1
4	DWS126	1943	Guy Arab 6LW	H56R	N Counties	1962	1
5	DWS127	1943	Guy Arab 6LW	H56R	N Counties	1962	1
6	DWS128	1943	Guy Arab 6LW	H56R	N Counties	1962	1
27-31	ASC311-5	1937	Daimler COG6	H53R	Met Cammell		2
33	ASC317	1937	Daimler COG6	H53R	Met Cammell		2
34	ASC318	1937	Daimler COG6	H53R	Met Cammell		2
36-8	ASC320-2	1937	Daimler COG6	H53R	Met Cammell		2
40	ASC324	1937	Daimler COG6	H53R	Met Cammell		2
42	BSC77	1938	Daimler COG6	H53R	Met Cammell		2
43	BSC78	1938	Daimler COG6	H53R	Met Cammell		2
45	BSC80	1938	Daimler COG6	H53R	Met Cammell		2
48-51	BSC83-6	1938	Daimler COG6	H53R	Met Cammell		2
52-61	BWS224-233	1938	Daimler COG6	H53R	Met Cammell		2
62	DWS82	1943	Daimler CWG5	H56R	Massey	1967	3,13
63	DWS83	1943	Daimler CWG5	H56R	Pickering	1967	3,13
64	DWS420	1943	Daimler CWG5	H56R	Pickering	1967	3,13
65	DWS421	1943	Daimler CWG5	H56R	Massey	1967	3
66	DWS422	1943	Daimler CWG5	H56R	Pickering	1967	3,13
67-70	DWS544-7	1944	Daimler CWG5	H56R	N Counties	1967	3,13
72	DWS929	1944	Daimler CWG5	H56R	Brush	1967	3,13
73-8	EFS128-133	1945	Daimler CWG5	H56R	Brush	1967	3,13
79-81	EFS554-6	1945	Guy Arab 6LW	H56R	N Counties	1957-60	
82-5	ESC131-4	1946	Guy Arab 6LW	H56R	N Counties	1957-8	
86	ESC728	1946	Guy Arab 6LW	H56R	N Counties	1958	
87	ESC729	1946	Guy Arab 6LW	H56R	N Counties	1958	
88-90	EFS914-6	1945	Guy Arab 6LW	H56R	Weymann	1954	
91-2	ESC207-8	1946	Guy Arab 6LW	H56R	Weymann	1954	
93-105	ESC920-932	1946	Guy Arab 6LW	H56R	N Counties	1957	4,14
106-110	FSC983-7	1947	Daimler CVD6	H56R	N Counties	1960	
111-2	FSF901-2	1948	Daimler CVD6	H56R	N Counties	1960	
113-7	FSC165-9	1949	Daimler CVD6	H56R	Met Cammell	1962	
118-122	GSF821-5	1949	Daimler CVD6	H56R	Met Cammell	1962	
123-137	FSC170-184	1949	Daimler CVG6	H56R	Met Cammell	1965-6	
138-168	GSF969-999	1949	Daimler CVG6	H56R	Met Cammell	1962-4	
169-184	GSG1-16	1950	Daimler CVG6	H56R	Met Cammell	1962-5	
185	FOF298	1939	Leyland TD7c	H52R	Leyland	1954	
200-214	GSG445-459	1949	Guy Arab 6LW	H56R	N Counties	1962	
221-237	HSG171-187	1950	AEC Regent III	H56R	Brockhouse	1960	
240-246	JSF655-661	1952	Leyland PD2/12	H56R	Leyland	1970	
247-250	JWS67-70	1952	Leyland PD2/12	H56R	Leyland	1970	
251-255	KFS942-946	1952	Leyland PD2/12	H58R	Leyland	1970	
256-260	KFS947-951	1952	Leyland PD2/12	H56R	Leyland	1970	
261-4	SWS261-4	1959	Leyland PD3/3	H72F	Alexander	1974	5,8
301-360	JWS581-640	1953	Guy Arab 5LW	H55R	Duple/Nudd	1967-9	
401-500	LFS401-500	1954	Leyland PD2/20	H60R	Met Cammell	1970-5	
501-600	LWS501-600	1955	Leyland PD2/20	H63R	Met Cammell	1973-5	
601-4	GSF334-7	1948	Crossley SD42/6	B34F	Roe	1957	
610	DSG965	1948	Daimler COG5	B36R	ECT	1952	
611	DWS928	1944	Daimler CWA6	B34F	English Electric	1953	
612	FS2160	1932	Daimler CH6G	B32R	Cowieson	1953	
613	FS2161	1932	Daimler CH6G	B36R	Alexander	1959	
615-9	FS2163-7	1932	Daimler CH6G	B36R	Alexander	1959	

Edinburgh Corporation Bus Fleet List
May 1951 to May 1975

Number	Registration	New	Make	Body	Bodybuilder	Withdrawn	Notes
620	WS637	1934	Daimler CH6G	B36R	Alexander	1953	
621	FS7033	1933	Daimler CP6G	B34F	English Electric	1952	
622	FS7036	1934	Daimler COG5	B30F	Weymann	1952	
623	DSG837	1934	Daimler COG5	B36R	ECT	1952	
624-643	WS9502-9521	1936	Daimler COG5	B36R	Weymann		2
644-6	ASC301-3	1937	Daimler COG5	B36R	Weymann		2
647	ASC304	1937	Daimler COG5	B36R	Alexander		2
648-653	ASC305-310	1937	Daimler COG5	B36R	Met Cammell		2
654-668	BSC15-29	1938	Daimler COG5	B36R	Met Cammell		2
669-687	BWS203-221	1938	Daimler COG5	B36R	Met Cammell		2
688	BWS223	1938	Daimler COG5	B36R	Met Cammell		2
689-698	FSC155-164	1948	Daimler CVG5	B35R	Met Cammell	1961	
731-740	ESG644-653	1948	Guy Arab 5LW	B35R	Met Cammell	1959-61	6
761	DSF987	1941	Bristol L5G	B34R	Bristol	1952	
762-776	FWS155-169	1950	Bristol L6B	B35R	Brockhouse	1960	6
801	JSF524	1951	Leyland Royal Tiger	B31R	Alexander	1968	7
802	JSF525	1951	Leyland Olympic	B32R	Weymann	1968	7
803-818	HWS768-783	1952	Leyland Royal Tiger	B40R	Leyland	1966	7
819-20	NFS748-9	1955	Leyland Tiger Cub	C41F	Alexander	1968	7
821	NFS941	1955	Leyland Tiger Cub	C41F	Alexander	1968	7
822	PWS822	1957	Albion Aberdonian	B43F	Alexander	1971	7
901-950	NSF901-950	1956	Guy Arab IV	H63R	Alexander	1969-72	
951-970	OFS951-970	1956	Guy Arab IV	H63R	Alexander	1969-72	
998	PWS998	1957	Leyland PD3/2	H72F	Alexander	1974	8
999	PWS999	1959	Leyland PD3/2	H72F	Alexander	1974	8
X 2	GWS465	1949	Bedford OB	C29F	Duple	1959	
X 4	DWS132	1943	Bedford OWB	C29F	Duple	1958	
X 6	DWS130	1943	Bedford OWB	C29F	Duple	1958	
X 7	DSG750	1942	Bedford OWB	C29F	Duple	1958	
X 8	DSG751	1942	Bedford OWB	C29F	Duple	1959	
X 9	GWS464	1949	Bedford OB	C29F	Duple	1958	
X10	DSG753	1942	Bedford OWB	C29F	Duple	1959	
X18	GWS465	1949	Bedford OB	C29F	Duple	1958	
X19-X21	DWS374-376	1943	Bedford OWB	C29F	Duple	1958	
X22-X25	GWS466-469	1950	Bedford OB	C29F	Duple	1959	
701-760	NSF701-760	1956	Leyland PD2/20	H63R	Met Cammell		
761-800	OFS761-800	1956	Leyland PD2/20	H63R	Met Cammell		
1-50	SWS1-50	1959	Leyland PSUC1/3	B44F	Weymann	1966	9
51-100	VSC51-100	1960	Leyland PSUC1/3	B47F	Weymann	1969-78	
101	YSG101	1962	Leyland PSU3/2R	B33R	Alexander		10
601-650	YWS601-650	1962	Leyland PD2A/30	H66R	Alexander		
201-203	201SC-203SC	1963	Bedford VAS1	C25F	Duple		
204-212	204SC-212SC	1963	Bedford SB5	C41F	Duple	1971-4	
213-218	213SC-218SC	1964	Bedford VAL14	C52F	Duple	1972	
219-220	219SC-220SC	1964	Bedford SB5	C41F	Duple	1974	
221	221FS	1964	Bedford SB5	C41F	Duple	1974	
222	222FS	1964	Bedford VAS1	C25F	Duple		
651-700	ASC651B-700B	1964	Leyland PD3/6	H70F	Alexander		
801	ESF801C	1966	Leyland PDR1/1	H74F	Alexander		11
802-825	EWS802D-825D	1966	Leyland PDR1/1	H74F	Alexander		11
826-850	EWS826D-850D	1966	Leyland PD3A/2	H70F	Alexander		
851-899	JSC851E-899E	1967	Leyland PDR1/1	H74F	Alexander		11
900	JSC900E	1968	Leyland PDR2/1	H82F	Alexander		
223-5	MSF223F-5F	1968	Bedford VAL70	C52F	Duple	1975	
226-7	MSF226F-7F	1968	Ford R226	C52F	Duple	1975	

Edinburgh Corporation Bus Fleet List
May 1951 to May 1975

Number	Registration	New	Make	Body	Bodybuilder	Withdrawn	Notes
228-230	PSC228G- 230G	1969	Bedford VAL70	C53F	Duple		
231-2	PSC231G-2G	1969	Bedford VAM70	C45F	Duple		
301-350	PSC301G- 350G	1969	Leyland PDR1A/1	H75D	Alexander		
351-400	SSF351H- 400H	1970	Leyland PDR1A/1	H75D	Alexander		
233-4	SSF233H-4H	1970	Bedford VAM70	C45F	Duple		
235-7	SSF235H-7H	1970	Bedford VAL70	C53F	Duple		
238-242	VSC238J- 242J	1971	Bedford YRQ	C45F	Duple		
243-247	AFS243K-7K	1972	Bedford YRT	C51F	Duple		
251-300	WFS251- 300K	1972	Leyland PDR1A/1	H75D	Alexander		
1-50	BFS1L-50L	1973	Leyland AN68/1R	H75D	Alexander		
102-105	BWS102L-5L	1973	Seddon Pennine IV	B25F	Pennine		
106-111	CFS106L-111L	1973	Seddon Pennine IV	B25F	Pennine		
204-208	NFS204M-8M	1973	Bedford YRT	C53F	Duple		
214-218	NSG214M-8M	1973	Bedford YRT	C53F	Duple		
901-918	OFS901M- 18M	1973	Leyland AN68/1R	H75D	Alexander		
919-950	OSF919M- 50M	1974	Leyland AN68/1R	H75D	Alexander		
112-121	GSX112N-121N	1975	Bedford YRT	C49F	Alexander		
401-450	GFS401N-50N	1975	Leyland AN68/1	H75D	Alexander		

Notes

1	Renumbered 81-6 in 1959, and 381-6 in 1960
2	Withdrawal dates:

In 1952 - 36, 38, 57, 59, 61

In 1953 - 29, 31, 48-9, 52, 54, 56, 625-6, 629, 631-3. 637, 639, 641, 646, 649, 653-4, 657-60, 667, 671, 673-4, 676-7, 679, 685, 687-8

In 1954 - 42, 51, 53, 55, 58, 60, 88-92

In 1956 - 27-8, 30, 33-4, 37, 40, 43, 45, 50

In 1957 - 664, 670, 678, 680-3

In 1958 - 642, 645

In 1959 - 624, 627-8, 630, 634-6, 638, 640, 643-4, 647-8, 650-2, 655-6, 661-3, 665-6, 668-9, 672, 675, 684, 686

3	Renumbered 362-378 in 1960
4	93, 95-7 renumbered 393, 395-7 in 1960 (others withdrawn 1957)
5	Renumbered 994-7 in 1971
6	Renumbered 831-840 and 862-876 in 1956
7	Renumbered 102-123 in 1966
8	Sold to Highland Omnibuses Ltd
9	Sold to Ulster Transport Authority (except 9 & 22 withdrawn 1963)
10	'Standee' bus with three doors - see text
11	'Panoramic' windows, standard from 1967 (also fitted to 802)
12	Withdrawal dates: 1969, 75; 1974, 77, 88-97; 1975, 99 & 100
13	New H58R Alexander body in 1954
14	Registration numbers of 102 & 103 were transposed.

In a few cases individual buses had differing numbers of seats from as shown, and in some cases the seating numbers were subsequently altered. Details are given in the text.

Edinburgh Corporation Support Vehicle List

The Corporation's lorry fleet is not within this history, but the tramway tower-wagons and breakdown wagons should be recorded.

Until November 1940 these were numbered in the lorry list, then a separate list, 1 - 7 was created as shown below:

Old No	New No	Reg No	Year New	Make	Type	Scrap Year	Notes
1	-	WS 194	1914	Halley	Tower	1929	
4	4	SG5431	1922	AEC	Breakdown	1945	
5	-	SG5077	1922	Tilling Stevens	Tower	1938	
1	1	SC5273	1929	AEC	Tower	1945	
5	5	SC3405	1929	Leyland Lion	Tower		1
17	-	SG7411	1922	Tilling Stevens	Tower	1939	
18	2	SF 899	1923	Thornycroft	Tower	1944	
-	7	SG2012	1921	AEC	Breakdown	1945	2
37	3	AWS682	1937	AEC	Tower		
-	6	SC3430	1929	AEC (Beardmore)	Breakdown		3
-	2	DWS528	1944	Austin	Tower		
-	4		1945	ERF	Breakdown		4
-	1	EFS743	1946	Austin	Tower		
-	5	FSF747	1948	Austin	Tower		

Notes:

1 Ex bus plus old tower, 1939

2 Ex bus 1932

3 Ex bus 1940; Leyland engine 1943

4 Used Trade Plates

The Edinburgh & District Tramways Coy had, for the Slateford electric line, a tower (possibly that later on SG5077) which was mounted on a small Albion lorry (51492) as necessary. WS194 was the former Leith Corporation tower wagon. The normal 'on call' wagon was SG7411, then AWS682, latterly one of the Austins. The two Tilling-Stevens were petrol-electrics.

AEC breakdown lorry, number 4 (SG5431) in Dryden Street with a selection of jacks. (EOC)

Leyland lorry number 3 (S9258) doubled as a charabanc. Seen here with rail-carrying 'janker'. (EOC)

Dryden Street yard with the Corporation fleet of eight Millars' dump trucks, and their uniformed drivers. Behind is the first bus garage (former horse tram body construction shop) and a Leyland bus showing route 'X'. (EOC)

The first tower wagon was this unstable-looking piece of equipment. An Albion lorry with the tower added, used on the Slateford electric line. (EOC)

Appendix 3

TICKETS

At the start of its operations in 1919, the Corporation introduced longer tickets with larger clearer print. They were still in 'fareboard' layout and in most cases both sides of the ticket were used but now without a centre column on the back. The wording on the centre column on the front read 'Edinburgh Corporation Tramways. Available only by car on which issued, and to station opposite punch-hole. To be punched in the presence of passenger, shown or delivered up on demand, or destroyed on alighting.' No printer's name was shown. Later 'Edinburgh Corporation Tramways' was replaced by 'Edinburgh Corporation Trams & Motors'. There were four sets of 1d and 2d for differing groups of tramway routes, A, B, C, and D, and another for buses. Later, as the bus services expanded, A, B, and C groups became necessary for 1d and 2d bus tickets too. The colours were: 1d white; 1½d (Cramond Bus route only) blue; 2d red; 3d pale brown; 4d green; 5d mauve; 1d child yellow; 1½d child blue. Transfers were green, 1d, the bottom half of this ticket having a wide panel worded 'Edin Corporation Tramways 1d Transfer Ticket. Valid to station opposite punch-hole and good only for continuous journey on day of issue. Not transferable. Issued subject to the Bye-laws.' Surrounding this and including the bottom and extending to the top of the right hand edge only were numbers 1 to 31 for the days of the month, and above the panel and without a centre column were the few stages concerned, headed 'From' and 'To' and shown separately in each direction.

A 1d ticket for dogs and luggage was brown, the wording on the centre column being amplified, the left hand column referring to dogs and the right hand to luggage weighing over 28lb. Workmen's return tickets were issued at 1d above the single fare, but available for return on the top deck of the car only. The 3d value was bright brown with green overprint 'Workman's 3d Return', the pale brown 4d similarly overprinted in red. There was also a Scholars' Transfer 1d ticket, white, with the hours 8am to 6pm down each side, respectively 'To School' and 'From School', with the wording in the centre column suitably amplified, overprinted Scholars Transfer in red. An annual permit purchased at the St James Square office and costing 2/- had to be shown before these tickets were issued.

1d tokens could be purchased in bulk and used for fares. These were Bakelite discs also used (coloured accordingly) by other Corporation departments, and the Post Office, for their employees, the latter green. The Portobello route retained season tickets as in Edinburgh & District Tramways Company days.

Through fares on the joint service with the Musselburgh Tramways Company were: Musselburgh 5d, Levenhall 6d, Prestonpans 8d, Port Seton 9d. The Corporation's fare to

Joppa was 4d but was reduced on 1 August 1923 to 3d and to Musselburgh 4d. Joppa to Port Seton then became 6d. The 2d through ticket King's Road to Ship Inn (Fisherrow), was white with a red stripe, the 3d King's Road to Town Hall (Musselburgh) brown overprinted B in red. The 3d through Waterloo Place to Ship Inn was pale brown overprinted A in red, and the 4d Waterloo Place to Town Hall (Musselburgh) green overprinted A in red. Stages were printed lengthways.

Tickets in the 'destination-punched' layout were introduced about this time instead of the 'fareboard' layout hitherto used. This new layout used both outer columns for the stage names in sequence, headed TO. The centre column showed only the fare, the series (A, B or C), the service numbers for which it was used, and '(See over for conditions of issue)'. Except for higher values, both sides were used, with no centre column on the back, across the bottom of which was printed revised wording: 'Available on Car on which Ticket is issued and to station indicated by punch-hole. To be punched in the presence of passenger, shown or delivered up on demand, or deposited in Ticket Box on alighting.' On the bus tickets the word Car was replaced by Bus and on the 6d bus tickets this wording was accommodated at the foot of the front. The title Edinburgh Corp'n Trams & Motors, and later Edinburgh Corp Transport Dept or Edin Corp'n Transport Dept was printed across the top of the front of the tickets beneath the serial number. Tickets were punched in the stage to which the passenger was entitled to travel. The earliest still carried no printer's name, but Bell Punch Co, Glasgow Numerical Printing Co and other firms later won printing contracts.

Soon followed the introduction of ticket-printing machines. After experiments, one hundred 'TIM's – were purchased and put into use from Tollcross depot in January 1933. Their use extended rapidly through the system, including by 1935 some bus services. Green ink (instead of purple) was used for bus tickets. To facilitate use of TIMs on bus services a 3d maximum fare was introduced on 5 December 1937 (except night services). 1½d, 2½d and 3½d fares on the Barnton route disappeared in 1934. Pre-printed coloured tickets thus disappeared – almost. It was still necessary for conductors to carry 1d, 2d and 3d tickets with stage numbers in case of failure of the TIM machine. Colours of the 1d and 2d were as before, but 3d was pale green. When these were used they were cancelled by tearing a small piece out at the stage number boarded. These tickets were printed by Colleys of London and the wording in the centre column was: 'Available only on Car or Bus on which Ticket is issued and From station indicated by punch-hole'. From was underlined, as these had to be consistent with the TIM tickets, reversing the 'destination punched' principle of previous pre-printed tickets. All tramway and bus stages were numbered, so to ensure universal stage numbers throughout the tram system. A scheme was adopted with the Post Office or Waverley as 12 in both directions on all services (except 20-23). A car leaving a terminus did not necessarily start at stage 1, but at a number to fit 12 at the Post Office. Thus Haymarket, and Tollcross were always 10 inwards and 14 outwards. This scheme came into use on 8 April 1934.

Appendix 4

CORPORATION TRANSPORT PASSENGER STATISTICS

Year ended			Totals
May 1922	Cable	67,986,467	
	Leith	12,632,560	
	Buses	20,407,736	
			101,026,763
May 1930	Trams	134,964,188	
	Buses	29,437,803	
			164,401,991
May 1939	Trams	145,972,840	
	Buses	60,306,416	
			206,279,256
May 1947	Trams	192,892,899 *	
	Buses	83,487,790	
			276,380,689
May 1950	Trams	186,005,463	
	Buses	100,611,294	
			286,616,757 **
May 1956	Trams	49,144,513	
	Buses	202,258,656	
			251,403,169
May 1958	Buses	232,603,302	
May 1975	Buses	151,675,505	

*   maximum year for trams
**   maximum annual total

ADAM GORDON
Publisher and dealer in transport literature & ephemera

If you have enjoyed reading this book you may be interested in some of the following titles, many of them being reprints; * = hardback; obtainable from bookshops or direct from the publisher (address below); add 10% for postage and packing up to £5 maximum. No post and packing charge for orders of £50 or over.

Tramways of Reading.* H. Jordan, 2nd edition, 96pp, £12

Kidderminster and Stourport Electric Tramway Co Rules and Regulations, 1899, 58pp, £7

My Life in Many States and in Foreign Lands, G.F. Train, autobiography of street railway pioneer, who claimed that Jules Verne based "Around the world in 80 days" upon Train's own voyage; over 350pp, £12

Tramways and Electric Railways in the Nineteenth Century* (Electric Railway Number of Cassier's Magazine, 1899), cloth, over 250pp, £23

Tramways – their construction and working*, D.K. Clark, 2nd edn of 1894, over 750pp, 12 plates and over 400 line drawings, cloth, £32

Edinburgh Corporation Transport Department, timetable of electric tramways and motor buses June 1930, c.2 ¾" by 4 ¾", 72pp, £6

London County Council Tramways guide to reopening of Kingsway Subway, 1931, coloured cover and map, 32pp £6

The Cable system of Tramway Traction 1896 – contemporary look at cable systems at home and abroad, 56pp, 6 photo pics and 2 line drawings, £10

The Feltham Car of the Metropolitan Electric and London United Tramways 1931, 18pp £5

The Overhaul of tramcars, London Transport, 26pp, 1935, £6

Tramway Review*, volumes 1 and 2, issues 1-16, 1950-1954, cloth h/b, includes articles on tramways in East Ham, Nottingham, Luton, Huddersfield, Barking, Sheffield, Oldham, Chester, Ilford, Wallasey, Leyton, Darlington, Cork, Lytham, Walthamstow, Isle of Man and Ireland, £23

Clippie, Z.Katin, a few months in the life of a tram and bus conductress in the war in Sheffield, 124pp £7

London Transport Bus routes, Central Area No 2 1943, folds out into c.11" by 17" – limited edition of 250 £5

Edinburgh Street Tramways Company Rules and Regulations for the servants, 1883, 56pp, limited edition of 250 £8

London County Council Tramways Motorman's Handbook, as from 1928, 32pp limited edition of 250 £6

The Training of Drivers and Conductors of Buses, Trams and Trolleybuses, London Transport, 1936, 20pp (250) £6

Double Century* by Stan Basnett and Keith Pearson. It comprises updated histories of the Upper Douglas Cable Tramway, and the Douglas Head Marine Drive Tramway. It also includes an appendix on the Cliff Lifts. Ch.4 consists of 'guided walks' along the routes today by Stan Basnett. It has 144 pages, including 8 in colour, and numerous illustrations; red buckram with gold lettering. £15.

My fifty years in transport – A.G. Grundy, 54pp, 26 illus, covers tramways of North Staffordshire, Blackburn, Potteries, Wrexham, and Stalybridge, Hyde, Mossley and Dukinfield. £10

Modern Tramway*, volumes 1 and 2, 1938 and 1939, reprinted and bound together in green cloth, sewn, gold lettering with original Light Rail Transit League logo on front, £38

How to go tram and tramway modelling – David Voice. Second edition of the title first published 16 years ago, now completely rewritten; coloured covers, 168 pages, 150 black & white photographs, 34 diagrams, and an illustrated glossary. £15.

Source book of literature relating to Scottish tramways – D. Croft & A. Gordon. Includes historical introduction and chronology, books, periodicals and major articles on specific tramway systems, legislation and accident reports, tramway museums and preservation, & rapid transit proposals. 48pp, £5.

The Twilight Years of the Glasgow Tram – Contains over 250 coloured pictures taken by Douglas McMillan, selected, prefaced and captioned by Alasdair Turnbull. 144 pages, £25.

All the above published by Adam Gordon, Priory Cottage, Chetwode, Nr. Buckingham, Bucks, MK18 4LB Tel: 01280 848650. [Trade terms, above prices less 35%, or more for multiple copies.]

Do you have anything of transport interest to sell? e.g. books, magazines, photographs, postcards, tickets, timetables, and ephemera – also hardware like ticket machines, racks and punches, enamelled signs, etc. Just ring or write to Adam Gordon above!